# *Paint Mojo, A Mixed-Media Workshop*

# paint mojo, a mixed-media workshop

## Creative Layering Techniques for Personal Expression

Tracy Verdugo

NORTH LIGHT BOOKS
CINCINNATI, OHIO
artistsnetwork.com

# contents

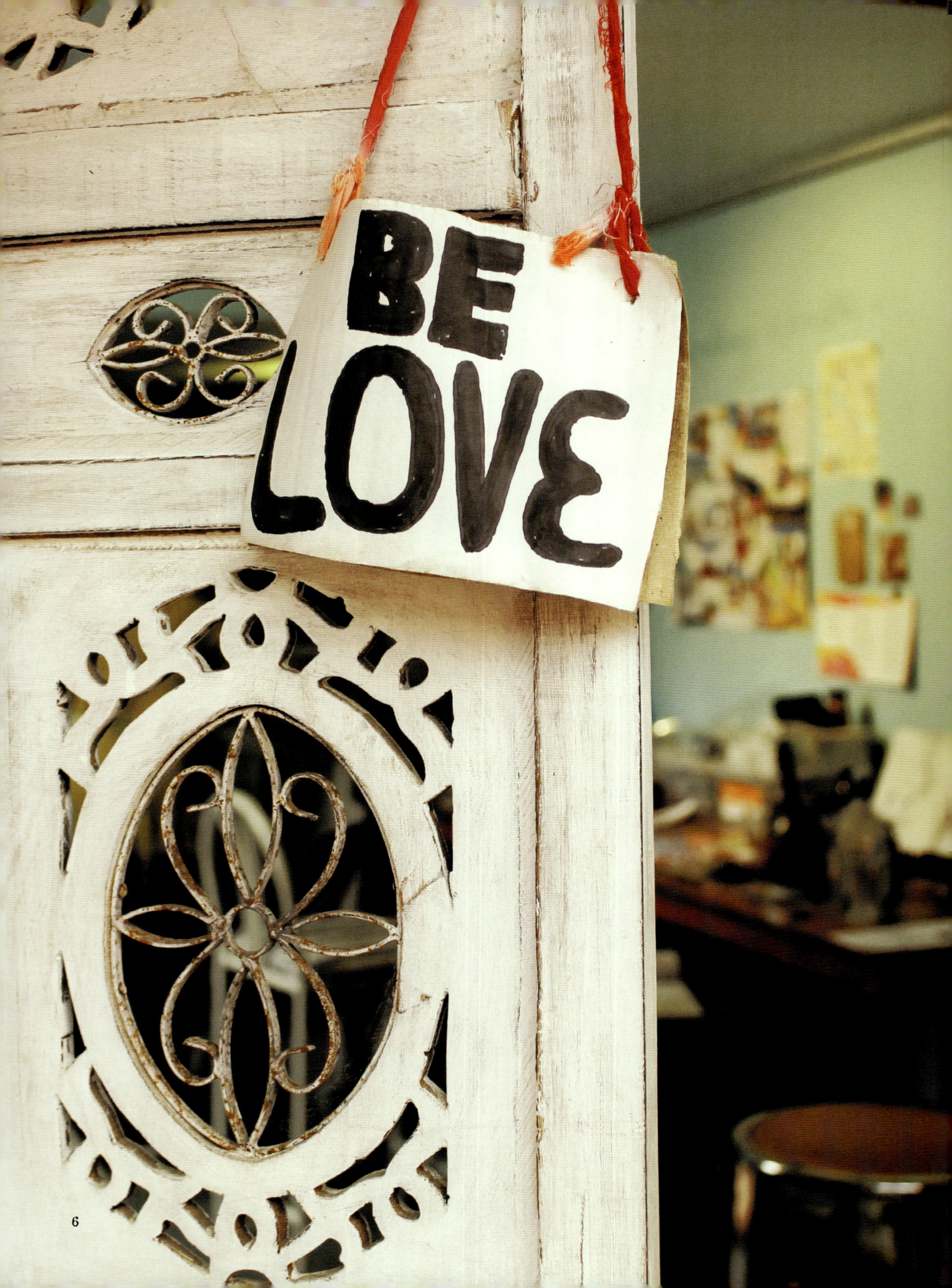
BE
LOVE

# introduction

This book is for the quiet one sitting way up in the back of the room,
hiding behind her big ol' canvas, hoping I won't notice her.
It's for the eager wide-eyed one at the front,
who jumps in with gusto and delight.
It's for the one who doubts his every stroke and color choice,
the one who listens and learns well for a while
. . . and then loses focus or gets impatient . . .
and does something on his canvas that sends him into meltdown mode.

This book is for the one who waits for instruction every step of the way, excited
to try new things but anxious to step out on her own.
It's for the one whose life is in transition or despair,
the one who feels stagnant or lost,
the one who is flying with joy.
It's for the one who has learned grace and patience through experience,
the one who has been painting for thirty years but still loves to learn,
and it's for the one who has never,
*ever*,
picked up a brush and dipped it into paint.

What an awesome, shiny, messy,
complex, perfectly imperfect bunch we are!

All parts of the bigger equation,
Tiny sparks of light from a far greater source.

**Necessary . . . Integral . . . Wonderful!**

You are all amazing sparks of divine love
with the unlimited potential to shine bright in this world.
You have a style and a presence that is truly unique to *you*.

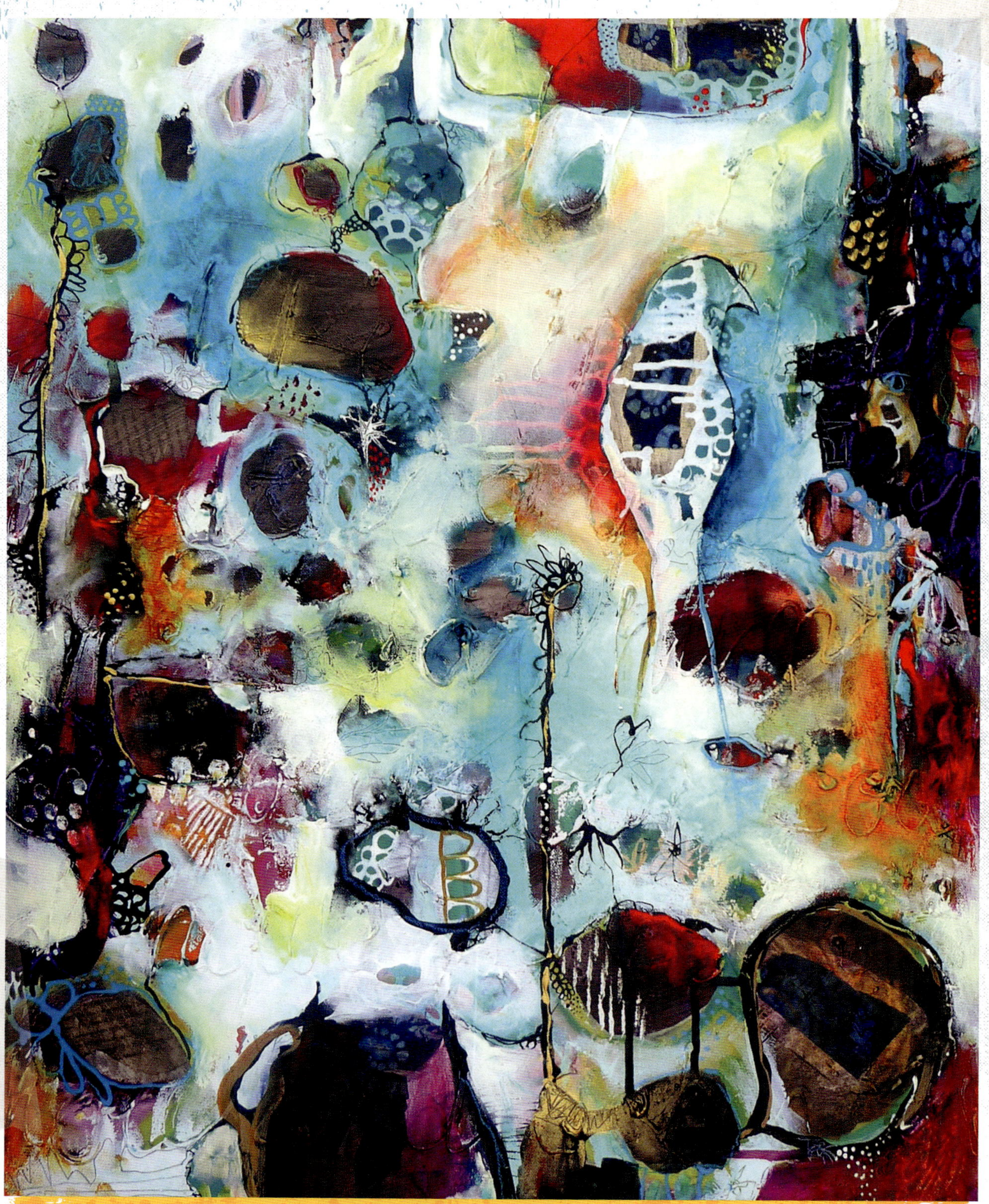

It was as if I'd entered a world of enchantment, of flowering cacti, nudged up against the base of palms, textured walls peeling in layers of magenta and turquoise, and everywhere, the aroma of Mexican spices.

Far away from the sounds of my suburban Australian upbringing, we wandered the cobblestone streets of San Jose del Cabo, Marco and I, in our first year in love, 1986. The familiar sounds of the lorikeets and kookaburras replaced by mariachis and street hawkers selling trinkets on outstretched, colorfully woven blankets.

Beneath a canopy of hanging plants we spied a rustic courtyard—tables set for romance beneath a sky dotted with stars, couples drinking margaritas and cervezas. Later that evening, we bought our first piece of art together; a beautiful woodblock print of a bird escaping its cage.

# chapter one: sacred marks

## Recognizing and claiming the beauty of your unique, authentic voice

Who are we if not a culmination of our stories? A kaleidoscope of ever-changing moments, minute story bites, in which we perceive the world and shape our reality according to our thoughts, our beliefs and the input of those around us. It fascinates me, this "infinite possibilities" universe, in which not one of us is the same as any other. Indeed, not one of us is even the same as our previous self from one moment to the next. Each breath, each thought, each moment set in motion, sets forth a shift within us on a quantum level, and we are, in a sense, reinvented again. Isn't that wonderful?

Each one of us made up of the same stardust and at our very core the same source and yet . . .

You are a totally unique expression of the Universe,
of the Creative Force,
an expression of a love so vast
that it is bursting in its enthusiasm to come
through you
and yet . . .
we doubt,
we compare,
we hide our light
and declare our smallness.

What if instead, we recognized that each one of us holds a story of such depth and beauty that to share it would be to enrich the world in such a number of ways that we could not even begin to fathom what effect it might have?

*There is a vitality, a life force, an energy, a quickening that is translated through you into action, and because there is only one of you in all of time, this expression is unique. And if you block it, it will never exist through any other medium and it will be lost.*
—Martha Graham

# stories

The stories of our lives leave marks on us and influence what we choose as our personal symbols. What stories have most left their marks on you?

I'm sitting with my grandmother, circa 1971. It's just Nanny and I in the back room of the small rented, dark-bricked Bondi flat, where she lives with her partner, Fred.

There is probably some dreadful seventies wallpaper adorning the walls  and a couple of vinyl chairs loudly shouting their era in lime green and orange, but even though I close my eyes to remember, I cannot see the details.

Just an image of my grandmother and me, sitting by the open window, intently watching the clouds float by and naming them in shapes of bunnies and chickens, flying pigs and hearts . . . just a feeling of love and belonging . . . and giggles.

Often, she takes my little hand and turns it over to trace the lines of my palm, predicting my long life span and the small troubles I might have along the way, how many children I will have and places I will visit. I look at her with eyes of total trust and my mind takes little leaps into possible futures. And then, as she has done many times before, she takes my small fingers in hers, gently strokes my fingerprints and says, "You know, love, this world really is a miracle. To think that of all the millions of people God has put on this planet, there is not one person that has exactly the same fingerprints as you. Think about that! What a wonderful thing! There is nobody else exactly like you. You are special and unique!"

Wide-eyed, I take in the wonder and magic of her words, until another puffy cloud catches our eyes and imaginations.

Some years ago I was mesmerised by an American TV show where the host would begin each episode by sticking a pin into a map of the United States while blindfolded. He would travel to the town or city, pick a name at random from the local phone book and call that person to tell him that his life story would be the feature of an upcoming episode. Invariably the astonished person on the other end of the line would be reluctant, protesting that his life was too ordinary, mundane or lack-lustre to be on TV. Usually the host would win him over, the film crews would arrive and, in every single case, something profound, inspirational and wonderful would unfold in the telling of each person's story.

Recently I was able to experience this magical phenomenon firsthand when I was involved in a community project linking the kids from our local high school's special education unit with residents of a nearby retirement village. Each week, staff and students would spend a morning interviewing these elderly gems with ages ranging from 73 to 103, focusing on how life was different when they were young, what kinds of jobs they had held and a myriad of other aspects of their lives. The effects of this collaboration were deeply impactful on both interviewer and interviewee; for the students, a chance to engage in a living, breathing glimpse into history; for the residents, a chance to shine in the retelling of stories their families had long since tired of listening to.

Irene regaled us with tales of a young, mischievous girl who once cut off her sister's braid and served it up at the dinner table to shock her mother. Ronald was the young soldier, who on his first deployment to South Africa, witnessed a brutal beating of a similarly aged black man who had done nothing wrong. Seventy years later he still teared up at the memory. And Iris, ninety-four and now mostly deaf and blind, became young again as she relived the wild dune buggy rides of her younger self across the dry, undeveloped hills of Cantamar, Baja California in the seventies, where my husband spent his childhood with his *abuelita*. We laughed together at the serendipity of lives and paths crossing, and as I sat holding Iris's hand in her tiny room, we pondered the miracle of life through shared stories.

At the end of the eight-week project, the kids had produced some extraordinary PowerPoint presentations, which were offered to their new friends at a special morning tea where the residents were awed and so proud to be the stars of their very own narratives, complete with all the technological bells and whistles that the kids had added to jazz up the show!

Sometimes our stories don't seem to go in the direction we would have them, but there is always a potential for growth, beauty and miracle.

Somewhere down the track I have heard a story that has stuck with me and made a huge impact on my beliefs and values.

For many years a woman with a rare talent for singing—the voice of an angel, some said—worked tirelessly to become a star. Although she performed in hundreds of shows and achieved many great reviews, she hovered beneath the level of greatness, never achieving the "big break" that could take her to the next level. Disappointed and somewhat bitter, she felt as the years passed by that she had lost her chance to shine, wasted her talent and not achieved her potential.

Then, one day . . . she found herself answering a call for volunteers in the neonatal ward of a local hospital. Her job was to hold these precious newborn babies who had come into the world, delivered by crack-addicted mothers and now suffering horrible withdrawals. As she held each baby, she would sing to it in her sweet voice and feel the energy of her song begin to relax the child in her arms. Maybe, she thought, I have it all wrong. Maybe this is the place my gift has always belonged.

And you see,
even in that moment,
when her whole story had been taken from her,
a new one had begun.
In the process of loss,
of being stripped away,
something new is created.
Something valuable and worthy,
always, in every moment.

Your story is important.
Honor its uniqueness.
Embrace its ordinariness.
Revel in its imperfections.
Paint it, sing it, dance it, write it.
The world needs your creative voice.

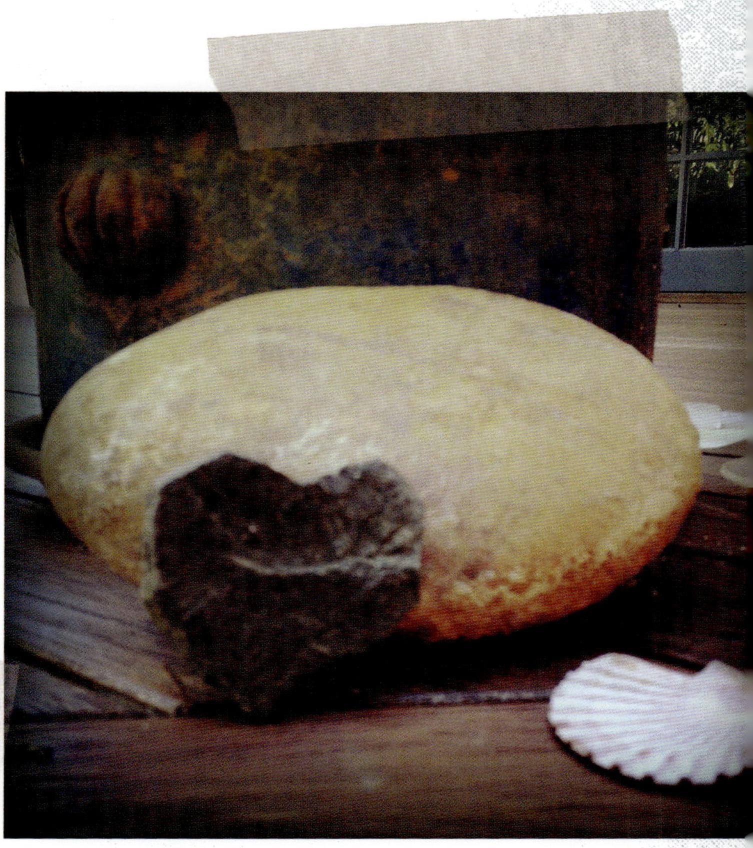

# symbols, style and serendipity

Students ask me often how I found my style. I have kept inspiration folders for years. Torn-out images from magazines crammed between plastic sheets—colors, fashion, faces, stories. From time to time I pull them out and notice what still speaks to me and what no longer does. It is an interesting way to monitor one's own evolution.

These days I keep an inspiration wall in my studio. Right now it is covered in images of elephants, some pics of new art that have caught my eye, love letters from friends and students, photos of my family and a dream board dedicated to traveling the world and teaching others to become creatively free believers of possibility and magic.

With the wealth of information available to us online, it is so easy and super-tempting to take every online class and devour all of the lusciousness that is out there. When I was first introduced to the world of blogging and mixed-media artists, I wanted to try so many new things each week that I sometimes felt like my head would explode!

Slow down and breathe, my friends; try one thing for a while and sit with it. Does it really speak to your soul? Or are you just excited to have learned something new on the journey to becoming your shiniest self? Do you want to embrace it wholeheartedly and explore it tirelessly until it speaks through your own authentic voice? Or is it just one little shiny pebble you are adding to your collection? Something that will one day become a part of a mosaic of such splendor that you could never even have dreamt it?

Take some time this week to create an inspiration board/folder/wall and begin to notice what it is that you are attracted to; are you a bold color person or do you resonate more with a soft, dreamy palette? Are you drawn to energetic, vibrant works or more ethereal, moody pieces? When you look at other artists' works, notice what they say about their process and begin to think about your own.

What is it you'd bring to the world with your art?

## Finding Symbols and Making Meaning

Look around your home and environment and make some simple, little sketches of the things you see. Sketch a bit of the woodgrain in your timber floor, a pattern of dots on a bedcover, an ornament you brought back from somewhere exotic long ago, a teapot on your kitchen counter.

Ask yourself, "If this was to mean something to me, what could it mean?" Try not to get too hung up on grand, life-changing meanings; jot down whatever comes to you and revisit your symbols often.

The ornament could conjure up a specific memory of taste or freedom or new experience, while the teapot could speak of slowing down and taking time, ritual and ceremony. Their meanings will change and expand just as you change and grow through your life.

Things that once held meaning will fall away and become less important while other symbols will appear, surprising you with their importance. I often tell my students to stop and wander around the room and find the symbols of others that resonate with them, to share and talk about them together and what they mean for each other.

I have a story around time that goes like this: racing against, running out, not enough. For some reason these are the connotations that time has for me. I rarely include clocks in my work and I don't wear a watch. I don't need the constant reminder!

Recently at a workshop, I noticed a clock featured prominently in a student's list of symbols. "What does that clock mean for you?" I asked, expecting to find a kindred spirit, a fellow lamenter.

"Oh!" Denise exclaimed, her face lighting up with a smile. "There is plenty of time! That's what it means for me."

I smiled back widely, delighted at this wonderful chance to reframe my relationship with time. "That's brilliant," I said. "Can I adopt that meaning?" "Sure," she said and I walked off happily with a slight shift in perspective and a new paradigm beginning to grow.

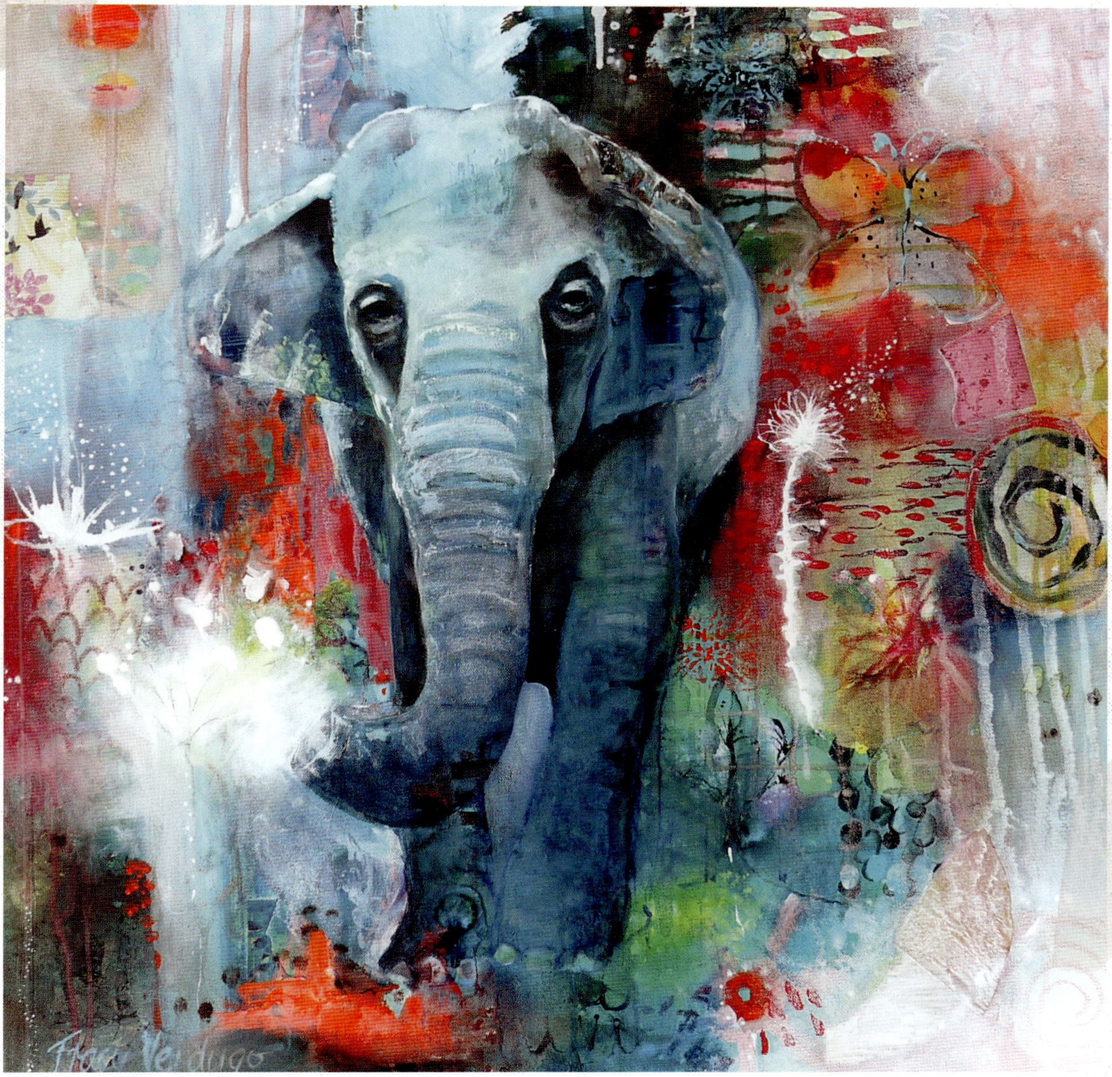

### Butterflies

Butterflies have long been a powerful symbol for me. Honored by many cultures as a symbol of transformation, the butterfly reminds me to keep growing, accept challenges and struggles and *know* that when I am on my path of growth and learning, quietly and gently aware and accepting of my forward leaps and backward falls, I will always emerge with greater freedom and scope for possibility.

Butterflies also remind me of the need to go within, and that quiet contemplation can lead to new insights that will rarely come through while my mind is in the throes of its regular, incessant chatter.

The butterfly speaks of miracles and surrendering to divine timing in our souls' growth, of expansion and elegance, celebration and resurrection, transition and vulnerability, beauty and faith.

### Elephants

Elephants have appeared in my work just recently, coming through with a power and grace that has astounded me.

Since the beginning of 2012 when I first communed with these beautiful creatures in Koh Samui, Thailand, I have been thinking of them, their quiet strength and ancient wisdom, loyalty, determination, power and capacity to love deeply.

In some Asian cultures the elephant is seen as a cosmic creature, carrying the Earth upon its back. In dreams, the elephant symbolizes our ability to overcome obstacles.

Which beautiful creatures on this planet do you feel connected to?

How can you bring them into your art?

# personal iconography

**by Jesse Reno**

When I look back at how I developed my iconography of symbols and beings, it feels a bit like magic because I was creating them without even knowing it. My first symbols—a circle, square, X and line—I'd been painting for one to two years before I thought or realized what they meant to me.

I'd been using them as elements in my paintings, thinking of them only as very comfortable marks to make among abstract fields.

I created layers and layers of circles over one another, squares, framed sections of the paintings I thought looked interesting—as if they were their own mini paintings within the larger piece—and a way of preserving pieces of what came before. I used Xs and lines as smaller decorative elements.

These repeating marks felt very comforting, so I never thought to question them. At the time, I was just beginning to paint and explore, trying to do what came most natural at all times, until one afternoon …

I was staring at a 4' × 5' (122cm × 152cm) painting full of these markings and it came to me: You can walk in circles forever; you will get nowhere. The squares were like an opportunity or a doorway you must take to see where it will lead. The X-like marks were reminders of the negative things that hold us from our goals. By crossing them out we can go farther. The lines held the idea of directness in your desire and communication as the world is confusing enough without riddles.

I realized these were the biggest things in my life that had been holding me back from my dreams and goals. This was the beginning of self-understanding coming from a place of self-exploration outside of telling myself what I was doing or planning what it would be.

I found—and still find—the best direction to come from, if you want to reach something true within yourself, is to come to yourself from mystery and contemplation rather than from preconceived ideas. It's too easy to hide from yourself when you choose the outcome first, when you move from a direction outside of your ideas about yourself and then analyze them.

It can take time but the messages are priceless if you learn something truly new about yourself or take responsibility for who you really are.

From there, I realized the power of what I had learned and began to keep track of the forms I would create and how they would change. I now always change directions in my work, starting with an idea and running with it, allowing it to change. The changes come when the idea is no longer interesting or a new visual idea seems more important.

Eventually I come to a place that feels potent and right in every way.

So I began to wonder, *Why do I start with a buffalo and end with a reindeer?* This actually happened three times in a row! The first time I decided to document my start and finish. After the third time, I thought I must really be desiring reindeer or the idea of a reindeer.

I sat and thought to myself, *What does a reindeer feel like to me?* Peaceful, walking or lying in nature, passively taking in the trees . . . a connection to trees with branches that are like antlers. Overall, I thought their place was with the trees.

Next I thought to myself, *I should go to the trees myself and relax.* I hadn't been to the woods in a long time.

This was the beginning of an understanding of the real potency of my work: the idea of the abstract narrative. A story told from abstraction, a place of following instinct to create a world that, in the end, is personal and correct in terms of expression and connection.

I began taking the time to analyze the elements—creatures, symbols and interactions—to find meaning in them.

If creation comes from within, it must represent a feeling of connection to those specific creatures, symbols and interactions. A connection that can be learned from or encourage ideas that are important to our core and self-desires.

Little by little I'd ask myself each time I saw a new creature or symbol, *What does this mean?* Eventually I came to a place full of dialogue between these animal beings and symbols that give me great insight into myself.

## Chart of Symbols

I discover much understanding through seemingly random shapes, colors and markings. I find myself writing words before I understand their meaning, trusting that I will be wise enough to understand them in time. Magic does not reveal itself easily. When trying to see the future, our eyes must be given time to adjust. To find our purpose we must ask many questions of ourselves. We must observe ourselves without judgment. To find something new, we must move without bounds. There are no hard questions for truth.

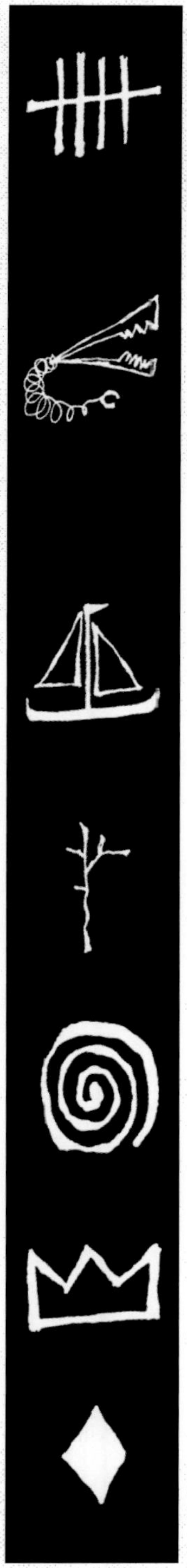

5 Dashes
Keep track of your accomplishments, but don't let them become you.

Bear Trap
A trap—something to be avoided. Man-made and mechanical. Something that happens when choosing diamonds over hearts.

Boat
Be aware of your actions when traveling. Respect the difference of others. Avoid conquest.

Branch
Growth. A branch is a wand to a wise man.

Circle
We can walk in circles forever; this leads to madness. We must make a choice.

Crown
The king will always seek to control.

Diamonds
Riches. Be aware that a diamond is just a sparkling stone of status. It's no one's best friend.

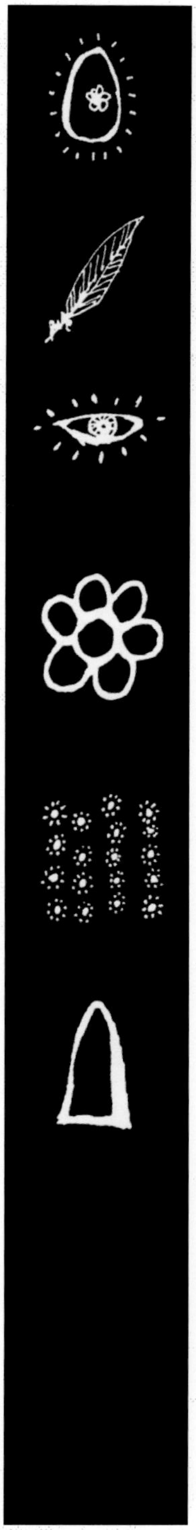

Eggs
Unknown potential. Something precious to be guarded.

Feather
Freedom.

Floating Eye
Being able to see what is beyond your vision.

Flowers
Random beauty. This is where connection can be made or ignored.

Flowers in a Grid
Many random connections are waiting.

Gravestone Window
An opportunity. We can look out a window. This is not the same as going outside. Don't wait until you die to achieve your goals. Don't fear death; let it motivate you.

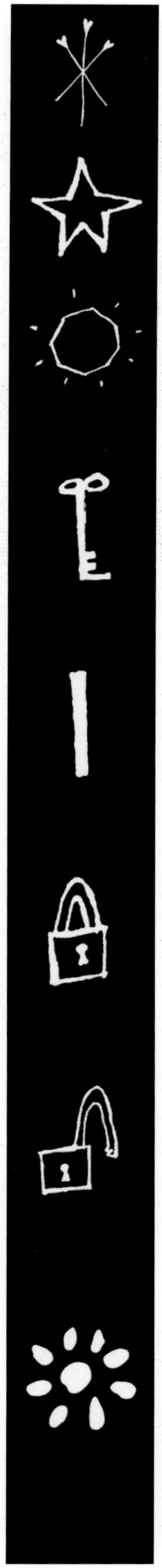

Hearts
Love.

Hollow Star
Accomplishment.

Honeycomb
Connection. One thing leads to another.

Keys
Use these to unlock restraint or understanding.

Line
Directness and clarity lead to achievement.

Lock - Locked
There is something that needs to be unlocked.

Lock - Unlocked
All is open to you. When the lock is open, you are free to move without restraint.

Magic
It is everywhere. You just have to look very close. Question what you see, not that you see it.

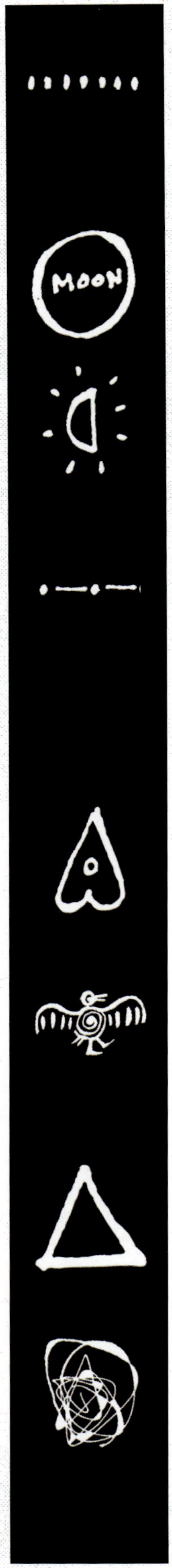


Measurement
Always measure yourself against your own dreams and accomplishments rather than those of others.

Moon
Natural signs.

One Half
Half of the story. Moving by oneself.

Orion's Belt
Something of power that cannot be denied. It can be seen and understood by all without argument. The power of stars.

Ouija Piece
Talking to spirits. Following your spirit rather than system logic.

Phoenix
Rising from nothing. Reborn. Always rising.

Pyramids
Empire. Pyramid schemes. A structure of control rather than order.

Random Energy
Energy. The potential of energy around you.

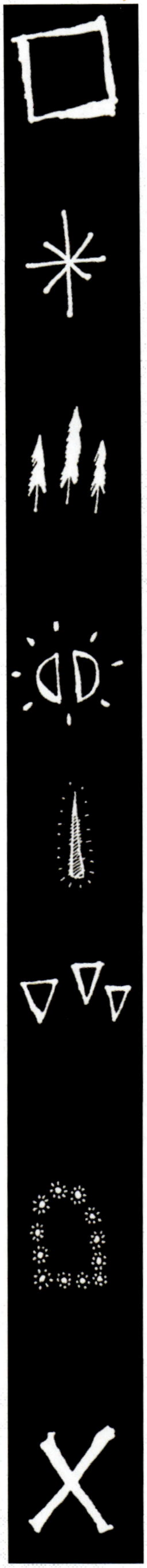

Square
An opportunity to be taken. You must move toward opportunity.

Star
Guidance. Something that cannot be denied. Recognizing your connection to the universe.

Trees
Growth. Being aware of what is around you and that it will affect how you grow. Connection to nature.

Two Halves
There is more than one side to everything. Both sides are equal.

Unicorn's Horn
Great purity and rarity. Something magical.

Upside-Down Pyramids
Turning the rules of empire upside down. Creating your own system, free of control.

Window Surrounded by Flowers
An opportunity with many random possibilities. Choosing to engage in random connection.

X
Something bad. Something to be avoided.

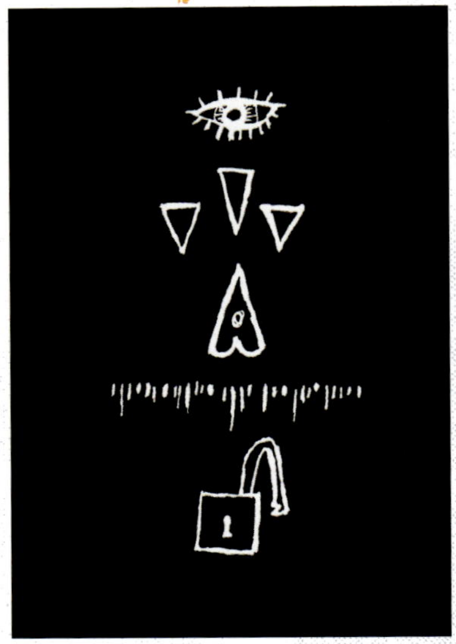

Symbols used in *Becoming a Chief*.

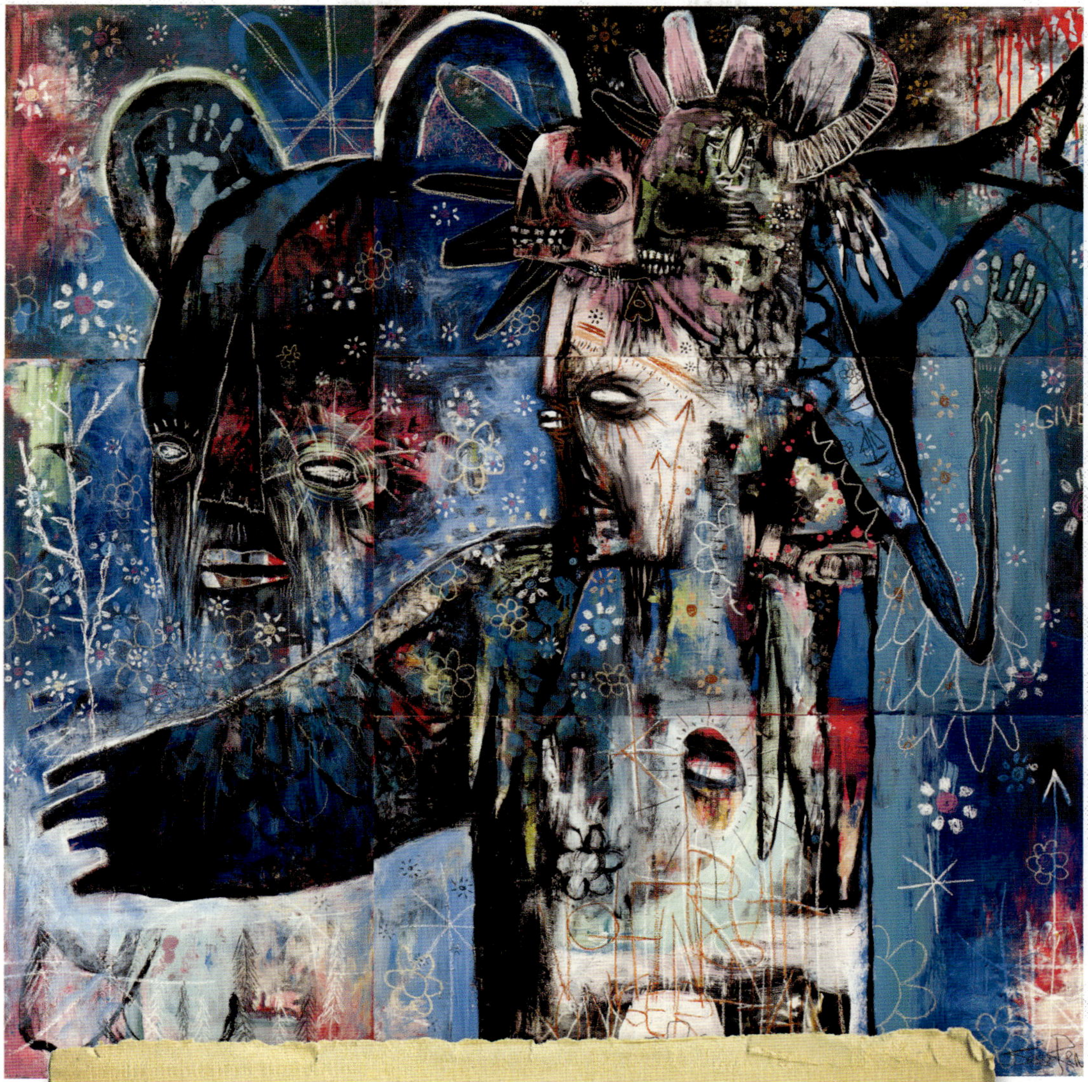

## Becoming a Chief

becoming a chief
impatiently waiting for
always rising
he reached into the ocean and befriended the captain of the sea
rings expanded from the center outward
if you're looking for godzilla he is in the sea
eggs from stones
transformation mask
the example only half erased
better than nothing
look inside
separate from boundaries
there is no edge for pure intention
no hard question for truth
nothing stronger than the truth
a branch is equal to a wand to a wise man give

# unique stories, free from expectation

**by Orly Avineri**

*A bird doesn't sing because it has an answer, it sings because it has a song.*
—Maya Angelou

Deep inside me lives my soul bird (a Hebrew phrase). She constantly reminds me of my boundlessness and I am glad she does, because I tend to forget. My soul bird is my art. She is my window through which I see farther than my own words and worlds, the opening through which I feel my freedom, loudly, clearly and oh-so sweetly. At times my soul bird flies out and brings back with her visitors to my soul to ease my casual loneliness. My soul bird is majestic.

I make art by way of visual journaling. It brings out the songs I have. I do it not because I feel the need to perform but because I feel the need to create, to create for the purpose of connection. Connection to myself, to others near and far, and ultimately to the space I occupy—the physical world I am a miniscule part of. There are countless magnificent invisible lines tying it all together. My intention is to recognize as many of them as possible and make them visible.

It is through the process of making art that I feel these invisible lines swaying me, moving me, enlivening me. I do it to feel the cyclical events that take place at any given moment, to feel that I am a sentient being. The actual physical process convinces me time and again that a creative block is merely the darkness from which all light originates. It is the crisis from which surrender emerges. Surrender soon brings about true freedom of raw and honest expression.

Contradicting elements of dark and light, such as ebb and flow, decay and bloom, war and peace, should be not only welcomed, but invited into our creative process. They should be allowed to become integral parts of a journey of self-discovery, growth and healing. They remind us to focus on our deep yearnings not to produce but to create. They remind us to break the structures that were meticulously built by us and by those who came before us, the forms that stifle our spirits.

We are here to unveil what we have veiled too long. To recall all there is to recall from deep within. To know that all we really need is right here in front of us and within us. When we start creating we need to first become completely hollow and empty—empty of wishes, expectations, pre-told stories and choreographed dances. We need to want absolutely nothing when we set out to create. Resistance or the willingness to fail will define the nature of our experience.

If we accept all that to be true, we should be able to let go of anything we've previously created, no matter how magnificent we believe it is. To disengage emotionally from it and instead welcome what comes to be next. To be able to cover up and start over. To stop seeing our creations as monuments. They are not, they are fragments of our souls that we brought forth. All we should be after is finding the songs that nourish and support us to no end, gently and steadily.

The creative process is one that blends our paradoxes. In it we give voice to what is obvious to us and to the mysterious as well, to our fear and our courage. Through it we express our tactile and visceral worlds. It's a state of self-love, trust and acceptance that manifests in a physical act. This act does not involve our intellect or what we call knowledge. Its nature is raw, instinctual, intuitive and improvisational. It meets our need to live rich and sensuous lives.

The storyboard here represents eight of the many phases one journal spread went through. Each one prepared the stage and made room for the next. The visual narrative was not told here by me but rather emerged on its own, facilitated or accommodated by my creative process.

*At bottom every man knows well enough that he is a unique being, only once on this earth; and by no extraordinary chance will such a marvelously picturesque piece of diversity in unity as he is, ever be put together a second time.*
—Friedrich Nietzsche

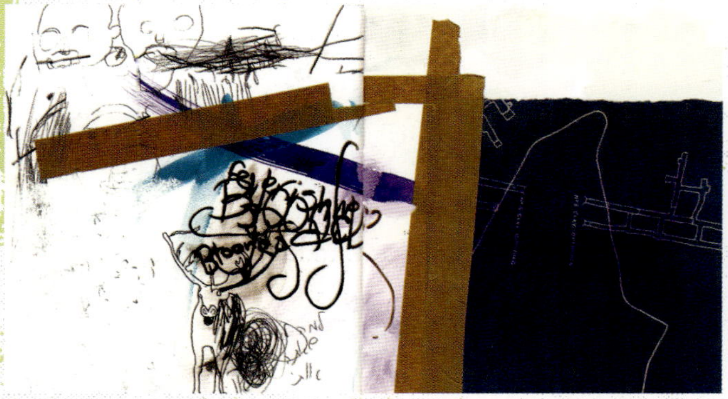

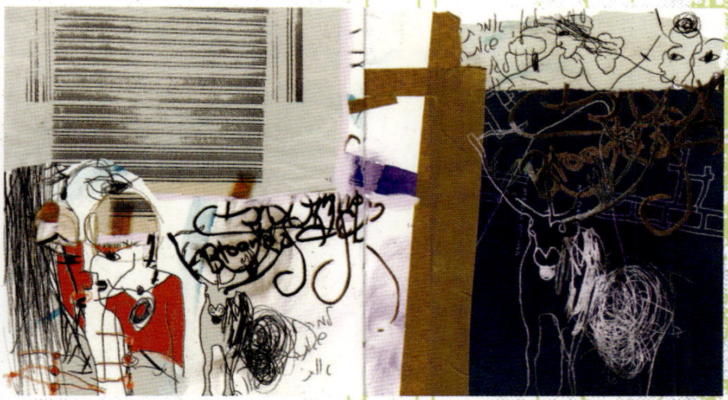

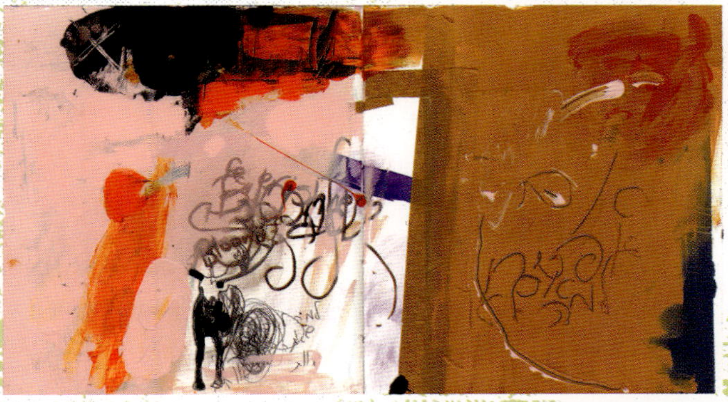

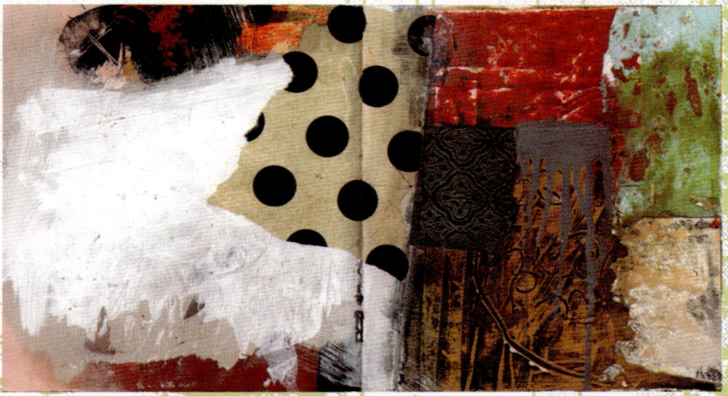

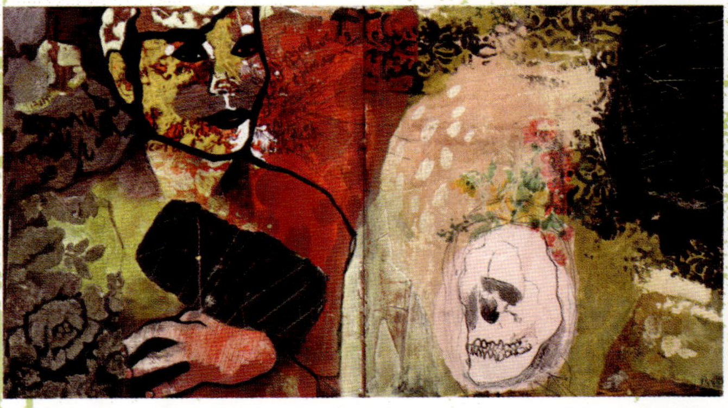

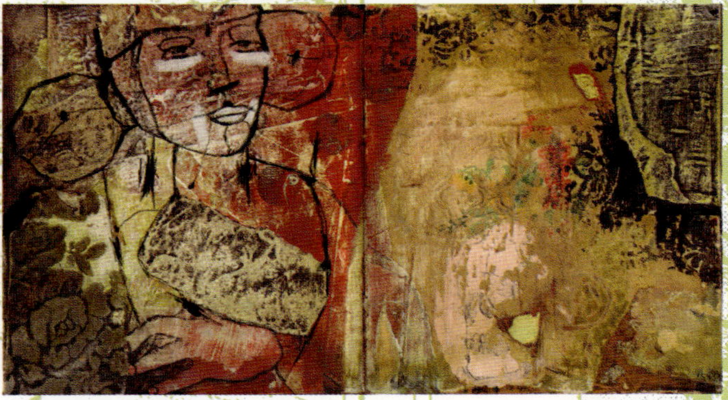

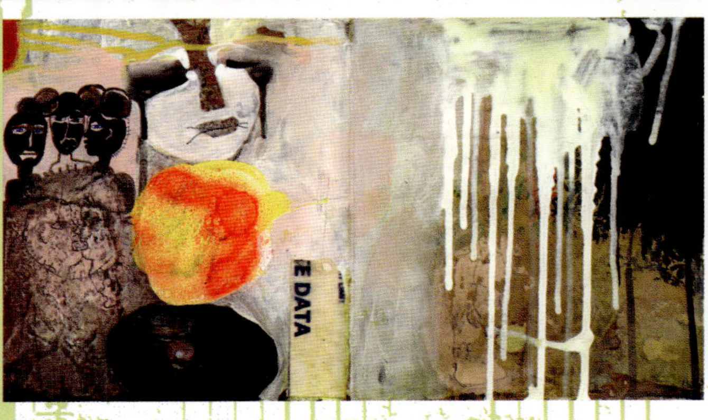
E DATA

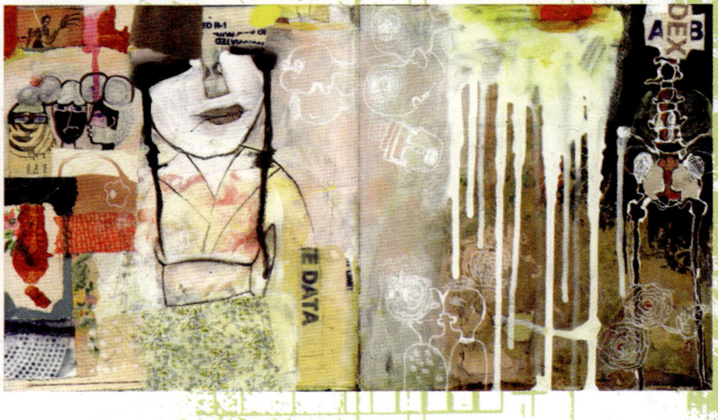
E DATA

# telling my story, a tapestry collaged

**by Roxanne Evans Stout**

I have always loved the way tapestry rugs look as they age, or how they look when they are overlapped in a room, each square or portion telling a different story.

When I was in New York City a few years ago, I saw a beautiful rug that seemed to be made of squares from different rugs. It was all sewn and pieced together creating beautiful color combinations and patterns.

### What You Need

- awl
- decorative papers
- fabric scraps
- matte medium
- needle and waxed linen
- paintbrush and water
- paper clips and small mementos
- ruler
- twine or wire

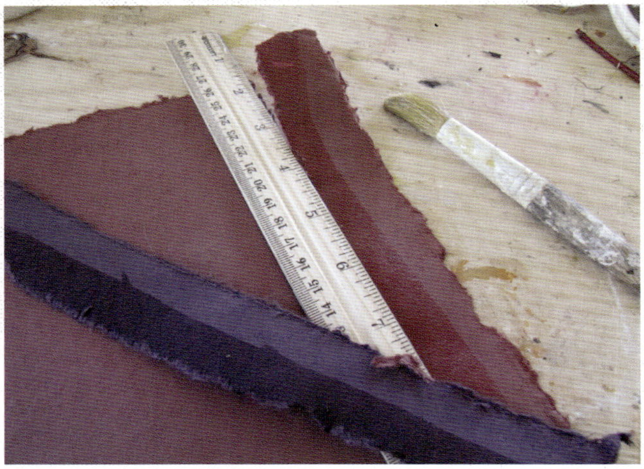

**1** When I began this project, I knew that I wanted to make a two-page spread in a book. I found the papers that I would be using for the background and tore them to the size that I wanted so the purple page was a little larger. To tear the paper, using a ruler as a guide, I painted two lines of water down the line that I wanted to tear. Then I carefully pulled the paper out so the edges looked the same as the original deckle edges. I learned and modified this method from artist Bee Shay.

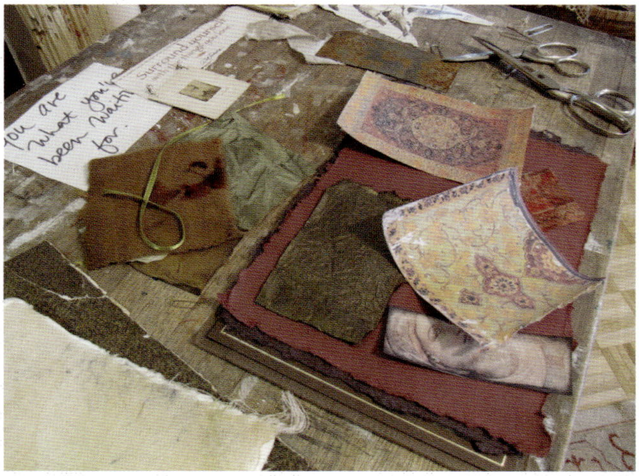


**2** I laid out various papers and fabrics that I wanted to use in this collage. I moved them around, playing with the design until it worked for me.

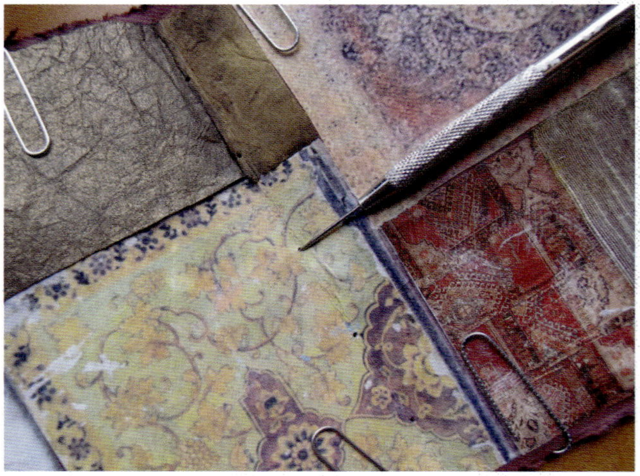

**3** After I adhered the papers with matte medium (and when it was dry), I folded them and poked five holes into the fold line with my awl.

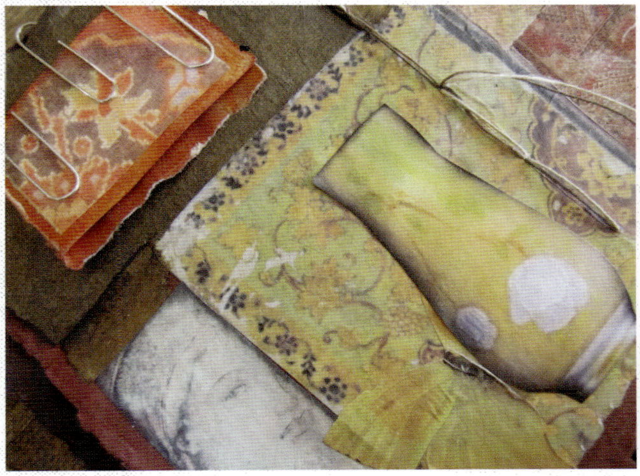

**4** I stitched the book together with a needle and waxed linen, using a modified pamphlet stitch.

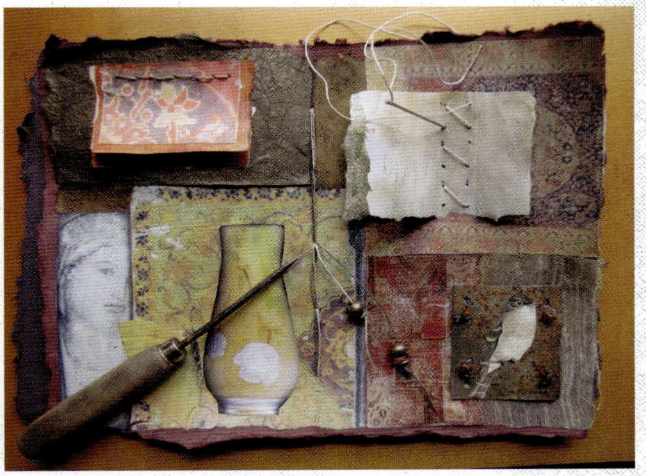

**5** I then attached the smaller pieces of art with paper clips—a tab, a small book and a metal piece—all things that I wanted to add to the collage.

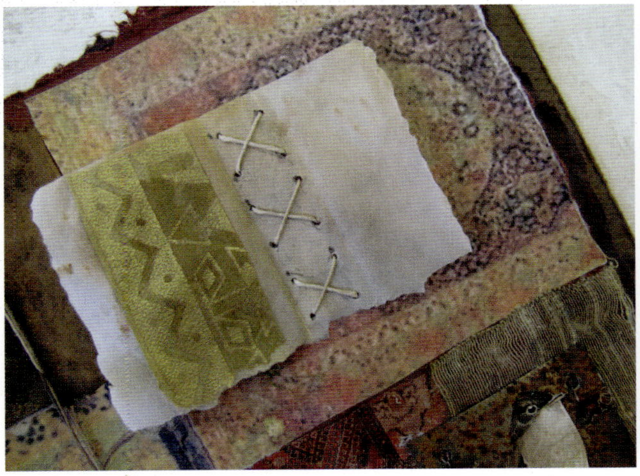

**6** I pre-poked holes and sewed the pieces to the book pages using twine or wire. Then I attached some small beads in some places.

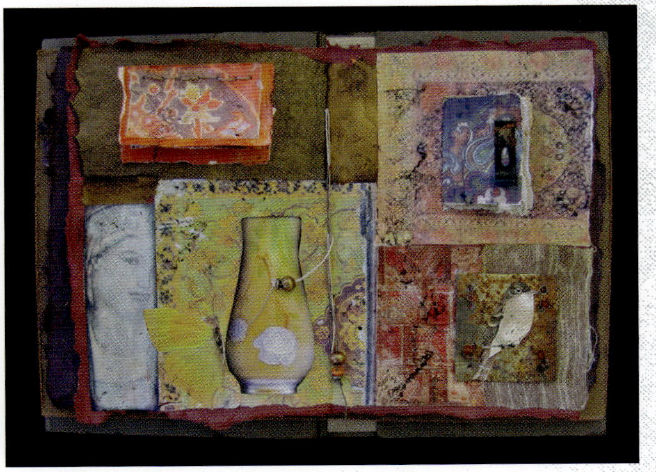

I had a rug in the back of my mind when I created this piece. In the piece, I am telling my story. I am sharing my love for warm and rich colors, for old patterns and textured papers, for fabrics and metal, and I am sharing my love for the natural world.

Alone each piece of this collage tells a story, but together all its parts become a whole—a tapestry of who I am.

exercise

# making marks, making meaning

Spend some time thinking about what symbols could be meaningful for you. Don't overthink it. A symbol you choose today might not be so important tomorrow or may have a different meaning entirely from one day (or moment!) to the next.

These are all techniques I use to loosen up and ensure a diverse and interesting variety of marks in my paintings.

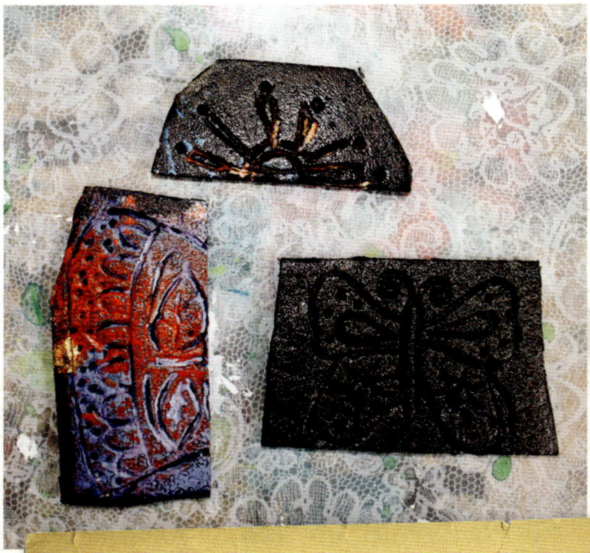

### What You Need

- cardboard scraps
- fine-mist spray bottle of water
- foam stamps
- Golden Fluid Acrylics
  - Turquoise (Phthalo) (optional)
  - Quinacridone Burnt Orange (optional)
- mark-making tools (skewers, eye droppers, etc.)
- oil pastels, including white
- paintbrushes
- paper (drawing or watercolor)

### Personal Stamps

One of my favorite ways to make personal stamps is to use the foam base of a pizza or meat tray, washed carefully and cut up into small pieces. Alternatively, you can also buy a product called Scratch-Foam at many art supply stores.

Draw your symbol or design onto the foam and once you are happy with it, use your pen to etch a deeper line, creating a stamp that is totally your own, that can be used multiple times!

### Symbol Journal

Start a symbol journal and spend time each week sketching designs and images you come across. Ask yourself, "If this design was to mean something to me, what could it mean?" Don't get stuck on trying to come up with something profound straightaway. Recognize that you are a beautiful, changeable soul and a symbol could mean something different to you today, tomorrow or next month.

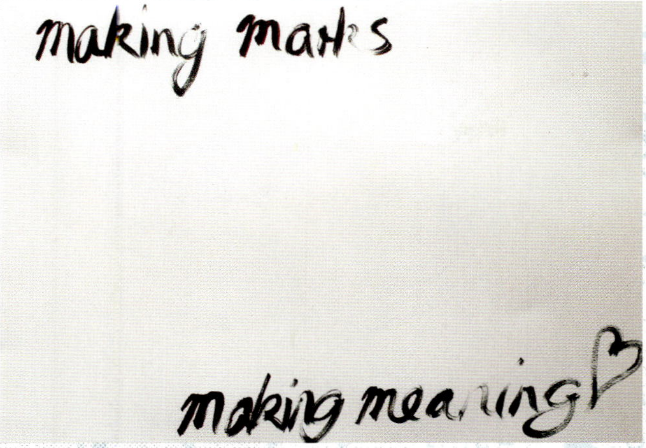


**1** Mix up a dark color, using two acrylic paints. I very rarely use black when I paint, and my favorite combo to make a dark is to mix Turquoise (Phthalo) with Quinacridone Burnt Orange. You could also mix any deep blue and deep red. Also choose two water-resistant oil pastels, one white and one in a color you love.

On a piece of paper (drawing or watercolor) loosely paint in the title of this project, "Making Marks, Making Meaning."

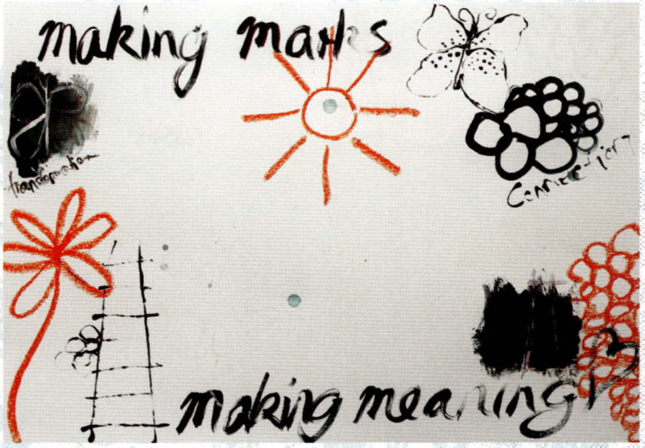


**2** Paint and draw your symbols using a variety of mark-making techniques. Experiment with a bamboo skewer to make delicate marks (e.g., the butterfly and ladder you see here).

Paint swatches of dark paint and scratch into them so the white paper shows, or paint your image in white over the top. Use a couple of different size brushes and play with the following: holding your brush loosely, varying the pressure of brush on paper as you paint the line, painting with your nondominant hand or painting with your eyes closed.

Draw in some of your symbols with the white and the colored oil pastels. Don't be afraid to overlap your images and work fast and loosely. Add in some words that speak about the meaning of your symbols and put it aside to dry.

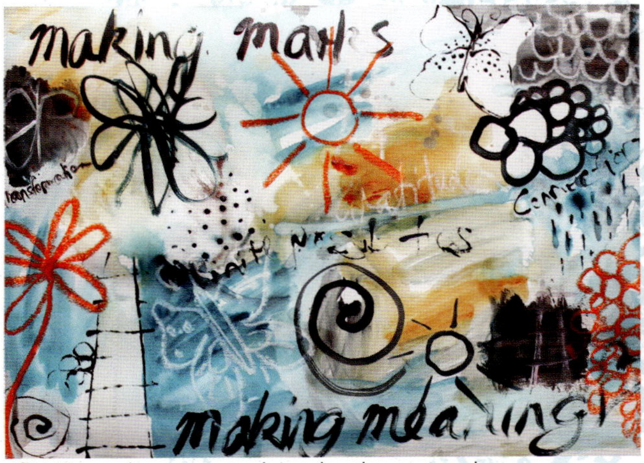


**3** When the paint is dry, take the two colors you used to create your dark, and drip them onto your painting in several areas. Spray with a fine-mist spray bottle to get the paint moving, and move the paint around with a brush in some areas. Leave a few places white for contrast and visual interest. The white oil pastel will resist the watery paint, and your symbols will pop through!

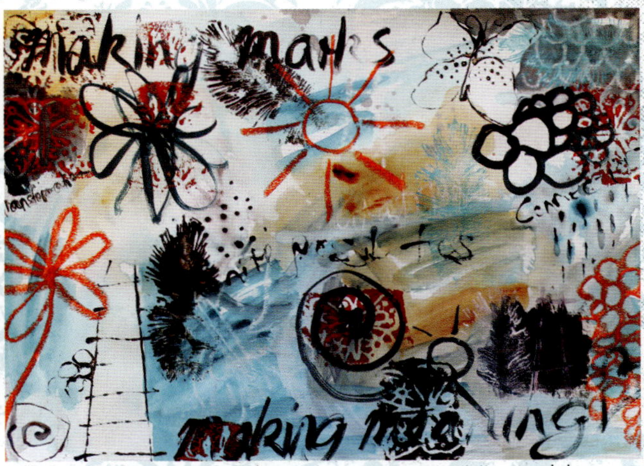

**4** Once the paint is dry, use some stamps to add some more fun symbols. Use variations of the colors that are already in your painting so the work is cohesive. I included one of my favorite feather stamps and used paints in white, Burnt Orange, Teal and my previously mixed dark shade.

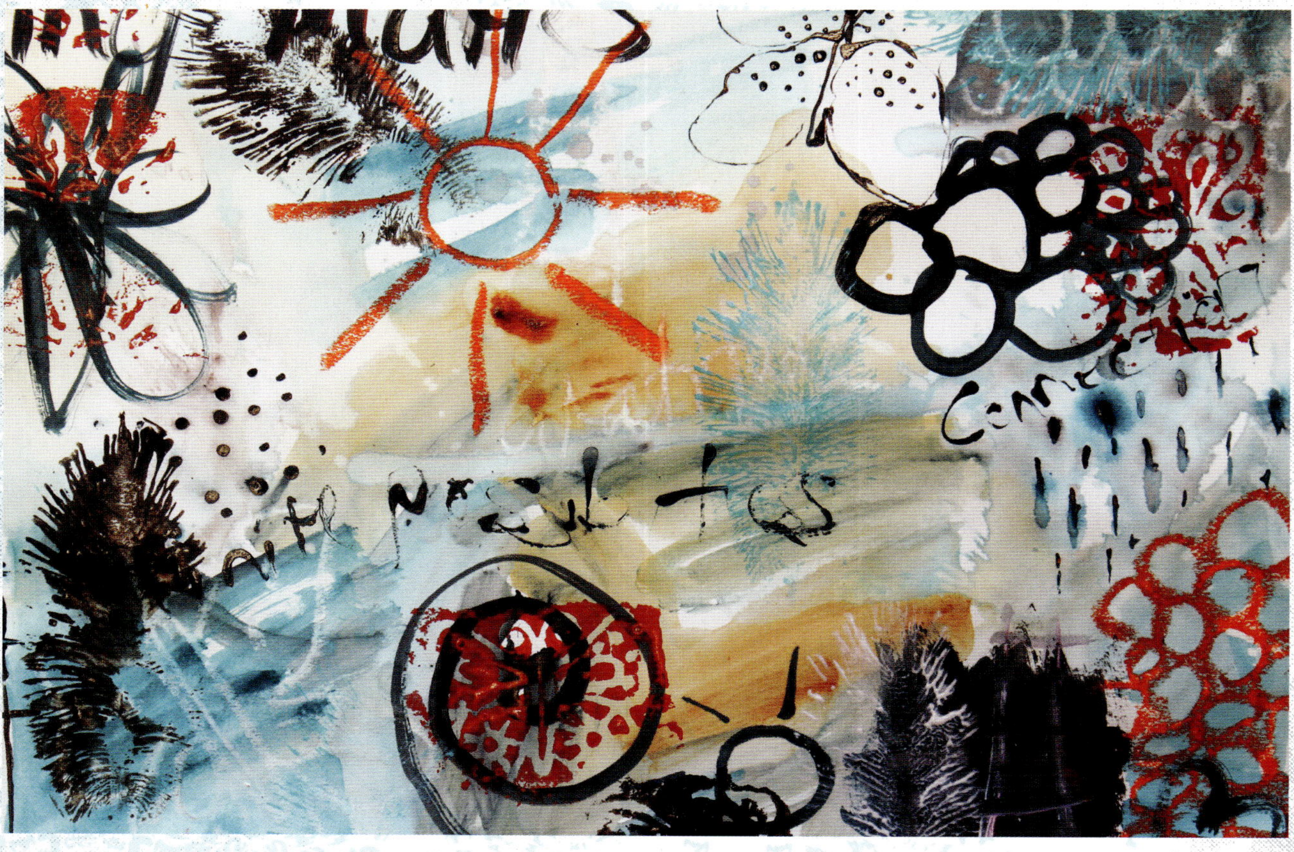

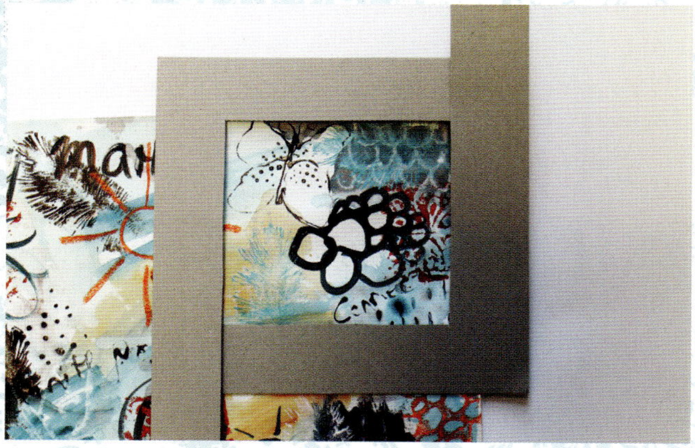

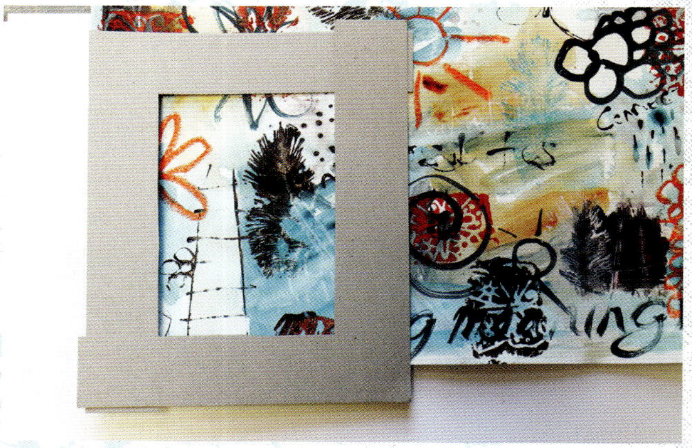

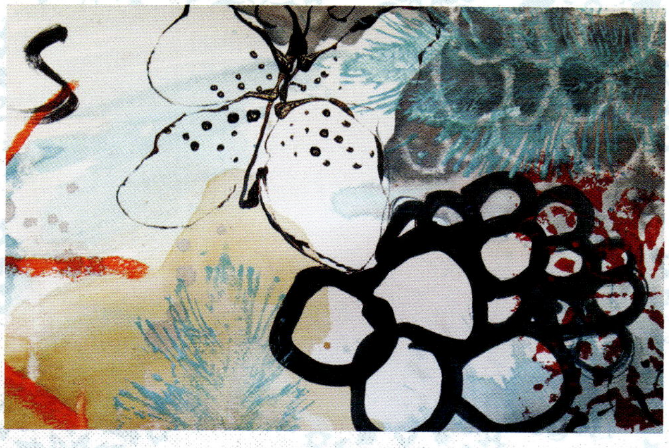

**5** Make yourself a simple viewfinder using two L-shaped pieces of cardboard. Move them around the painting, looking for interesting compositions.

This is a fantastic way to train your eye to see what works in your paintings and why. Make visual notes and try to understand why you instinctively feel that a cropped area works. Is there a strong contrast? A balance of shapes? A diversity of mark? Find several areas that feel right and mark them with a pencil.

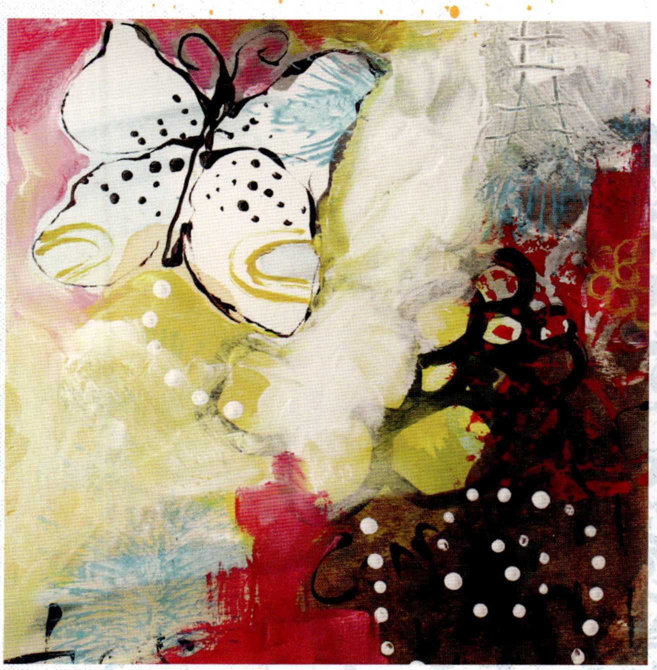

**6** Cut out your mini paintings and play with them! Use these small works to explore and experiment. You don't have to be precious about it. It's just paper!

Here you can see I added two totally new colors: Quinacridone Magenta and Green Gold (with a little white thrown in). I skimmed the colors around my butterfly and over the other symbols in various degrees of opacity, then scratched in another ladder in the top right corner.

The little white dots, added with the end of the bamboo skewer, and the ladder, help to lead the eye around the painting. Fun!

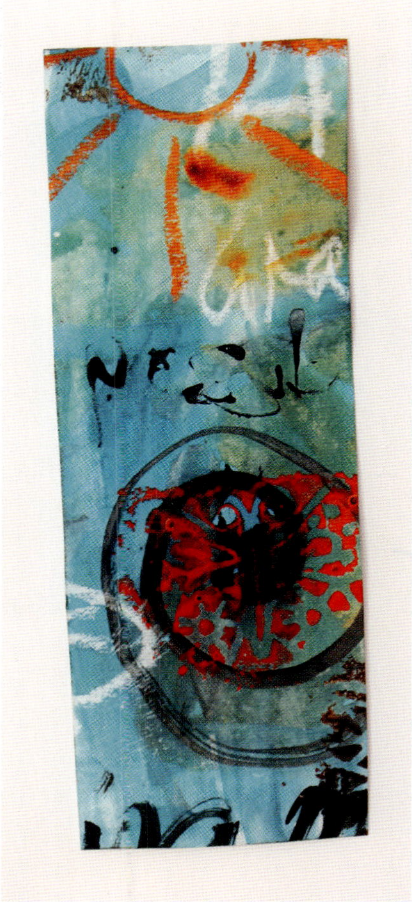

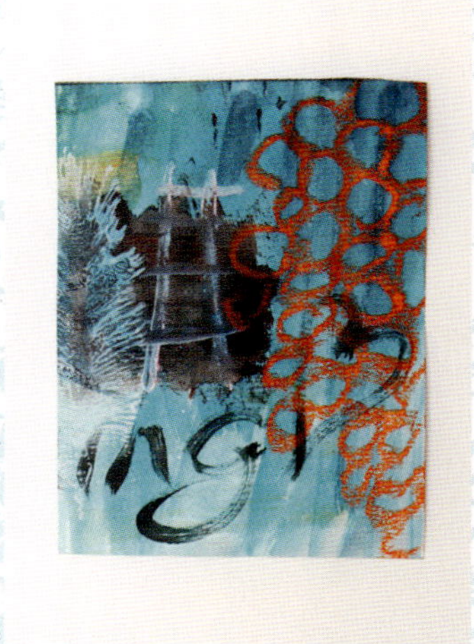

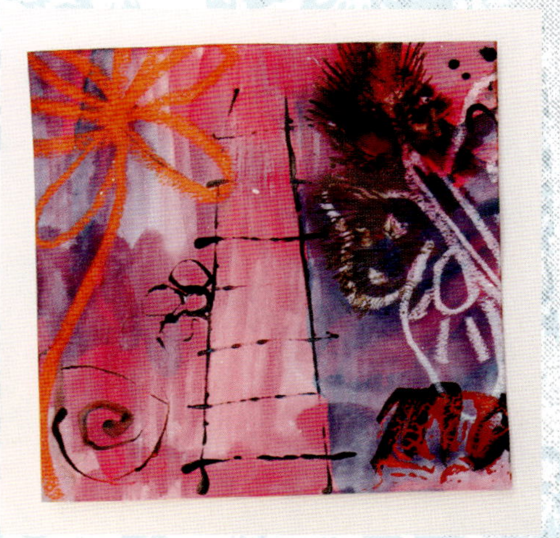

**7** You can also create some striking mini paintings by glazing one color only over the entire work.

In these examples, I used Turquoise (Phthalo) and Quinacridone Magenta. You can use a glazing medium or thin a paint down with water to a consistency that allows all of the lovely variations to show through.

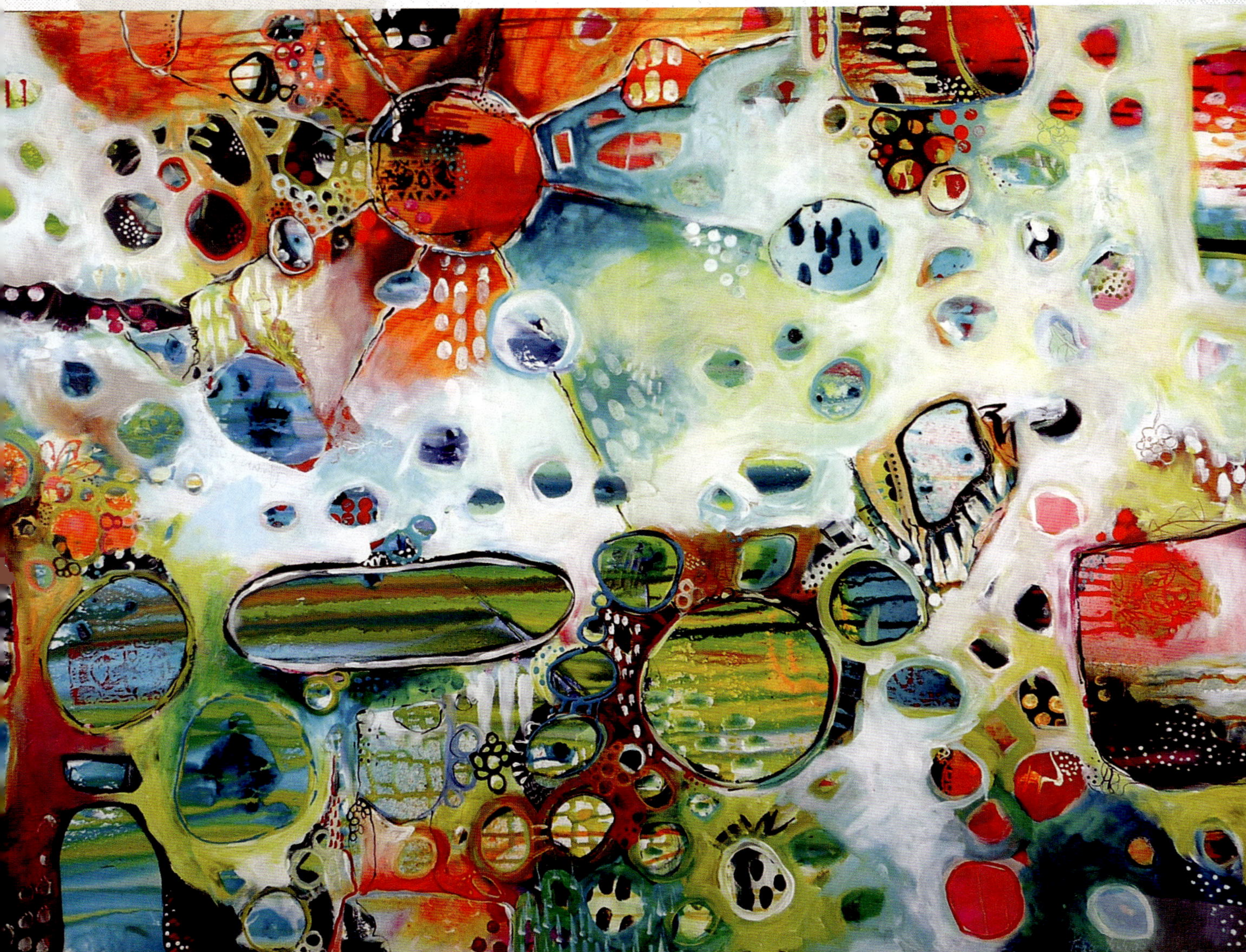

# chapter two: the spaces between

## Listening to the brilliant beauty within

Why are we all in such a hurry? Where are we going, why do we need to get there so fast and how much are we missing along the way? (I have to admit I get a little kick out of seeing crazy, impatient drivers overtake me only to find themselves right there in the lane next to me, up the road a bit, stopped at the next red light.)

I started painting at the turn of the millennium, clumsy, naïve paintings of ideas formed from our travels in Mexico. I was totally inept with acrylics, had no clue how to make them work and nine times out of ten would end up super-frustrated at my inability to get what was in my head out onto the canvas!

I remember seeing other artists' works—beautiful, layered, energetic abstracts, blended with realistic elements—and would scrutinize them endlessly, looking for some clue as to how I could make such wondrous things appear from the end of my brush.

One November day with the magnificent bottle-brush tree in blossom and a late spring breeze blowing, I felt a spontaneous rush of creative energy and dragged the biggest canvas I had ever tackled out to the back garden.

Grabbing a big brush and a shade of bold lime green house paint, I approached the canvas like Jackson Pollock, wrenching the lid from the can of paint and flinging its contents across the canvas. With my brush I made deft strokes this way and that, letting my gut guide me and revelling in the sploshing and dripping! Then, striding back into my studio, I grabbed a can of hot pink spray paint and let it fly as well!

This is how it happens, I thought! All you need is the confidence to do what you feel and the masterpiece will appear!

*Even after all this time, the Sun never says to the Earth, "You owe me." Look what happens with a love like that. It lights the whole sky.*
—Hafiz

When I was done I put down the spray can, looked at my canvas and in one second, my exuberance was replaced by an overwhelming feeling of depletion, followed quickly by a barrage of self-doubt.

My canvas looked like crap!

It was many years before I tried another abstract. Some six years later, however, fueled by knowledge and experience gained from three years of studying for a fine arts degree and many hours spent exploring workshops and artists' practices online and in person, I was ready!

So many times we are attached to the end result instead of enjoying the process. Will our art be liked, salable, popular, published, licensed? Will our art-making bring us peace, health, happiness, restoration? What value can we place on these things?

I'm learning to slow it down, breathe in the moment, recognize when I need to take a break, to lie on the grass and watch the clouds or walk on the white sand beach across the road. Things don't go well when I ignore that need.

While I wasn't happy with the end result of my painting on that spring day six years ago, I do remember the bliss I felt of creating in the moment. I can see now that I possessed the passion; all I was lacking was a bit of practical skill.

With the instruction and self-guided learning I have given myself over these recent years, I can now enjoy the process not the end result! (Most days!)

Close your eyes for a moment and just listen. What do you hear? Birds, cars, voices, your breathing? Listen more deeply to the exclusion of all else, and you will find yourself becoming still.

Listening can be a form of meditation. Many of my students tell me they find it hard to meditate, to find that quiet, still space amongst the plethora of thoughts (most of them on some crazy repeat cycle) racing around their heads. When you listen in a deeply focused way to the sounds around you, you will find your thoughts dropping away, slowly allowing you to feel more centered, more in the flow, more in the moment.

The more you can experience this stillness, the more you will be able to recall the way it feels to be in this place. The more you can recall that feeling, at will, the more you will be able to bring that peace with you, both when you are living your daily life and when you are in your creative zone.

The more you are in a deep state of peace while you are creating, the more the art you make will come from a place that is at once made up of your individual stories and connected to a place far greater than yourself. When I really feel that I have been in that place of quiet stillness, I can stand back from a painting when it is finished and say, "Whoa … Where did that come from?"

In his book, *The Spell of the Sensuous*, ecologist and philosopher David Abram describes an experience in which he is trapped in a cave in Bali when the first monsoonal rains of the season erupt. Unable to leave as the cave entrance transforms into two tumbling waterfalls, Abram becomes transfixed by the spider sharing the cave with him, rhythmically weaving its web. With his focus only on the spider's creativity, he ceases to even hear the torrents of water pouring down just steps away.

From this focused intent, this slowing down and being at one with whatever is around us, happening to us right now, Abram suggests we are tapping into a form of magic used by indigenous healers over thousands of years.

In her poem "The Stillness and the Waiting," aboriginal artist and writer Miriam-Rose Ungunmerr-Baumann speaks of the concept of deep listening:

"Our aboriginal culture has taught us to be still and wait. We do not try to hurry things up. We let them follow their natural course—like the seasons."

It was important to the aboriginal people to practice deep listening, as this was the way in which their Dreaming Stories were passed from generation to generation, through music, dance and ceremony. The stories and spirits were also within the landscape, connected to each person through the lineage of distinct song lines. These song lines could be traced over forty thousand years of habitation in this vast country and encompassed law, culture and spirituality in a living, interconnected web.

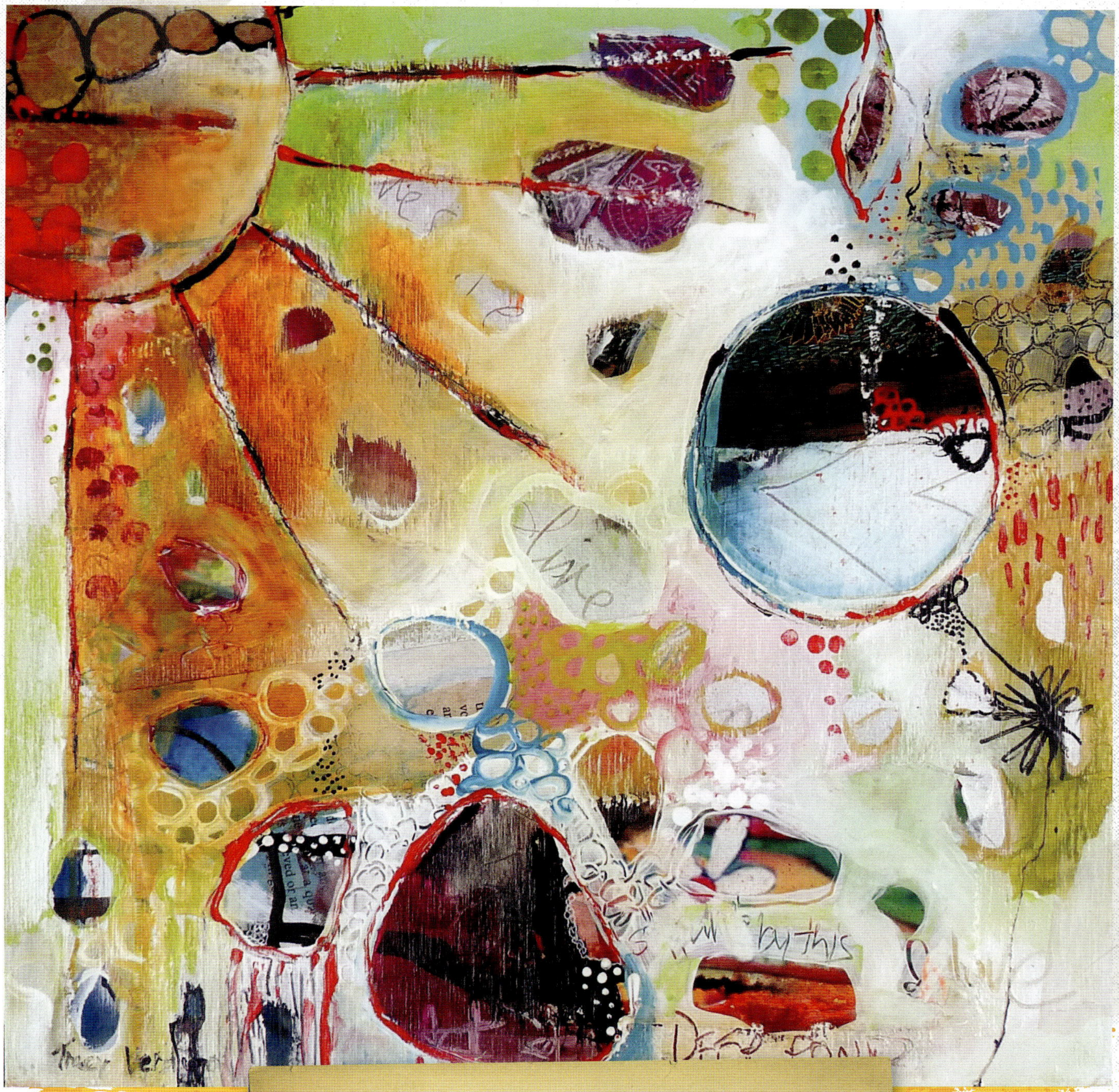

*For a day, for just one day,*
*Talk about that which disturbs no one*
*And bring some peace, my friend into your beautiful eyes.*
—Hafiz

It was incredibly important to really listen, to be in the flow, to be connected to the wisdom of past, present and future. Miriam-Rose speaks of deep listening as being a gift from the aboriginal people to all Australians. I would like to see it spread out as a gift to the entire planet, a call for centeredness and connection in a world that is sorely in need of such healing.

So many of us try to fill every second with noise or clutter or thoughts that clammer to be spoken even before we have finished our last sentence of before we have really listened to the one speaking to us.

Tapping into the stillness or "getting into the gap," as author and inspirational speaker Wayne Dyer calls it, allows us to enter the magical space where possibility lives and our most beautiful, creative ideas can flow through us.

When you slow down enough to regularly experience this flow, you will find that serendipitous moments begin to happen more often, and your intuition leads you to the people and places you need to connect with.

It's wonderful to dream big but it's also easy to get ahead of ourselves. Creative people are often buzzing with ideas, jumping ahead of themselves with excitement over an epiphany, only to wish later that they had slowed down a little, thought things through or waited for the right opportunity to let their idea bloom.

Sometimes our brilliant ideas are like little rough stones and we need to polish them for a while to see the fiery opal inside. I know about this kind of impatience because I've lived it—many times.

Maybe Ira Glass says it best:

"For the first couple years you make stuff, it's just not that good … We know our work doesn't have this special thing that we want it to have. We all go through this … It's gonna take a while. It's normal to take a while."

Patience, grasshopper, patience. I feel your creative yearnings, dear reader. I feel them in my heart. It's all about the timing. Keep painting and learning and painting and learning and painting and learning. Cultivate the stillness within and know that it's all possible. Your season will come.

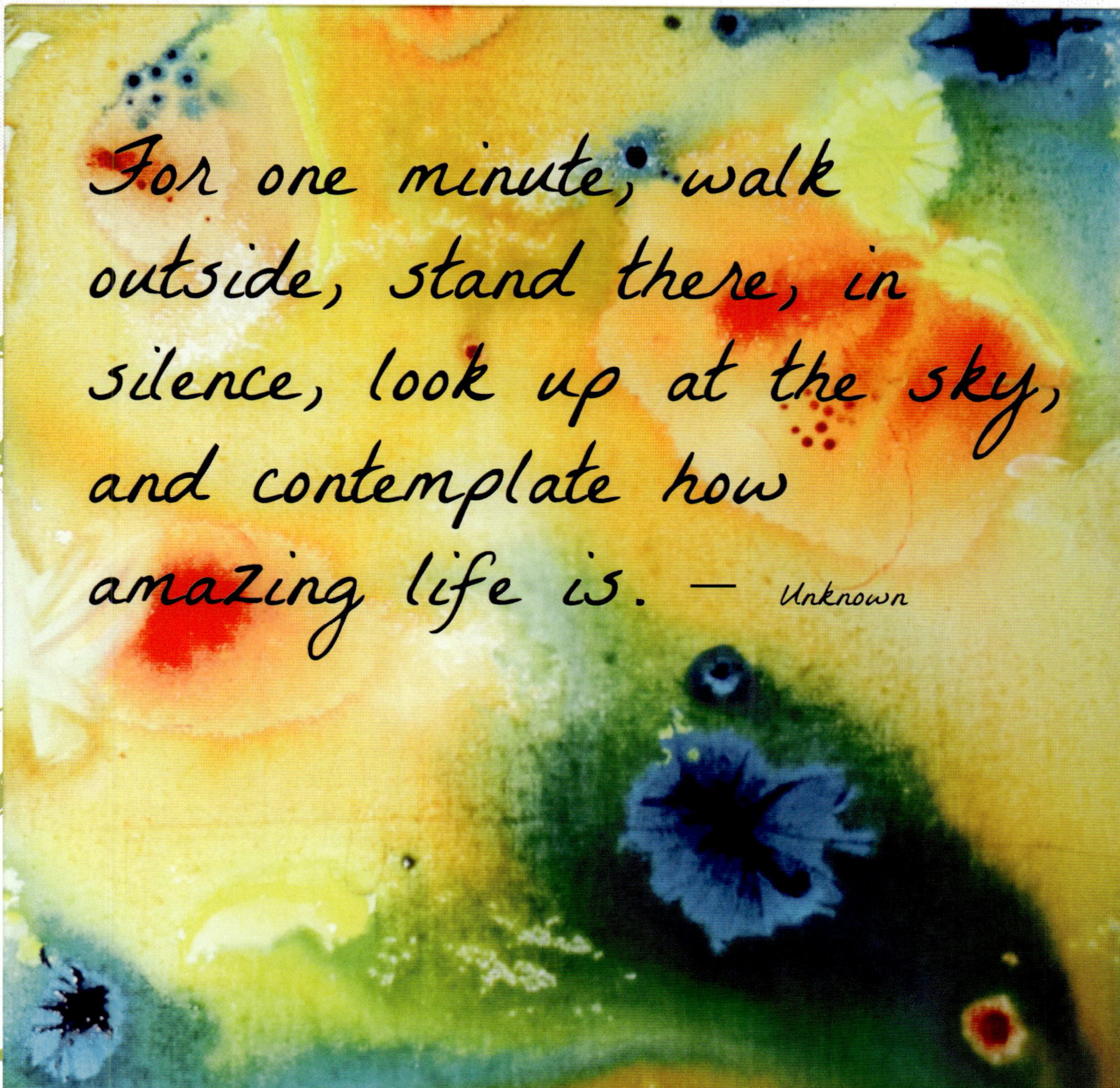
For one minute, walk outside, stand there, in silence, look up at the sky, and contemplate how amazing life is. — Unknown

# personal narrative

by Juliette Crane

I've learned to get out of my own way whenever I create. This allows the true beauty in the process to come forth, and to know that it's not always about trying to create something specific on a given time line. Following my instincts and allowing things to emerge in unexpected ways reveals the story in my heart.

A few years ago I wrote a three-hundred-page manuscript about a girl who could jump into her drawings. I wasn't painting at the time. I hadn't painted in years. All of my artwork had ended up in the basement. I didn't see any point in painting anymore and locked away that part of myself.

Yet I had to create something, so I started writing my novel.

I was one of fourteen writers accepted into a six-week writing workshop on the East Coast. I even flew out to Washington D.C. to meet with my literary agent.

But then I stopped writing.

My creative spirit was stunted from all of the writing critiques and constructive criticism. I had been convinced that because my voice was different, it wasn't right. So I'd written a novel that boxed my imagination in to fit a story that had already been told rather than letting my own unique strengths flow free.

I wasn't ready to share my story.

To get my spirit back, I returned to what I loved as a child: painting in my backyard. I dragged out all of my old art supplies and spread everything on a blanket in the grass. I still had the red plastic lunchbox filled with my Crayola crayons. I bought giant Masonite boards such as the ones I had loved painting on in college.

And I played.

That's what started all of my whimsical paintings and blossomed into a business I love. A year later, after I'd been painting lots of owls and girls, I felt paralyzed with my artwork. To get unstuck, I again went back to something I loved as a child: chalk drawing. I took my box of neon jumbo sticks and drew, sketching little characters on the bike path, sidewalks and our backyard patio.

I fell in love with one character with a big head, boxy body and little wings and feet. But my mind immediately thought it looked too goofy to be a painting. When I saw that same goofy character in the India ink splatters of one of my backgrounds, I completely resisted it. After a few failed attempts to make the character into something else, I went with my first instinct.

I moved the eyes higher up on the face and defined a long nose where I saw them in my background. I found vintage wallpaper in my paper collection and added it to the wings. I defined the hair and body with black India ink. Then I added my top coat and a beautiful mistake defined the body.

When I brushed the Mod Podge over the art tissue paper I'd used in my background, the color bled and despite loads of layers of acrylic paint, oil pastels and ink, the bright paper showed through and made the character look luminous.

It was then I realized, I'd painted a character from my novel.

I'd painted Snooter of the Backwoods, one of the characters my protagonist is told never to talk to or trust. Once I painted one Snooter, I couldn't stop. I fell in love with each one and their unique personalities.

Seeing each of these Snooters in my paintings reminded me to get back to writing my novel. After four years of setting it aside, my paintings helped me know the characters and gave a new depth to the story in ways I never could have planned. I knew then that these Snooters needed to play bigger roles. They may even lead me to write a second book.

Either way, I am excited to see just where my creativity takes me.

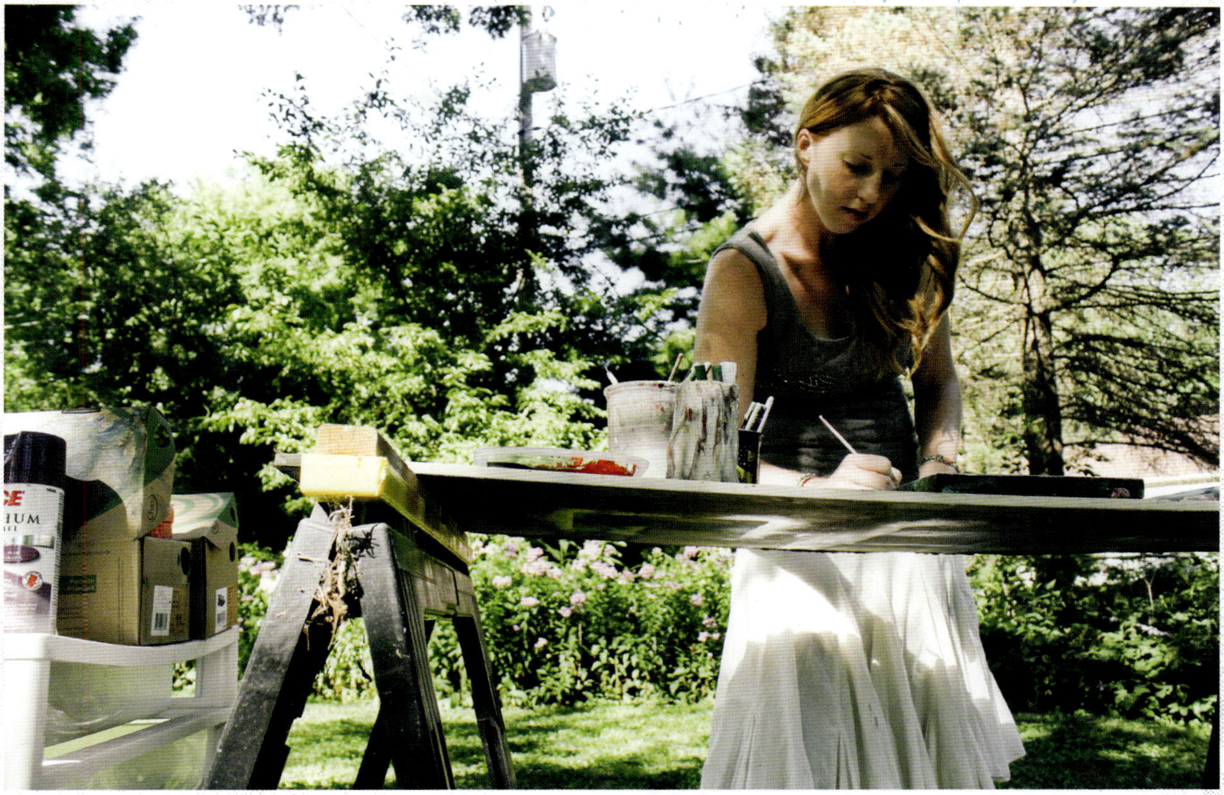

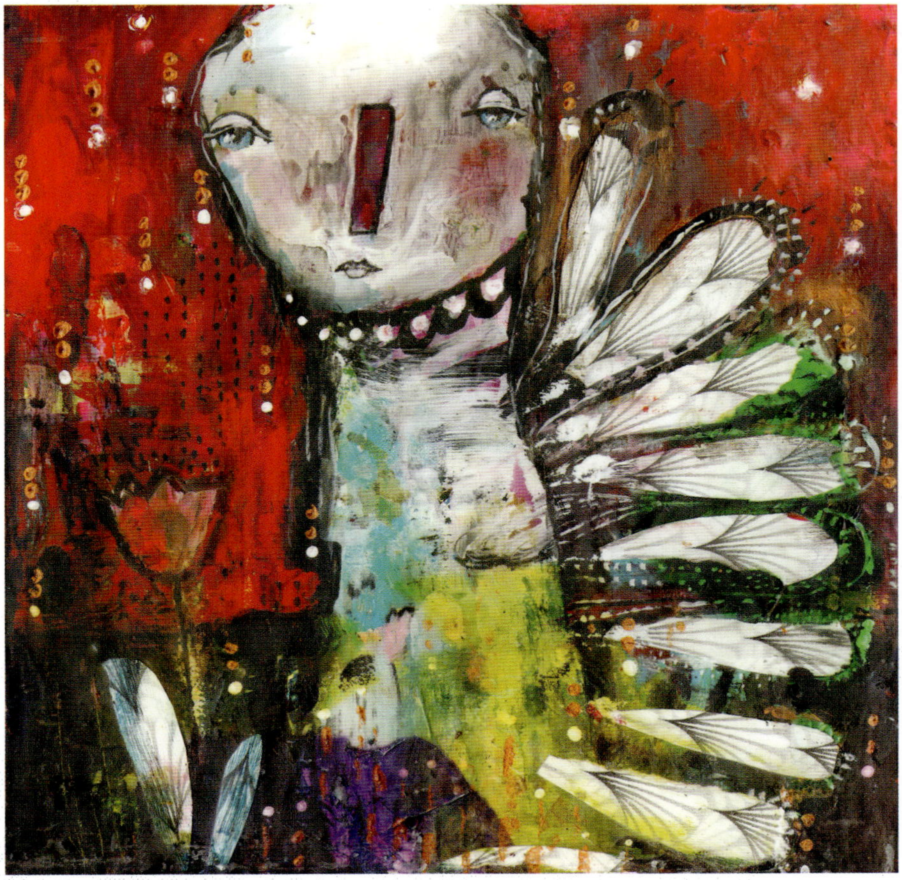

# the stillness of waiting

**by Judy Wise**

When Tracy gave me the subject for my painting, I was *deep in the stillness of waiting* myself. All my creativity felt shut down, the well of joy run dry.

I wrote this in my journal:

*How do I help others through this dark passage beyond advising them to wait and stay expectant? To do other things (clean the studio, journal, cook, visit other artists in person or online) and to survive any way you can until the muse returns. Not working is painful for any artist.*

Maybe it helps to know that it happens to all of us at times. We find ourselves feeling uninspired, maybe even depressed and out of sorts.

So we curl up and wait. We fill our hours with compassion for ourselves and practice being gentle within the process. We reassure ourselves that it always passes. My strategy is surrender and acceptance. I have, over the years, developed an unshakable faith in the cycles of abundance and renewal.

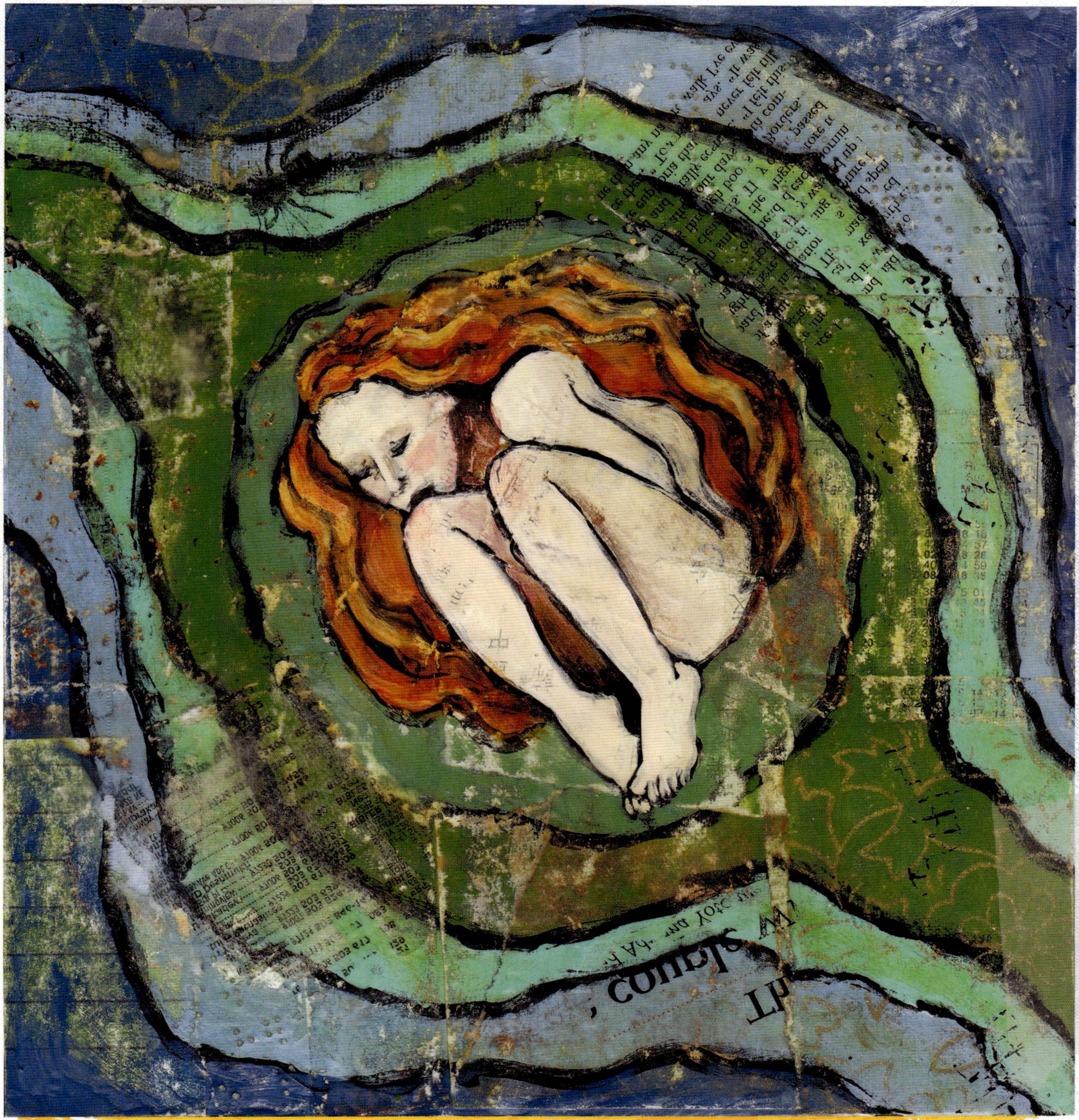

exercise

# sacred transformation painting

Before you start this exercise, put a timer on for twenty minutes and spend the time reflecting on the things that make you uniquely you. Get your thoughts down on a piece of paper or in a journal. Try not to think too much, just keep your hand moving and your pen writing.

If you get stuck, write down the words *I am* and see what comes. When you have finished, look over what you have written and highlight some words or sentences that really encapsulate the essence of who you are.

You might also like to light a candle or some incense or play some soft music during this exercise.

**What You Need**

- 12" × 12" (30cm × 30cm) canvas
- acrylic artists inks, either a warm or cool palette (I chose warms: pinks, reds, oranges)
- acrylic paints, your favorite colors, including white
- bamboo skewer
- fine-mist spray bottle of water
- gesso
- ink dropper
- oil pastels: white, silver, one other color
- paper towel
- small brushes, 2

**1** Begin with the dark shade of acrylic paint you mixed for your symbols in the exercise from Chapter One. Very loosely paint across the entire surface of your canvas the words and sentences you jotted down. Forget about perfection, just paint away.

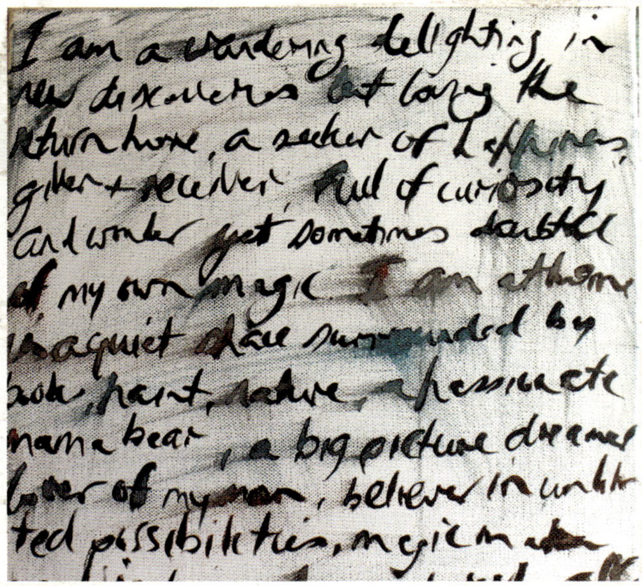

**2** Then with a paper towel, wipe away the excess paint to get ready for the next step. YES it looks messy and YES that's OK! Sometimes life is messy and that includes the real us!

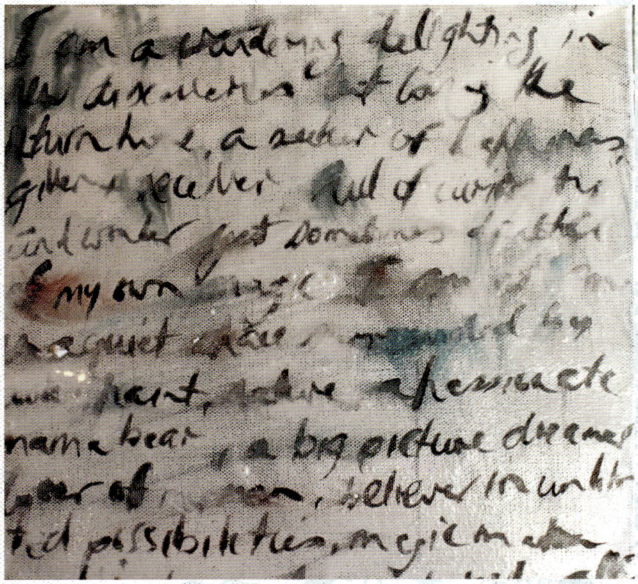

**3** Using some gesso thinned down with water, paint a layer across the entire canvas. This will make the words appear to be pushed back, but still be visible.

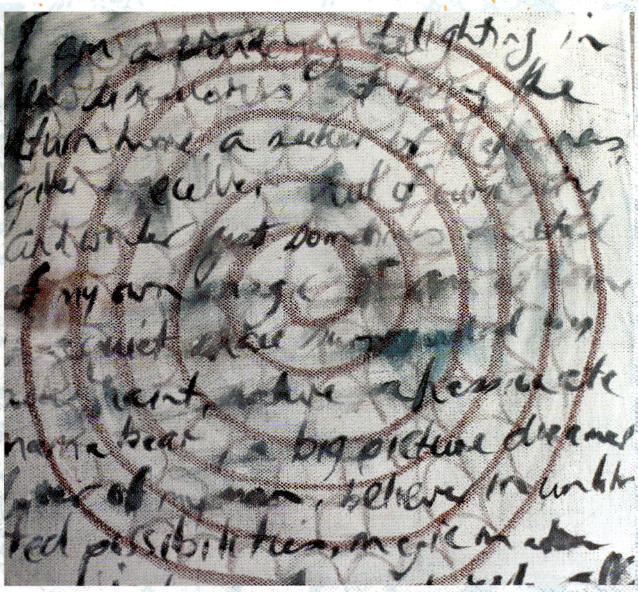

**4** Using a colored oil pastel and starting from the outside of the canvas draw a spiral, moving inward. Draw it slowly and deliberately with an intention of coming into your center, to the truth of who you are. Repeat the spiral with a white line next to the colored and then add a pattern over the top with the silver pastel. Think of it as a personal mandala spiraling in toward your authentic core.

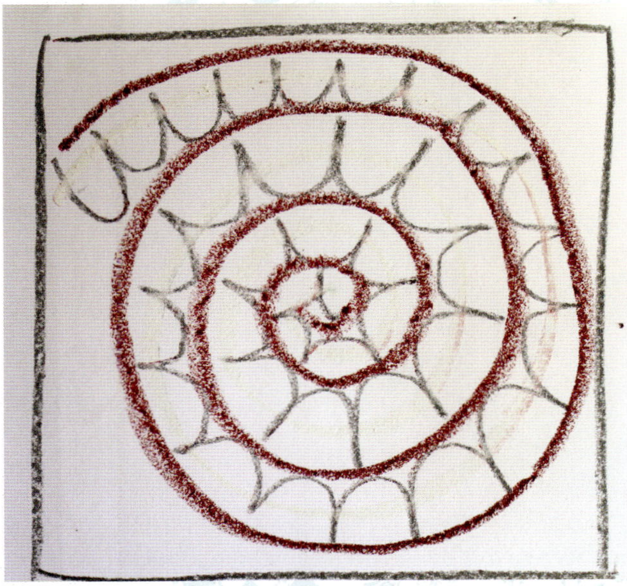

Here is a more clear representation of the design I used over my writing. Feel free to create your own patterns within your spiral, using marks that speak to you.

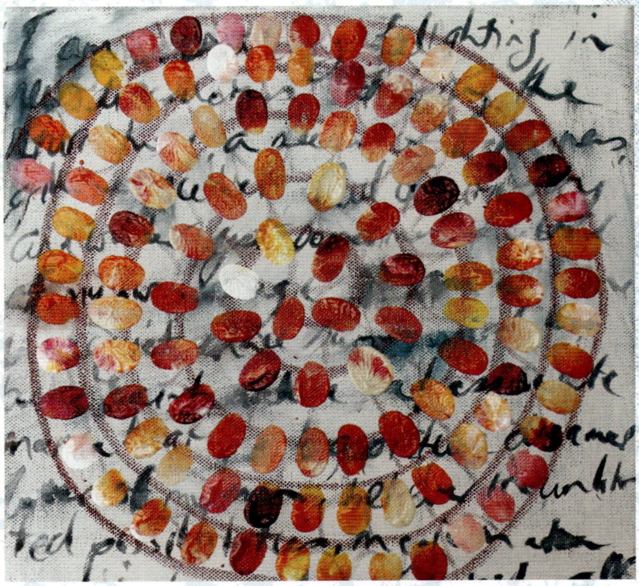

**5** Using four or five harmonious colors (colors that are close together on the color wheel) plus white, use your thumb or finger to mix different colors and apply your unique sacred mark to your canvas, repeatedly and slowly, contemplating the miracle of you and following the spiral from the edge of the canvas inward.

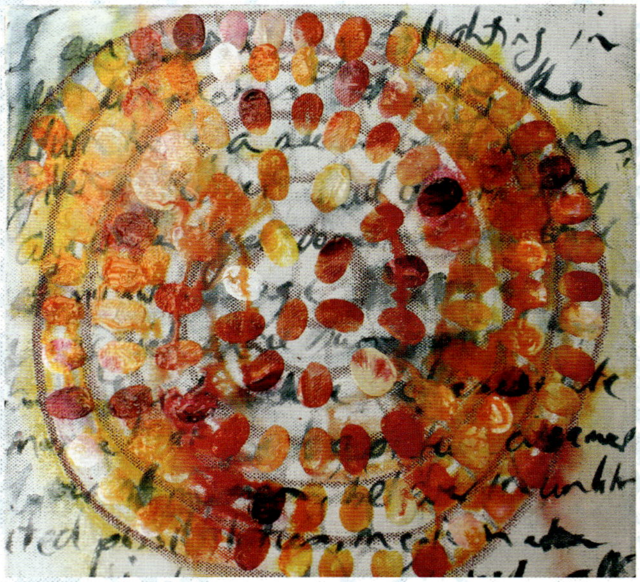

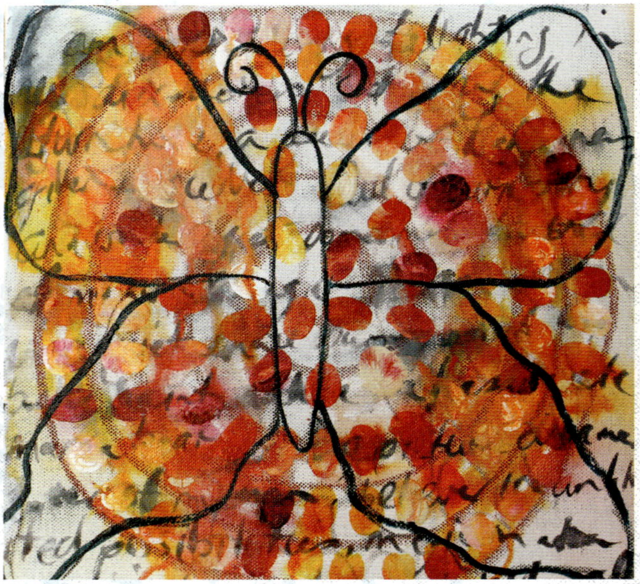

6 And then . . . just so we don't get all caught up in perfection again, give each quadrant a spray or two and let those marks loosen up and drip into each other. Remember, each move is a contemplation. Work slowly and don't overdo it.

7 Using your dark color, paint the outline of a butterfly or an alternative symbol that speaks to you. Use a pencil first if you like.

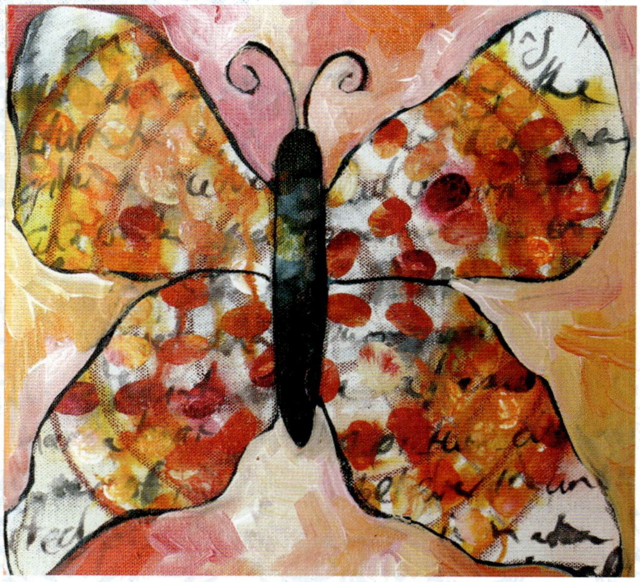

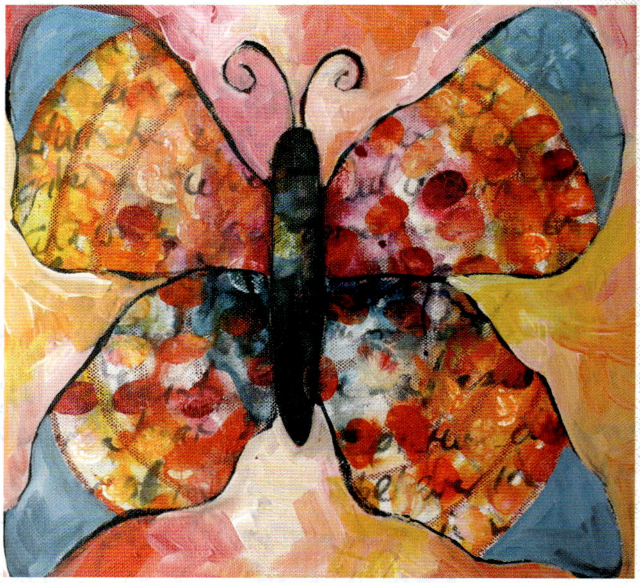

8 Water down a little of the dark acrylic and paint the body of the butterfly so you can still see through to the patterns beneath in some areas. Using the colors on your palette and white, roughly paint in the area around the butterfly, using bold and expressive strokes—transformation is exciting stuff! Allow the colors to meet and blend on the canvas! You could choose to finish your painting here or . . .

9 You might like to introduce an entirely NEW color! Here I used Turquoise (Phthalo) that made up half of my dark, mixed it with a little white and filled in the tips of the wings. I also used a little Phthalo thinned down with water to glaze across a section of the bottom wings (toward the body) and did the same with Quinacridone Magenta in the top wings.

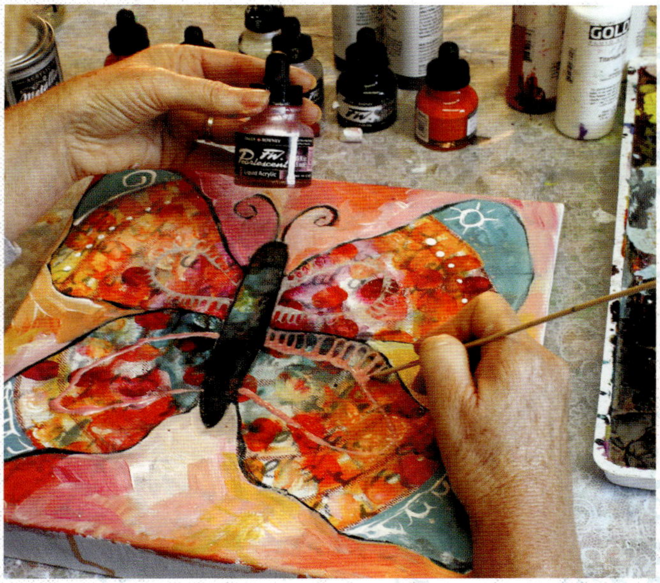

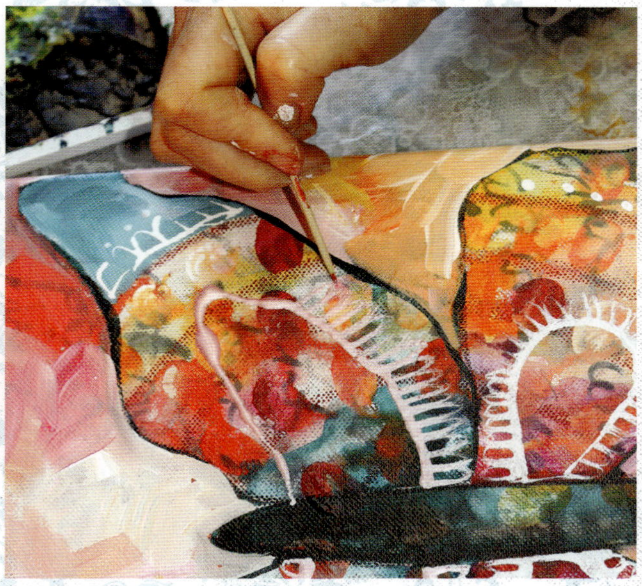

**10** Inks can add a beautiful layer across the top of acrylics, either dropped on and sprayed with water for a transparent glaze or to create intricate designs as I am doing here. Use the ink dropper to draw your main designs, and then play with a bamboo skewer to pull the ink away in more detailed patterns. I have used silver ink in the top wings and a rose-colored metallic on the bottom.

**11** I added in some more designs with white ink and my favourite color Flame Orange, and my Sacred Transformation painting is done!

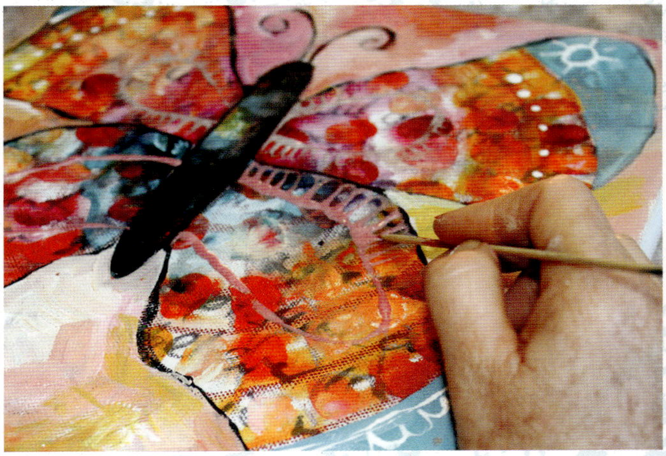

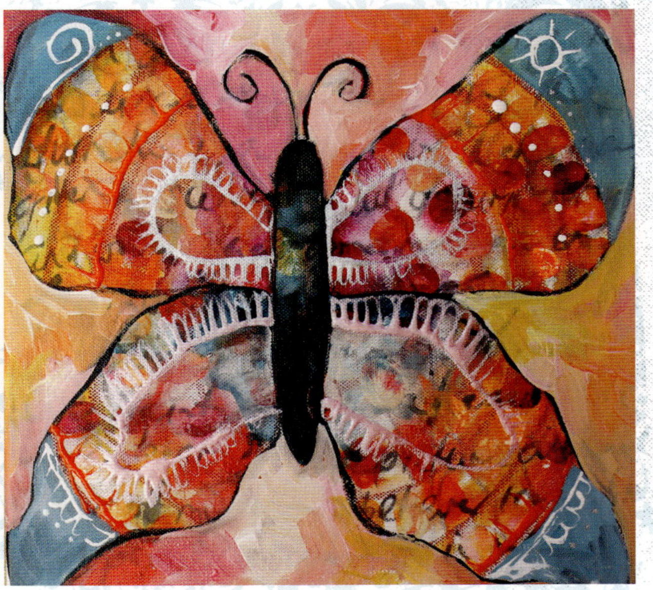

*Thanks to impermanence, everything is possible.*
—Thich Nhat Hanh

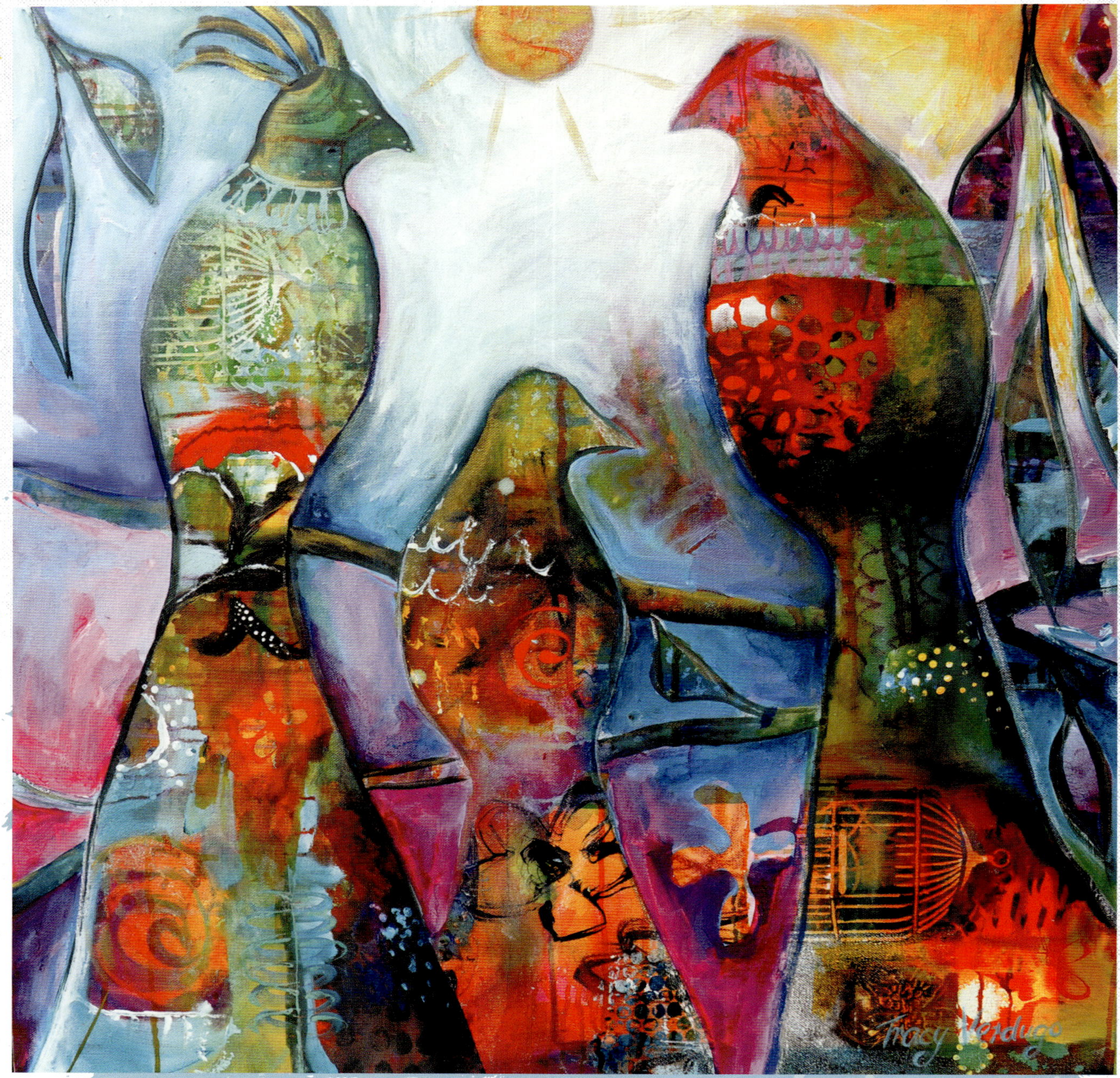
Tracy Verdugo

# chapter three: loosen up, lighten up

## Breaking free of our comfort zones and self-imposed restrictions

May I suggest something outrageous? Something that may seem to be a ridiculous idea in this world of schedules and traffic and terrorists and high cholesterol and ADHD, political correctness, GM foods and pharmaceutical ads for every ailment under the sun?

May I suggest that we are on the verge of a great remembering, a yearning for something so deep and so necessary that it is the number-one thing students say to me when they come to paint at my workshops?

May I suggest that we are wound so tightly in our collective striving for acceptance and belonging and attainment and recognition that we have almost forgotten how to relax, how to play, how to laugh, how to be silly?

"I want to loosen up," they tell me, one after the other, while the others in the group nod their heads in understanding and empathy. "I want to feel more free, less restricted."

It didn't take long for me to realize that I was in the game of teaching self-acceptance, to breathe through self-criticism and to release the need to compare ourselves to others, far more than I was teaching people how to blend colors and apply paint in diverse ways. I was teaching them to loosen up and lighten up.

At what age do we begin to censor ourselves? Little by little, bit by bit, we fall into the trap of comparing ourselves to those around us, vying for attention, competing for love, adapting our behavior to attain the greatest share of both.

*Freedom is not given to us by anyone; we have to cultivate it ourselves. It is a daily practice.*
—Thich Nhat Hanh

# wild abandon

Not long ago, my sister and her family came to stay. It had been several years between visits (Australia is a *big* country and we are spread out all over it). For the first time I got to hold my cute little nephew, Andre, all expressive eyes and coy glances, pudgy cheeks and Cupid's bow, pucker-up mouth. His face lit up when I asked if he would like to draw. At two years old I thought it might keep him busy for a few minutes.

Picking up the nearest thing I could find in my studio, I brought in a large sketchbook and a set of pencils, never anticipating the whirling dervish of creative fire that would emerge next. Small chubby hands gripped the pencils with passion and fervor, attacking the page with color and sprawling line, totally immersed in the doing.

At some point the drawing would be deemed finished and with barely a glance at what he had created, a total nonexistence of self-judgment (*hmmm, should I really have put that purple right there next to the orange?*). He was onto the next page, racing through that entire sketchbook with an intensity and joy that I have rarely encountered.

Totally in the moment, sprawled out on the patterned green and red Navajo rug in our adobe-walled lounge room, his face close enough to eat the page, sometimes with two pencils gripped tightly in one hand. His little arms moving with deliberate intention, spreading rainbows across the waiting white expanse.

When was the last time you allowed yourself to feel such abandon, to skip along the beach or play on the swings of the local park? What would the world look like if we stopped worrying about what we are *supposed* to do, stopped thinking about appearances and allowed ourselves to experience moments of play, silliness and abandonment?

And if you think for a moment I have it down pat, think again! I'm the girl who was so desperate for acceptance and approval most of my life that ten years into our marriage I would still casually leave the vacuum out in the hallway seeking approval and validation when Marco arrived home from work!

Even while I sit here today writing notes for this chapter on laughter and loosening up, I am competing with a noisy and incessant inner dialogue, which goes something like this:

*You can't say that! What are your credentials?*

*You need to go get some facts and figures to back that up!*

*Who are you to write a book? You're no Patti Digh/Anne Lamott/insert best-selling author here.*

*Really, people are going to think you're frivolous, making light of the things that are serious in their lives!*

Blahdity, blahdity, blah …

Loosening up requires a willingness on our part, a daily practice that first begins with being gentle to ourselves. Think about the ways that you are kind to the people around you, compassionate to the mistakes of others, encouraging and willing to see the beauty in the unfolding practice of a friend. Can you begin to treat yourself as well as you do others?

When we allow ourselves the privilege of unwinding, of softening into self-compassion and imperfection, we also begin to feel lighter, to laugh more and to appreciate how wonderful it is to make regular excursions into silliness.

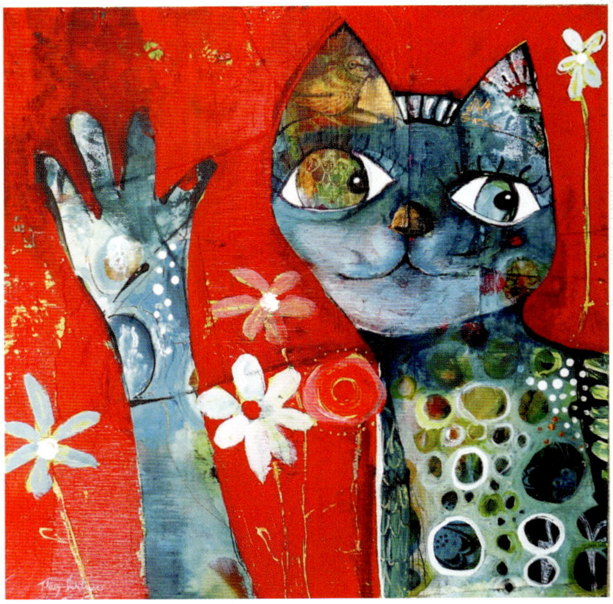

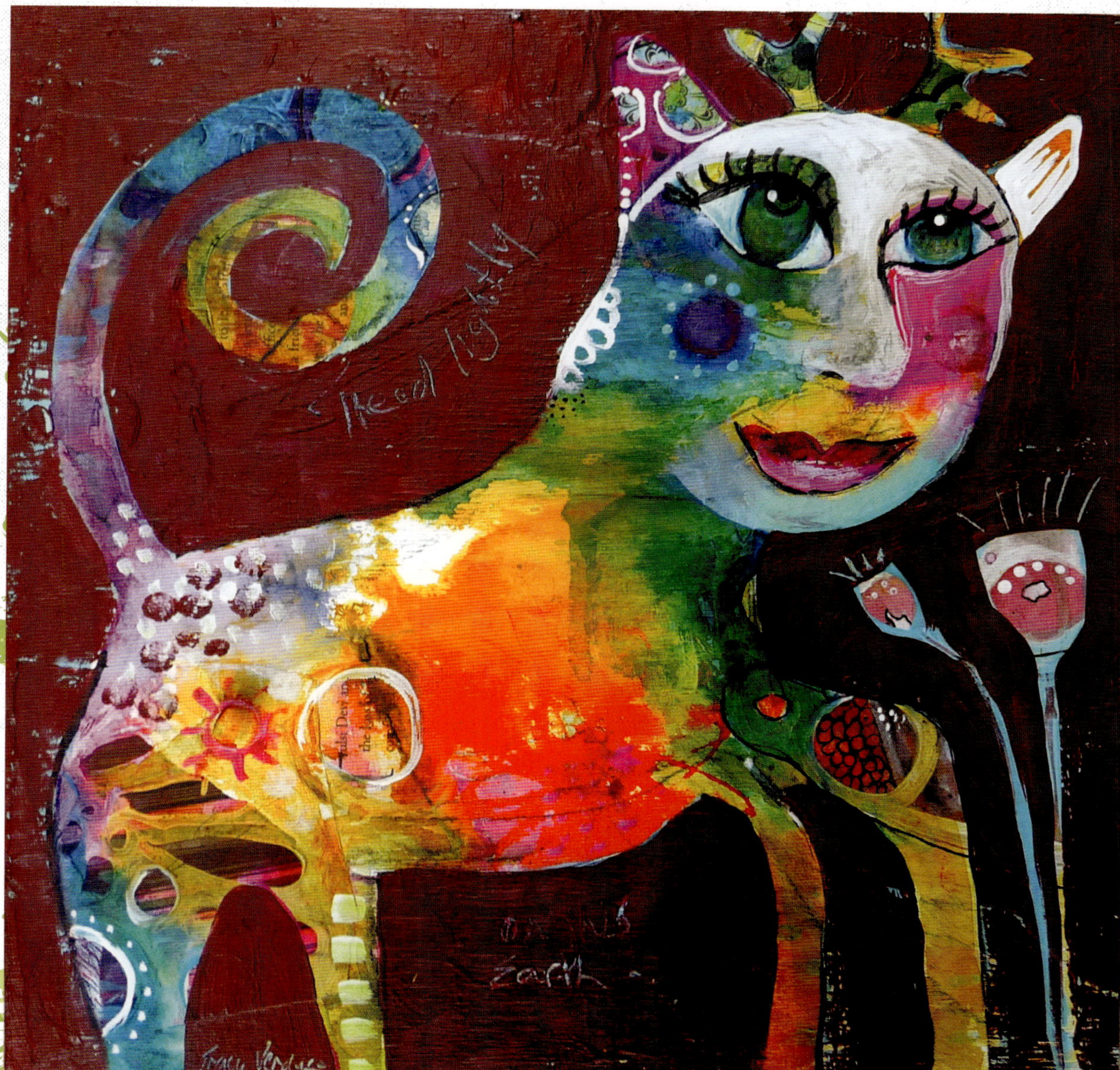
tread lightly

# the sublime and the ridiculous

I may be biased but I truly believe we live in one of the most beautiful places on the planet, just steps away from pristine turquoise waters and white, white sands. Jervis Bay is surrounded by a state forest and, farther inland, rolling green hills, which give way to the rocky escarpments of the highlands. The land around us is lush and productive with an abundance of dairy, wine, strawberry and veggie farms. The sky, more often than not, is a clear azure blue, punctuated here and there by wisps of clouds and flocks of cockatoos.

A couple of years ago, on one such perfect day in paradise, Sienna and I were headed home after indulging in a girly day of shopping at the nearest large mall (about an hour away from our home). At fourteen she had just begun to enter that eye-rolling, mother-disparaging stage of teenagehood. Having survived the same period with our eldest daughter Santana, I was holding onto the small moments of childhood-mother-adoring love as I watched them disappear a little more each day.

I feared I was in imminent danger (for the second time) of becoming She Who Knows Nothing Worth Hearing About, the formerly loved and adored mama whose meaningful advice and motherly words of wisdom were now, more often than not, greeted with disdain or a sullen glare or worse still, silence, not having been heard at all by those sassy ears filled with headphones and music and hormonal righteousness!

In that moment, however, the air was light as the verdant Kiama countryside whizzed by us, rolling hills of emerald on one side and a deep blue ocean stretching to the horizon on the other. We chatted sporadically about school and life and our new clothes. I felt a bubble of joy in my center and love and contentment in my heart.

Out of the corner of my eye, I took in the patchwork cows, some slumbering beneath the sprawling figs, which have stood watch here far longer than I, others nonchalantly standing, nibbling at the greenery below them, willy wagtails perched cockily on their backs.

I giggled and surprised myself with a low and bellowing mooo. It was a risk you see, it could have gone either way with Miss Newly Become Cool Teen. She glanced at me with a sideways smile, parted her lips and let out her own mooooo to top mine, slightly louder, slightly longer, slightly more dramatic.

I countered with a sound that came from deep within my belly and tickled my lips as the vibration of mmmmm passed between them. With a glint in her eye Sienna gave back as good as she got and for the next five minutes the car was filled with the sounds of two competitive, overbearing, baleful, constipated cows interspersed with fits of belly laughs and giggles.

We slid into silliness and hilarity with the ease and finesse of two six-year-olds, and when it was over we pondered the thoughts of the people who had overtaken us, catching us mid-moo, a look of surprise or bafflement frozen to their serious faces.

We drove on in silence, but happy, our moment of lighthearted silliness reminding us that with each other we are safe to be whoever we want to be. That not only is it safe to abandon ourselves to the ridiculous, it is necessary for the soul to flourish.

How often do you allow yourself the freedom to be silly and with whom do you feel safe to play? *Or . . .* do you play it safe too often?

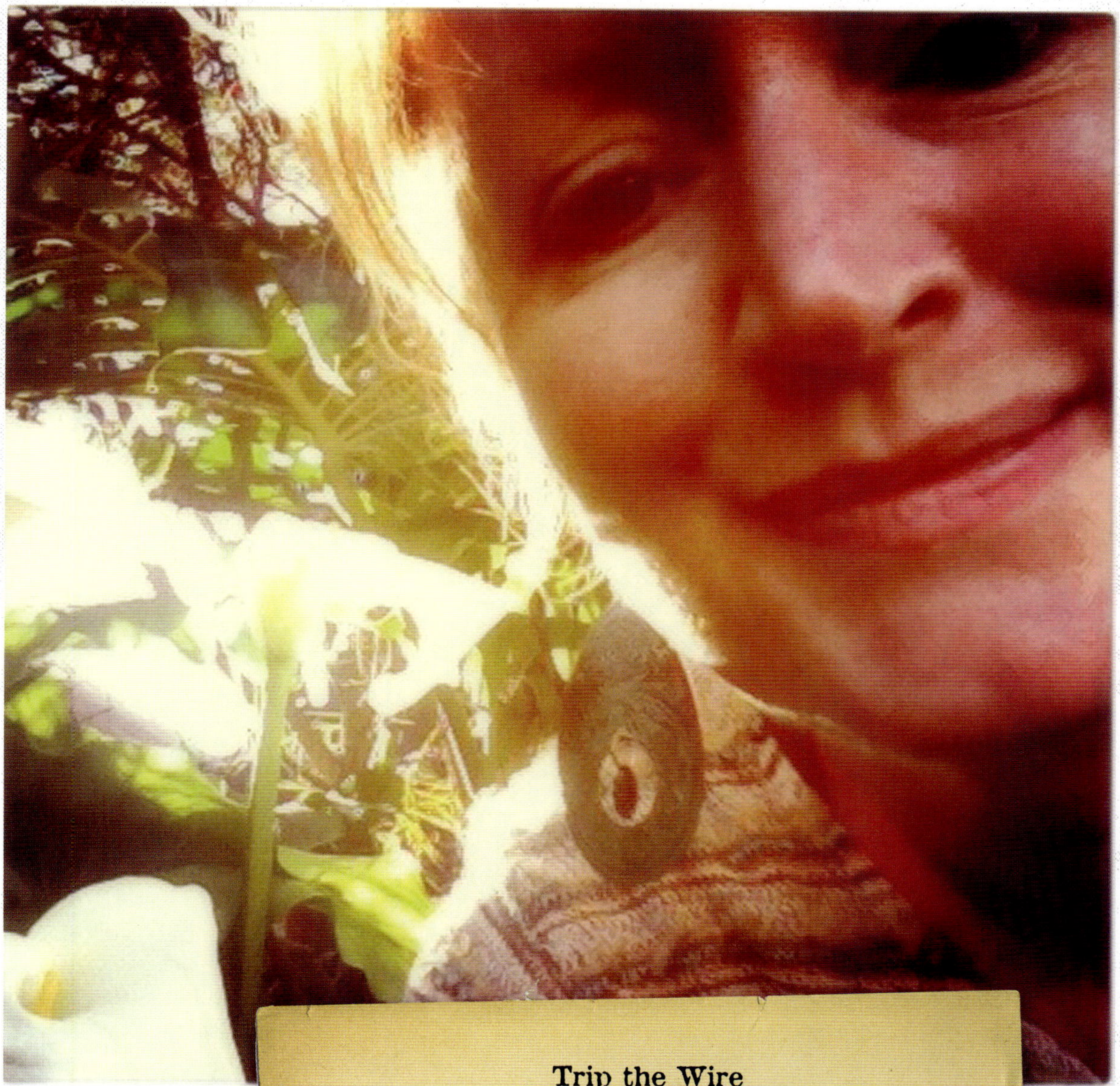

**Trip the Wire**

*Won't you chose a silver trail, like a butterfly in the air*
*Well, it's like invisible ink,*
*on a delicate sheet*
*It can make you think . . .*

(Lyrics by Tracy Verdugo. Go to youtube.com/watch?v=husjUeBk7uU to hear this song.)

# technique to free your creative spirit

by e'Layne Koenigsberg

This exercise is effective because the amount of materials used is minimal. This means there are not so many decisions to make, freeing you to just play and experiment and have no attachment to the end result.

**What You Need**

- 10" × 10" (25cm × 25cm) or so Masonite or plywood board
- #4 soft pencil
- decoupage medium
- fluid acrylic paint, a few colors including white and Burnt Umber
- laser copier
- old credit card
- paintbrush
- photo (instructions below)
- sandpaper (optional)
- various scrapbook papers

1 Take a walk and snap a picture of something you find inspiring, or use a photo you already have that you love.

2 Make a 4" × 6" (10cm × 15cm) laser print of the photo.

3 Put on music that represents a time in your life when you felt really happy and creative.

4 Paint the board any color(s) and let dry.

5 Sand the edges or any part of the surface.

6 Tear up scrapbook papers, maps or dictionary pages and decide placement for them randomly on the board. If some overlap, that is fine.

7 Adhere the papers with a generous amount of decoupage medium, both underneath the papers as well as over the top. Use a credit card (or your fingers) to get out all air bubbles.

8 Continue this process until you have all your papers glued down and let it all dry.

9 Next adhere your photo the same way you did the paper.

10 Now the fun begins. You can paint over some of the papers and let other parts peek out; you can make a wash with Burnt Umber to tone down the look; you can pencil in circles or scalloped edges; put in words or sayings; dip paint bottle lids in paint to make circles. At this point if your art "tells you" to add anything from your studio—a piece of driftwood, bottle caps, a button—do it. Let your wild child play!

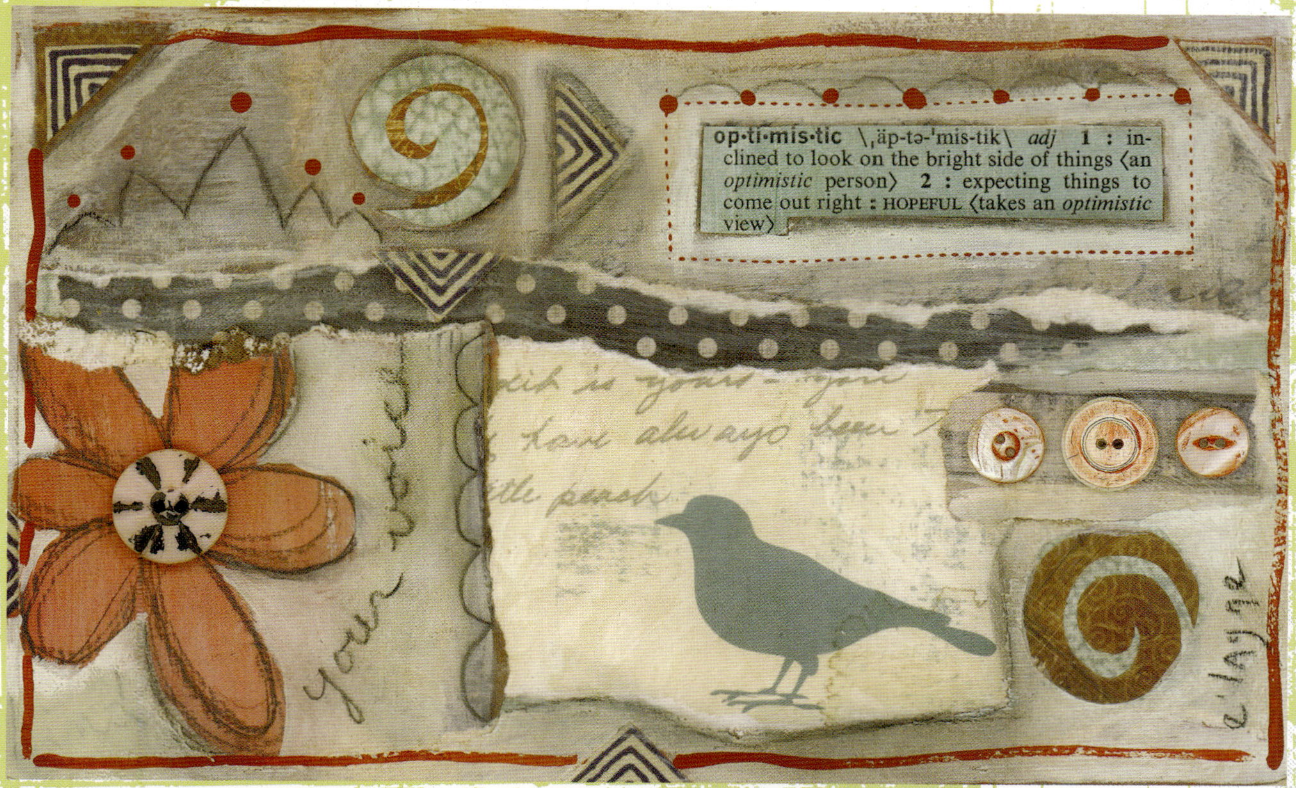
op·ti·mis·tic \ˌäp-tə-ˈmis-tik\ adj 1 : inclined to look on the bright side of things ⟨an optimistic person⟩ 2 : expecting things to come out right : HOPEFUL ⟨takes an optimistic view⟩
your voice
e'layne

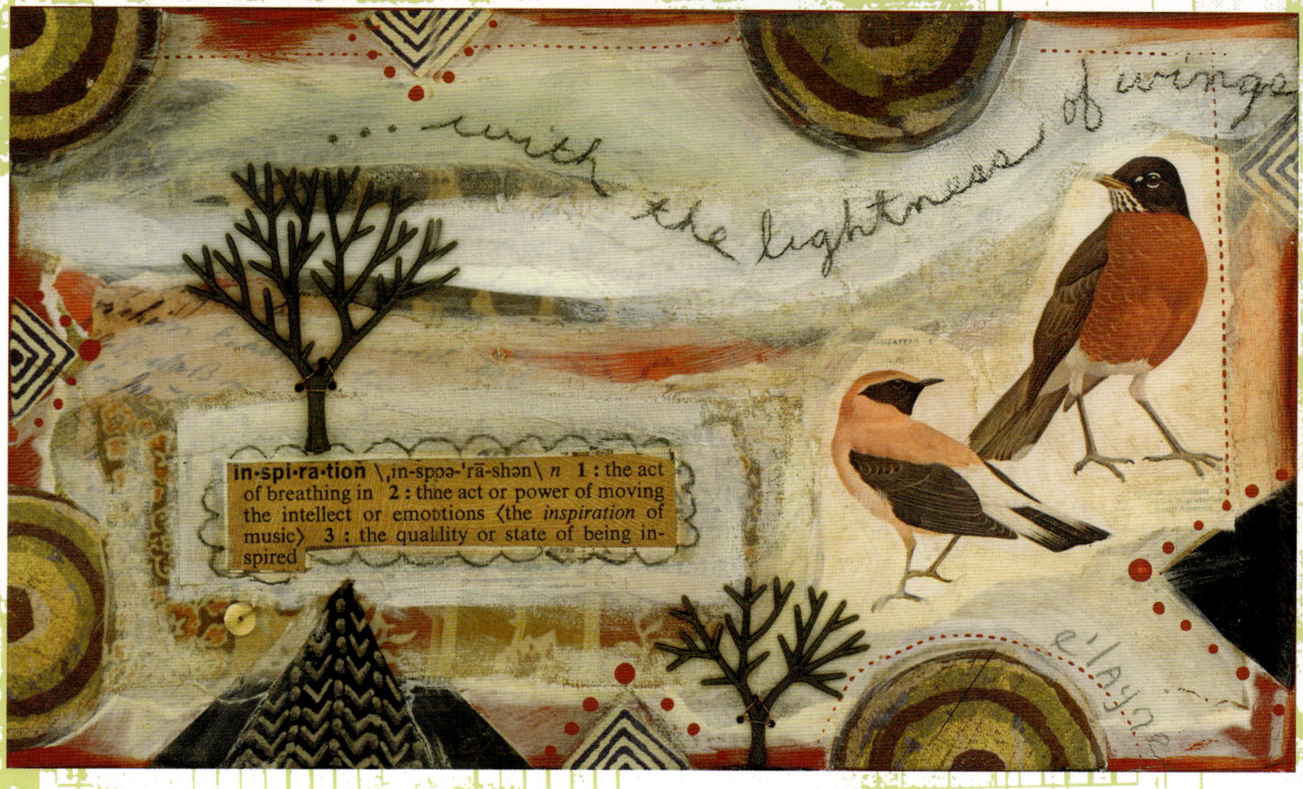
...with the lightness of wings
in·spi·ra·tion \ˌin-spə-ˈrā-shən\ n 1 : the act of breathing in 2 : the act or power of moving the intellect or emotions ⟨the inspiration of music⟩ 3 : the quality or state of being inspired
e'layne

exercise

# outside the square!

The grid is a representation of the Western way of thinking, where everything has to be "just so," rigid and compartmentalized. In this artwork we are going to embark on the beginning of a journey to let go of this rigid structure and step bravely but tentatively into the unknown. Almost as soon as we create these boxes, we are going to "go outside the lines" and escape them!

**What You Need**

- 12" × 12" (30cm × 30cm) plywood board or canvas
- acrylic paints, favorite colors including Titanium White, Metallic Gold and Raw Umber
- collage glue or gel medium
- collage papers (text, scrapbook papers, magazine images)
- disposable gloves (optional)
- paintbrush
- pencil
- ruler
- stencils/stamps
- watercolor pencils (optional)

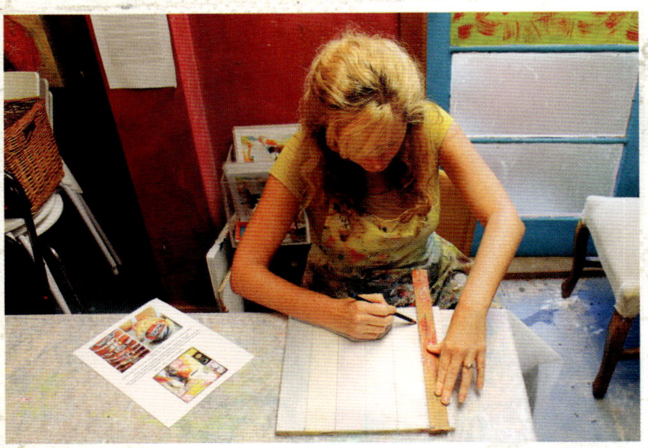

1 Draw up a grid of twenty-five equal boxes on your board.

On a piece of text that speaks to you, lightly sketch an image you feel aligned with. You can use one of your symbols or something in your environment that speaks to you. I used a Derwent watercolor pencil to sketch with so it would blend in easily once I began adding paint.

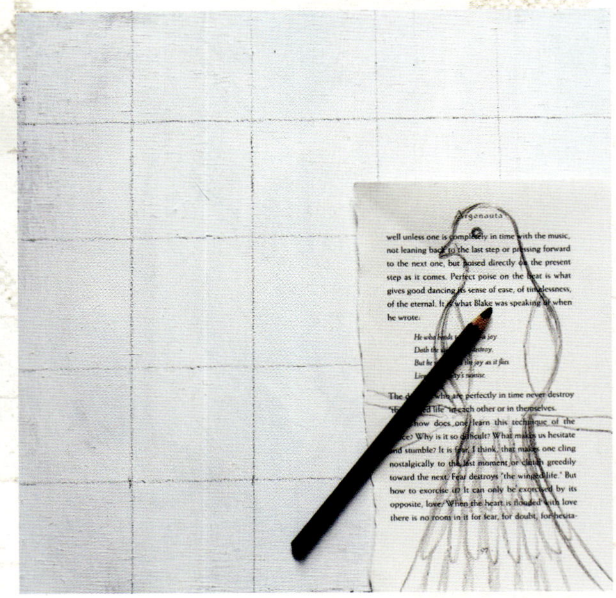

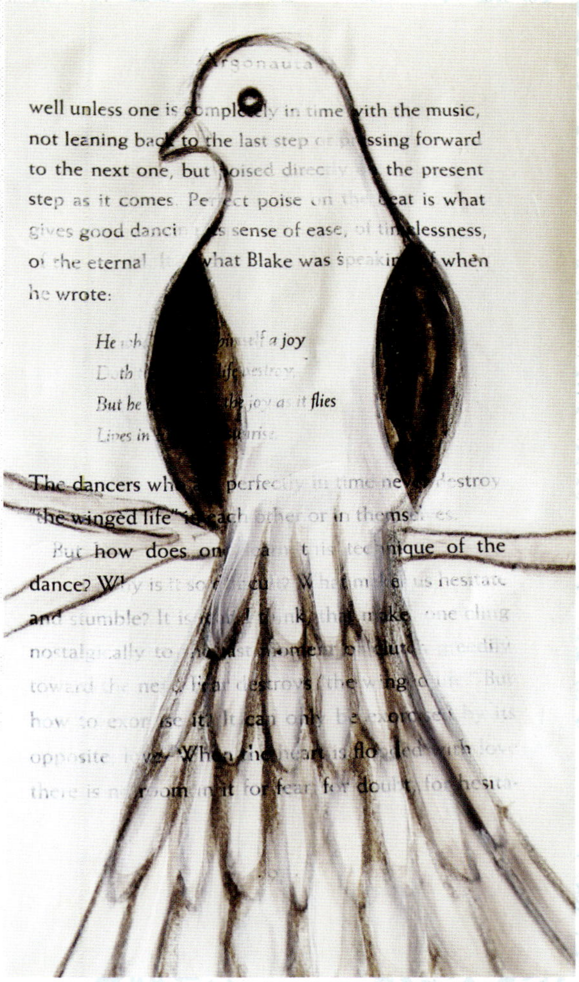


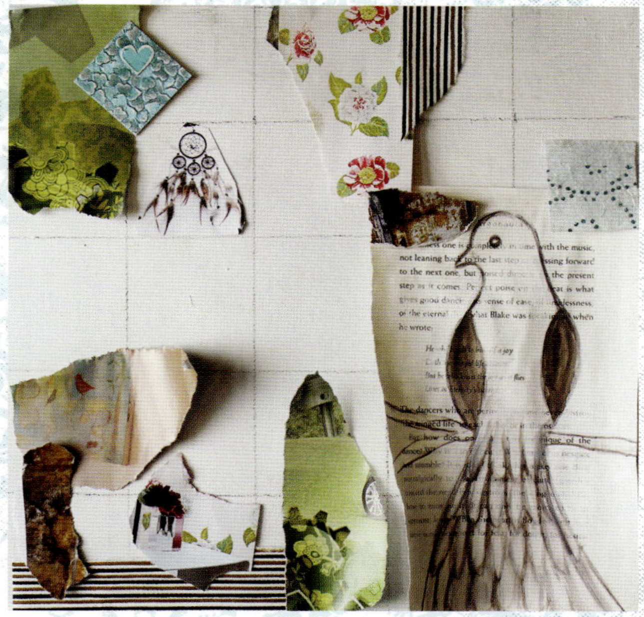

**2** Mix up a wash using Titanium White acrylic and water. Brush lightly in and around your design. Watch for serendipitous moments whenever you are painting. As I filled in the white, the words *joy* and *flies* popped out at me in the heart area of the bird. Love! I decided to leave them visible.

These wonderful occurrences will happen more and more as you feel yourself in the flow and they will often direct the next step of a painting.

Add in a dark tone in a couple of areas, too.

**3** Gather your collage elements together and begin to think about a color palette. Try to limit it a little so you don't get overwhelmed with possibilities. I decided upon soft greens and magentas with a hint of aqua and gold. Move them around the board, trying out different placements until you are happy with the layout. There is no need to stay in the boxes. Remember we are breaking out! Overlap some elements and also think about repetitive themes to connect the elements of your painting.

I have several images and patterns that link back to the main bird symbol. Can you find them? Glue the images in place using collage glue or gel medium. Add a thin layer of glue over the top. Don't worry about small creases and bubbles. These add character and we are moving away from a need for perfection.

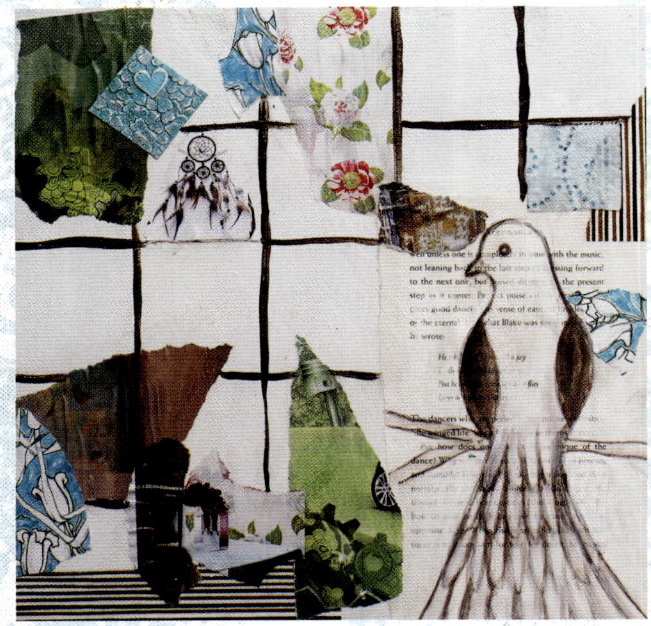

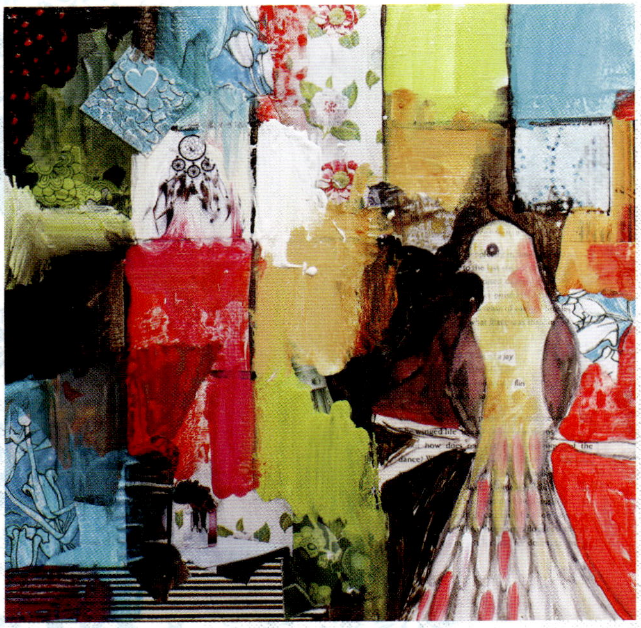

**4** With a thin brush and some Raw Umber paint, roughly paint in the grid lines that are still visible. There should now be an interesting balance between structure and a more playful placement of your collaged elements.

**5** Place the paints you have decided upon on your palette along with some white and some Raw Umber. I personally avoid using black to mix dark colors, but you should experiment to see what appeals to you when mixing colors.

Begin to fill in areas with your paints, loosely and intuitively. Placing darker colors against lights will add a pleasing contrast. Don't be afraid to be messy and definitely go outside the lines! You may want to cover some collage pieces up and leave some peeking through.

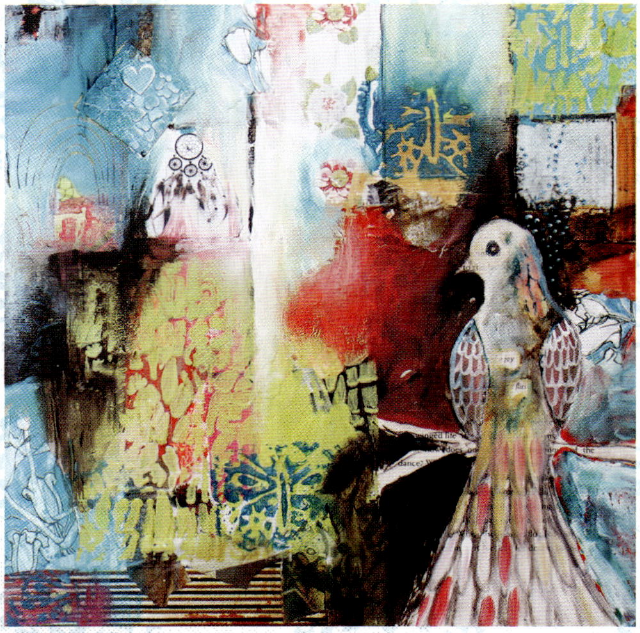

**6** Add a stenciled design to create more texture and surprise, and repeat the design in another spot.

Using one of your own personal foam stamps, continue to layer in more color, scratching through some of the layers with designs and symbols to show the colors underneath. Push some of the colors around with your fingers (disposable gloves are optional) and watch what happens when the colors mingle. Try to maintain an attitude of curiosity and wonder and stay aware of those moments when you are about to slide into panic or critical mode.

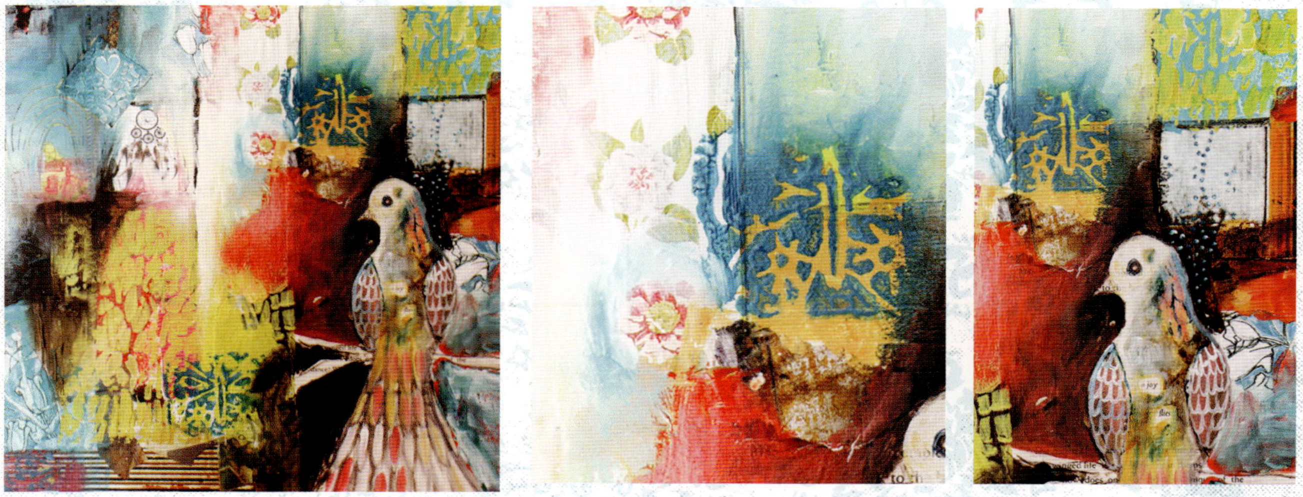

7 Look for ways to connect areas, for example, the turquoise paint on the top left, lightly smeared over the Raw Umber to almost meet the collaged blue flower element. Or the tiny blue dots I painted in from the neck of the bird up to the square piece of collaged paper, which carries the same design.

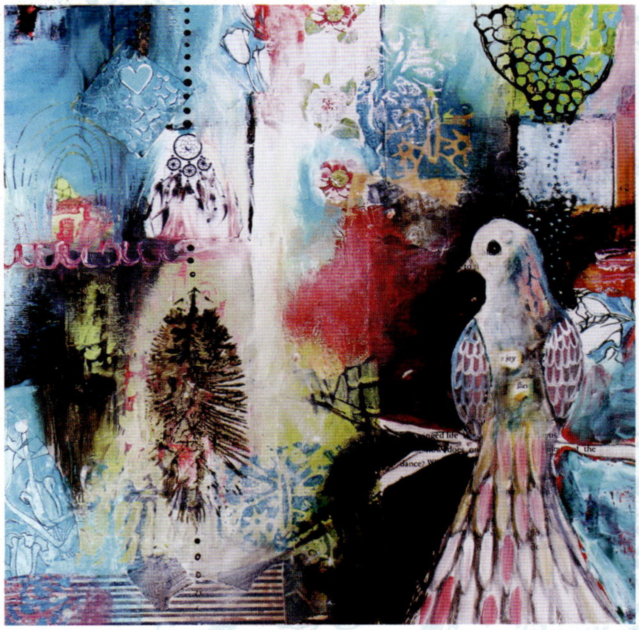

8 Continue to find ways to refine the color placement and add cohesion to your painting. Here I added some magenta and turquoise tones to several areas including the bird, a feather stamp (more repetition) and dots to connect the feather to the dream catcher above and anchor the painting below.

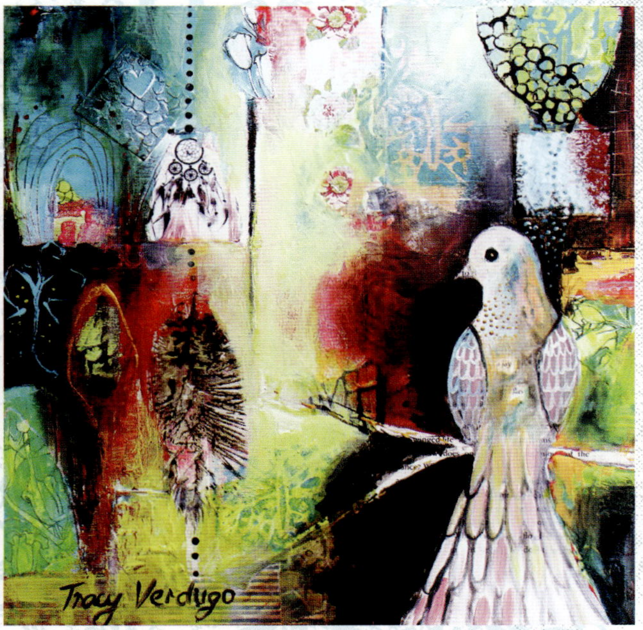


9 A few Metallic Gold highlights for a bit of oomph and an added butterfly symbol in the dark area to the left and it's time to say *Done!*

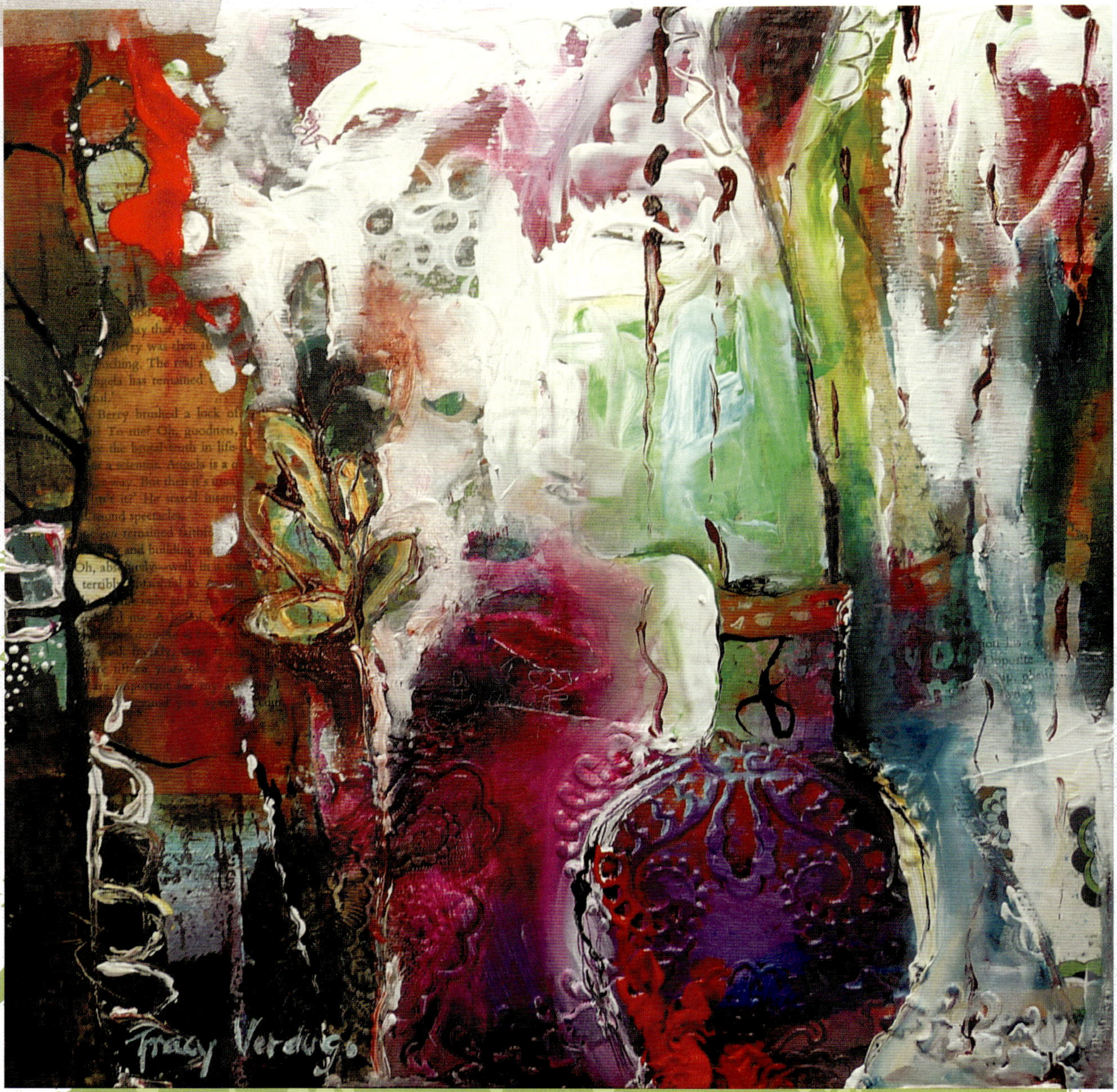

There is a quote by Anaïs Nin that I love, which talks about the solitude of a dream and the possibility of pleasure.

I painted this painting while slowly reading the quote out loud, feeling the emotion of each line and painting a response until the painting was finished.

# chapter four: dimensional language

## Sharpening your senses to perceive the world around you

Sometimes a passage in a book I am reading is so beautiful, I could roll the words around on my tongue and almost taste them, savoring the pleasure of the images they paint, not wanting to move on from their evocative lushness.

Sometimes the colors and emotion in a painting reach out to me with such succulence I am transported, and my imagination awakens to a thousand new possibilities.

Sometimes a song can break open my heart, pulling down the barriers I have erected to protect me from feeling too much, and in this release new marks and expression are able to pour forth onto my own canvas.

We are sensory creatures and there is much beyond the five physical senses.

In these moments of connection, this intermingling of the senses, something is born that is completely unique, something primal and new, captivating and fresh. Works inspired by a collision of the senses, of the body and the heart and everything beyond, outside the logical boundaries of the mind, yield a beautiful result.

*We die containing a richness of lovers and tribes, tastes we have swallowed, bodies we have plunged into and swum up as if rivers of wisdom, characters we have climbed into as if trees, fears we have hidden in as if caves.*
—Michael Ondaatje

# each our own language

During the years I spent working in special ed, I had the privilege to be with a group of awesome teenage boys diagnosed with Asperger's syndrome. Equally wonderful was the fact that the two main teachers I worked alongside, Mr. Jones and Mr. Lee, were empathic, progressive, innovative and totally committed to the boys. Often we would talk with them about how their brains processed the world differently than the neurotypical—not better, not worse, just differently. Sometimes we studied other conditions to better understand the multitude of different and amazing brains that exist among people in general.

One of these that really caught my mind and imagination was that of synaesthesia, a fascinating condition. In simple terms, it is best described as a mingling or union of the senses in which two or more of the five senses that we usually experience on their own are merged involuntarily and automatically. Sounds or words can be linked with certain colors or tastes. Musical notes can conjure up letters or numbers. An apple could have a feeling of purple or yellow when touched. In fact, any of the senses could blend in any combination without any thought or direction from the person experiencing them. Many synaesthetes are highly creative and many could not imagine their lives without their unusual sensory perception.

Sometimes I wonder if this might be part of human evolution. Perhaps we are all heading toward an opening and blending of the senses, a time of greater creative exploration and connection.

### Mixing It Up to Stimulate Creative Thinking

One of my favorite games I used to play in my kids' art classes was a twist on the Australian show *The New Inventors*. In my class I played the host and introduced each "inventor" to come showcase their new invention. I called out the name of each student in random order, and the idea was for each child to quickly choose an item from somewhere in the room when they were introduced to the "stage" and improvise while announcing their new invention. The skits were hilarious! An empty cardboard roll became an instant teleporter essential for every household for easy interplanetary travel! A jar of glue became the newest in hair gel technology guaranteed to hold your style for days or weeks! A red bucket could be the latest in haute couture headwear from the Paris fashion runways. Sometimes the next student would grab the prop from the last inventor and reinvent it into something completely new! The fresh associations were endlessly clever and entertaining and always got us in the mood for some great creative outpourings!

### The Language of Nature

Nature itself is one of my biggest inspirations, and I try to pay attention to the nuances of the unseen world within it, the mysteries of a reality that lies beyond our basic human senses.

Walking along the beach one day with Marco and the girls, we marveled at the low-tide hieroglyphics of the tiny clams moving in the wet sand, this way and that, in circles and jagged lines, gliding smoothly forward then abruptly changing direction, incising the sand and leaving deep indentations.

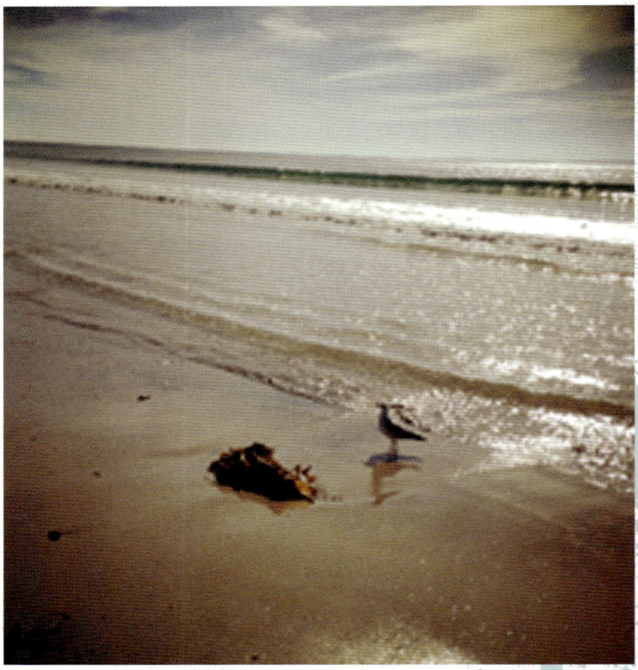

Musing about language, creatures and our human assumption that we are the highest order on the planet, we wondered out loud if there was perhaps some form of communication inherent in their movement, so similar do the marks look to human forms of writing. *Wouldn't it be funny*, I wondered, *if they were actually trying to communicate with us but we weren't advanced enough to understand them*?

Moving forward just a couple more steps, we were stopped in our tracks, astounded to see in the sand at our feet three perfectly formed letters:

I C
U

In my garden, one balmy summer's day, I became aware of a butterfly flitting around me. It would circle me, then fly away a bit, then come back and circle me again, each time flying off in the same direction before returning. Inclined as I am to talk to butterflies and other sentient creatures, I asked if it was trying to tell me something. It continued its pattern of circling and flying away toward the back of the garden, and I began to move in the direction it was heading. It seemed happy that I had noticed and led me to a large spiderweb about twenty feet away, out of sight, behind the tea tree and bottlebrush trees. In the spiderweb another butterfly had just become entangled but was still flapping its wings trying to escape. Luckily it was barely caught. I helped it on its way and the pair flew off together out of sight.

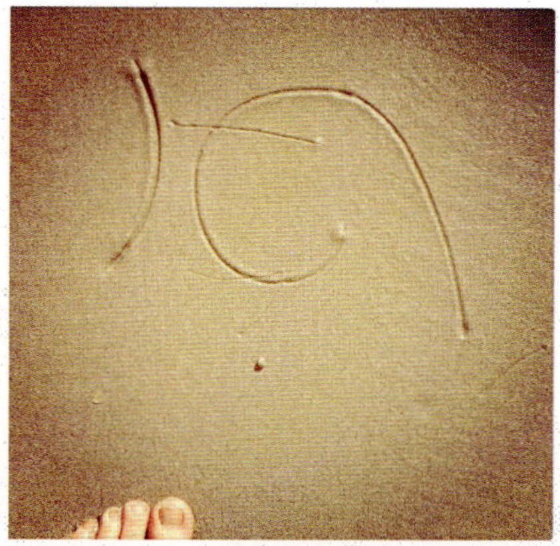

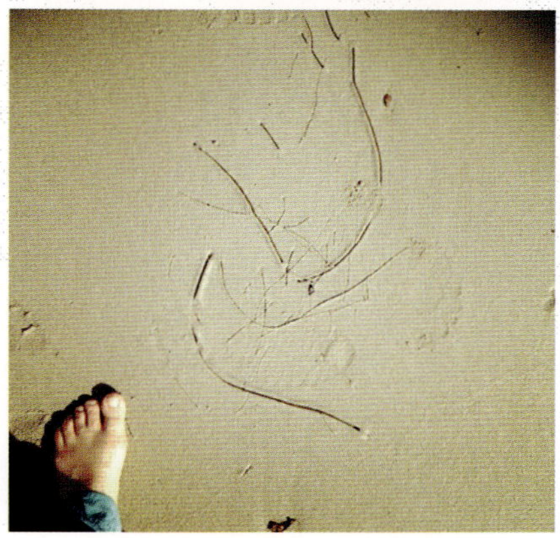

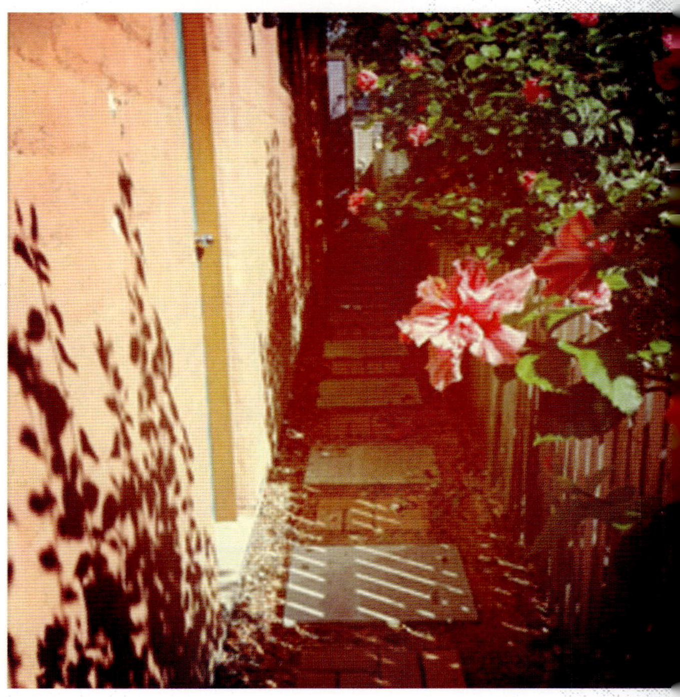

# mingle your senses

Here are some additional ways to grow your creative originality and allow your senses to intermingle to create new and original ideas.

- Listen to music while you paint and allow yourself to flow with the rhythm and emotion, making marks to match your feelings with no thought to outcome.
- Hold an image in your mind—a woman, an elephant, a tree, a bridge—and with your eyes closed draw a series of these on paper with a felt-tip marker. Don't peek and don't worry about how they look when you open your eyes.
- Collect images and photos that really speak to you and create a haiku for each one.
- Get out some paints and a canvas and read yourself a favorite poem, stopping after each line to paint the feeling that comes to you, reaching intuitively for the colors and tools to express that feeling. Keep building up these "feeling" paintings, overlapping one onto another until your poem painting is complete.
- Pay attention to nature. Talk to your plants. Listen to the wind. With a sense of wonder, observe small creatures.
- Explore other cultures with an open mind. Suspend your belief systems for a moment and look with the mind of an anthropologist.
- Create happy faces and rainbows with the food served on your dinner plates even if your kids are all grown up.
- Lie on the earth with your hands and feet bare, and listen to the sounds around you.
- Make paint-blot papers from the leftover paint on your palette and find creatures within the paint shapes.

### Textures of the Heart and Senses

- On a piece of paper, draw up a grid. You can use any number of squares. Using your imagination, collect a diverse array of items with different textural qualities, cut to size, and glue each item inside a square.
- Texture can relate to our senses of sight and touch but equally to our heart-centered senses, evoking memories and associations. In my grid I included wool, chili seeds, lace, vintage wallpaper, film, small twigs, sprinkles, an old kitchen sponge, wire mesh, aluminium foil, a dead leaf, shellac, fabric and feathers.
- On a separate piece of paper grab a pen and engage in some free association. Looking at the contents of each square, write down whatever comes to mind that you feel or associate with the item in the square. For me the kitchen sponge evoked the following words: *sanitary, home, clean slate, clarity, dust-free, porous*; while the sprinkles conjured up: *childhood, sweetness, party, friends, anticipate, belonging*; and the wire mesh brought to mind: *trapped, barrier, rigid, unspoken, fear, withheld.*

This exercise not only allows us to better understand ourselves and our responses to the world around us but also helps to build a vocabulary of colors, textures and symbols that will inspire and inform our own art-making practice.

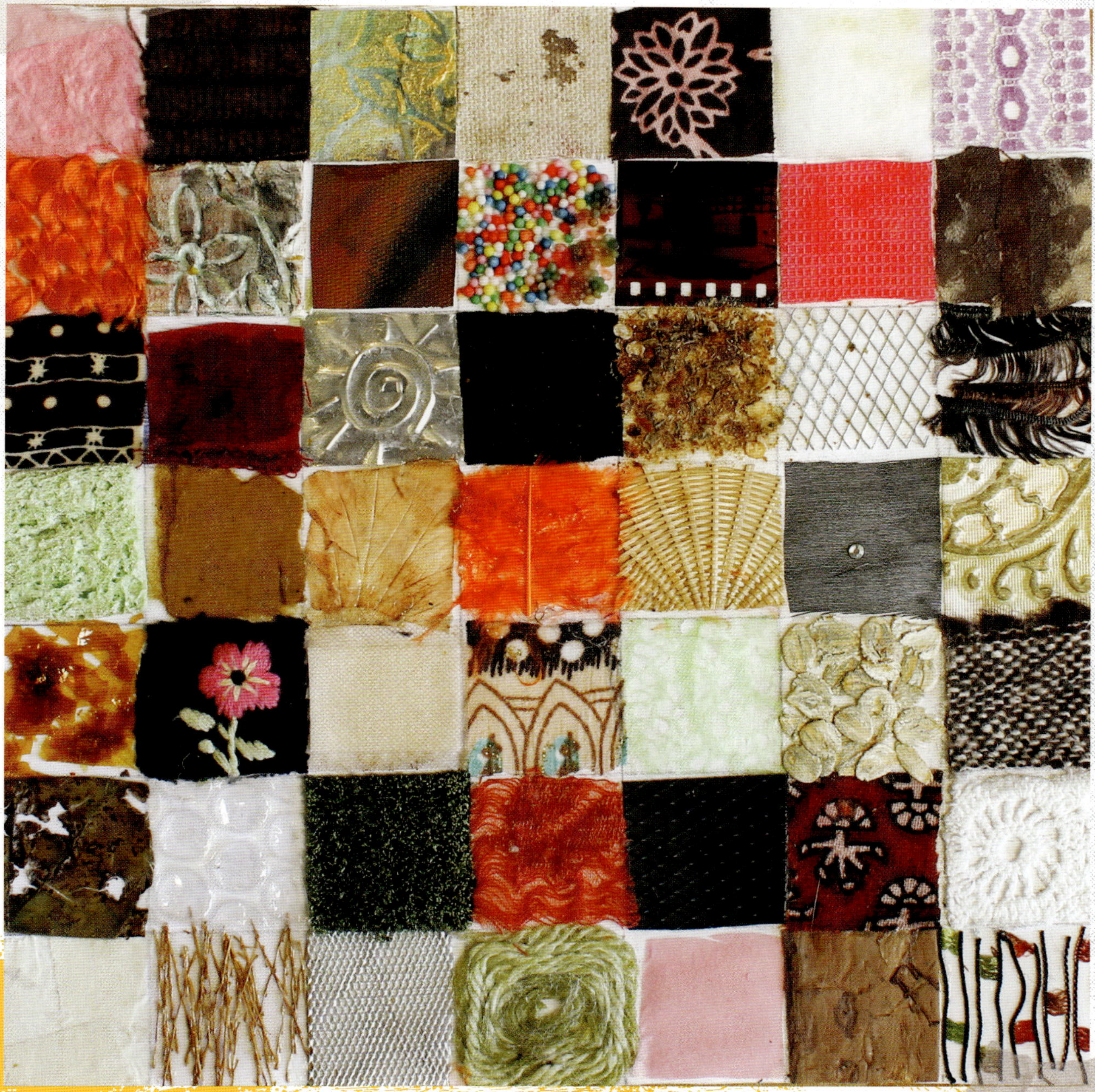

# exercises for coloring your senses

by Louise Gale

Energy is everywhere and color has its own energy makeup that affects how we see the world, ourselves and everything around us.

Color is essential to our lives. The colors you are drawn to and love are stories of who you are and the world you would like to create. We often have our go-to colors when we create—ones that make us feel safe. Using those colors in your creative life and day-to-day is the ultimate form of self-expression.

Some colors may challenge you more than others, and these are the ones that, when you explore them, open up a whole new world creatively.

These get-started exercises will help stimulate your senses and awaken your creative mojo to take you on a journey with color—an adventure that will continue for years to come.

### What You Need

- acrylic paints and watercolor pencils
- camera and printer
- crayons or any favorite art materials
- fabrics, textured paper and other items in various colors
- glue
- hole punch
- large clear envelopes to collect bits in
- magazines
- paintbrush
- ribbon
- rubber stamps and inkpad (dark brown or black)
- sketchbook/journal
- watercolor or acrylic painting paper

### Create Your Own Color Journal

Creating a journal dedicated to color is a wonderful tool. Use it to collect images, photos and paint samples from the hardware store, and make color studies to refer to and explore throughout your life as an artist.

Altered journals are also fun to play with, so create embellishments, page cutouts and pop-outs, and let those colorful creative juices flow.

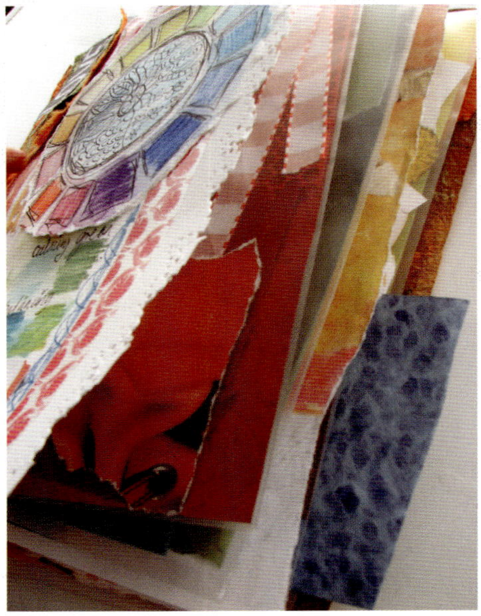

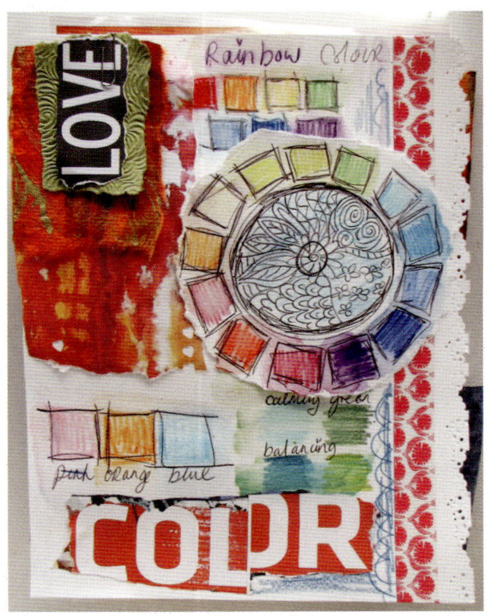

### Get Started by Collecting Color Inspiration

Use your clear folders or envelopes to collect magazine cutouts, fabrics, ribbon and other images in each color.

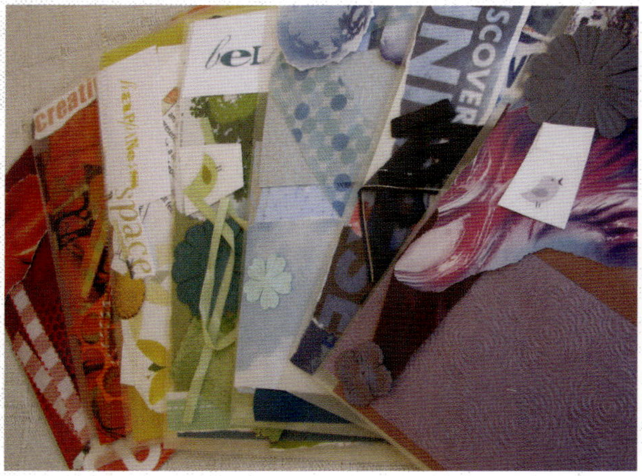

### Take Your Camera on a Creative Exploration

Capture the different shades and hues in the colorful world around you. Take your camera out with you and you will start to notice color everywhere! Pop your images in your journal and study the different shades in your images. It won't be long before you notice the variety of colors around you in every little detail. The world is a beautiful colorful palette.

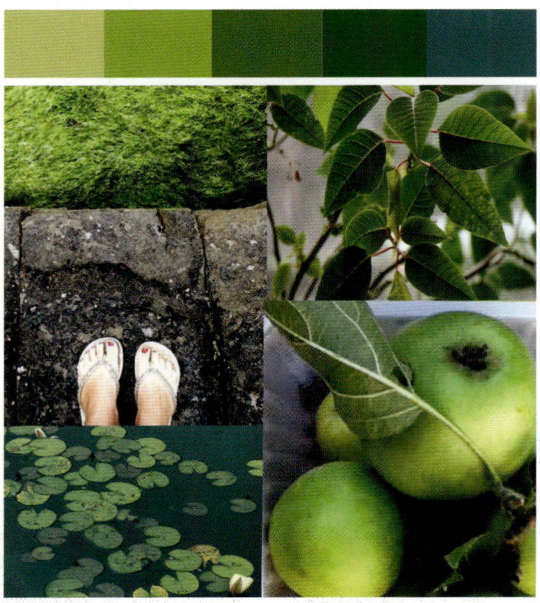

### Color Sensing Exercise

This is a fantastic dive-into-the-senses exercise, which you can reuse over and over again. Color is all around us and sometimes we don't even realize how much of a particular color we are drawn to or even colors that we avoid. When we have every color of the rainbow represented in our lives, we are more balanced and our creative energy can flow more freely.

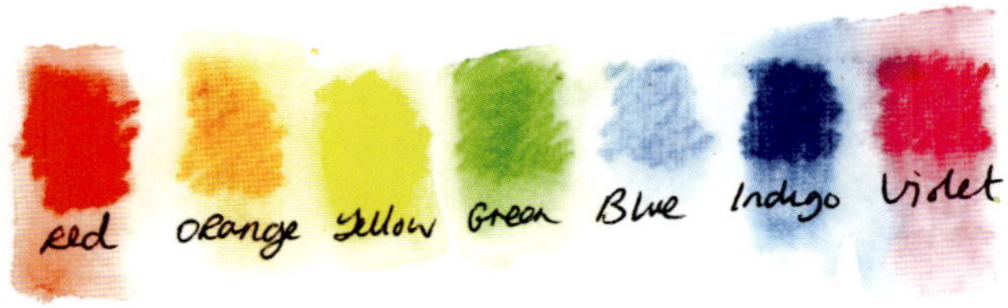


Take a look at the colors of the rainbow. Which one are you drawn to today? Can you think of a reason why you are drawn to this color? What comes to mind when you think of this color? How does it make you feel? Using you own color journal or sketchbook, explore your senses using the following prompts:

- Color your page with this color and shades of this color to really submerge yourself into its energy. Write the following on your page:
- What words come to mind when you think of this color?
- How does it make you feel? Does this color relax you or energize you? Does it make you feel hot or cold?
- What are some of the items, objects or even clothing in your own environment and home that are in this color? Is it missing from your environment?
- What foods do you consume in this color? If none, how can you begin to integrate a food item in this color?
- What songs come to mind?
- What scents or smells do you associate with this color? Does it make you think of a particular season? Or spark a childhood memory?
- Is this a color you usually like to create with? If not, what do you think is holding you back?

### Create a Color Studies Page in Your Chosen Color

Start to fill your color journal with color study pages. Journal and create a color page in your sketchbook with as much detail as you can related to this particular color, and really submerge yourself into its energy and how it connects to your world.

Focusing on all the things you write down in your senses exploration, dive more deeply into the energy of this color by creating pages for your color journal. For this exercise we are going to use orange as an example.

Pull together your folder of items you have collected and let your intuition guide you around the page.

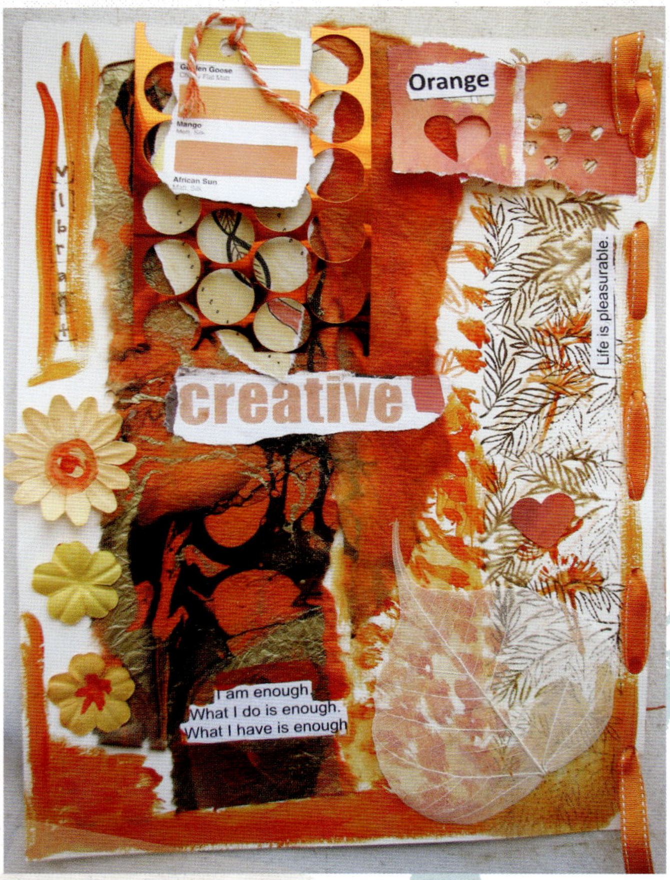


**1** Start building your background by placing a large piece of colored paper to create a strong area of color.

Use your watercolor pencils or crayons to add more color to the paper, then using a rubber stamp and an ink pad, stamp some pattern into the color.

**2** Start creating layers by adding paper, drawings and any other colored paper and items that resonate with you. Move them around the page to see what feels like the right position for you, then glue them down once you are happy with their placement.

**3** Mix your paint to create your color. Use any paint that you have or prefer to work with. You can use crayons or pencils instead.

**4** Smother color into your page. Go with the flow and let your intuition guide you in how much you want to add; you can always add more later on.

**5** Add some more variety to your page by hole punching. Use a regular or craft hole punch, or create the holes using an awl or any other tools you have available.

Thread your ribbon or fabric through the holes to create a beautiful embellishment.

**6** Gather the words that resonate with you for this color and add them to your page. Tearing them from magazines or creating a perforated edge adds lovely dimension to your page.

**7** Finish off your page by using letter rubber stamps to add any additional words to your page.

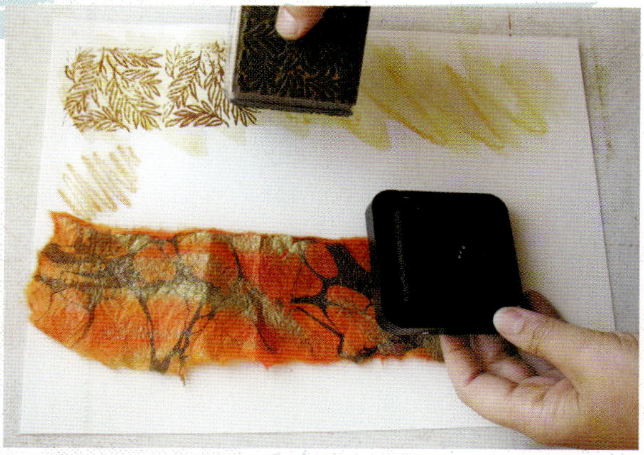

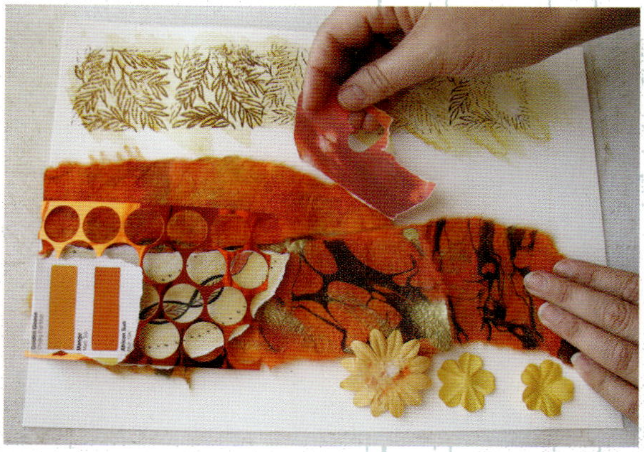

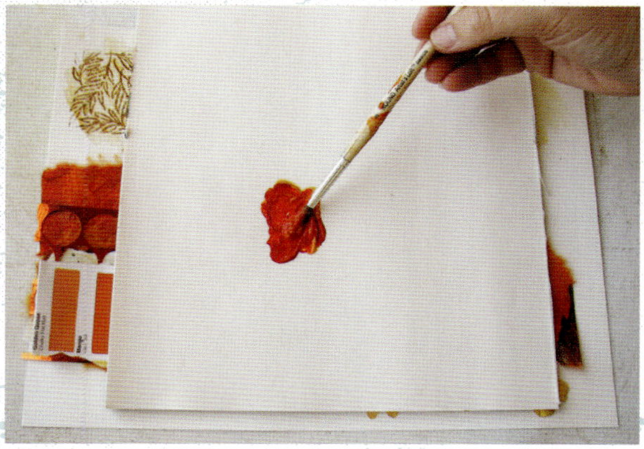

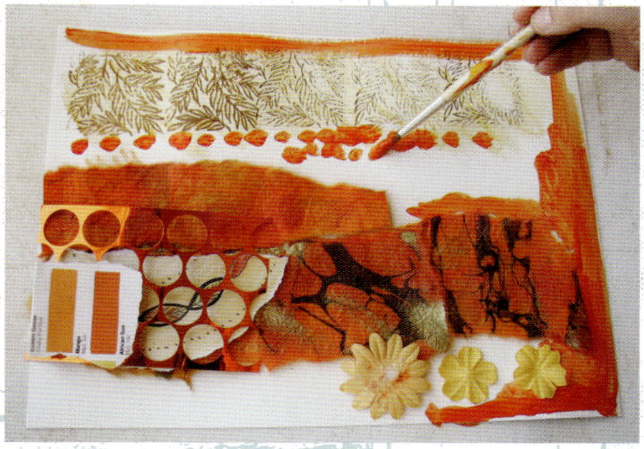

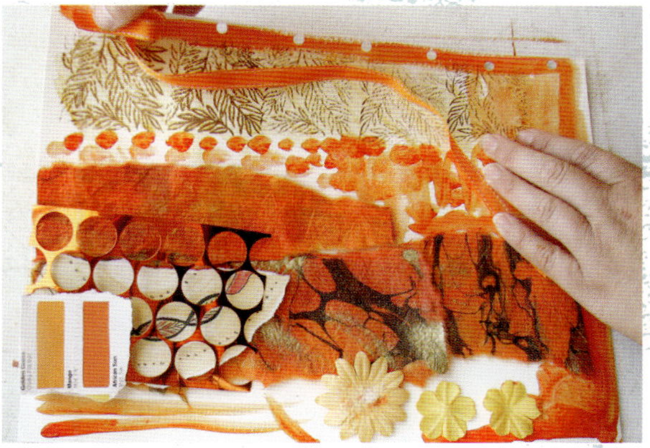

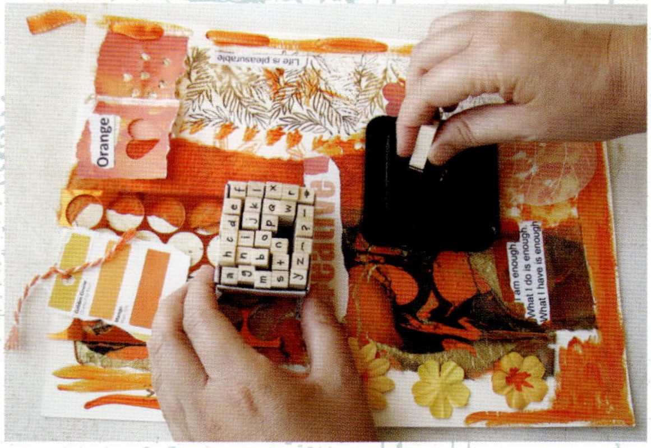


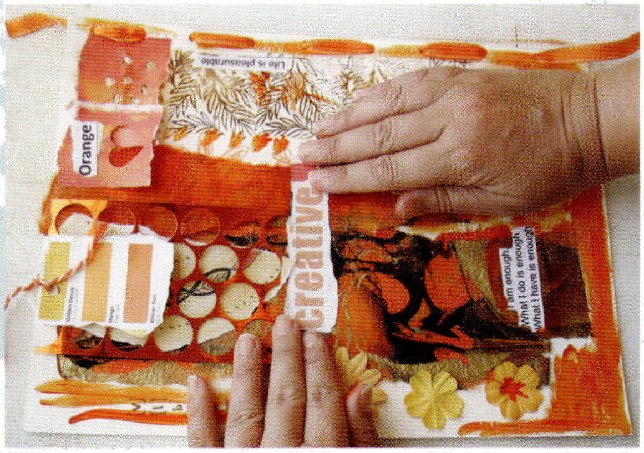


Enjoy exploring the energies of color and in no time you will have beautiful inspiration and resources in your color journal to revisit and play with for years to come.

Art and color is the conversation we are having with ourselves and the story we are telling the world.

exercise

# paint a memory

Like most of you, I bet, I am an avid taker of photos. I like to capture snippets of time through the window of the car as I drive through a new town or city. Sometimes I have to do it furtively like the time I spied an old man who looked exactly like Santa Claus on summer vacation, and I proceeded to embarrass Sienna by hiding amongst the foliage in Old Town San Diego until I was happy with my snaps! Or the time I took a beautiful photo of a woman deep in prayer outside the Basilica of Guadalupe in Mexico City. The scene was so moving and evocative I just couldn't resist!

Back in my studio I rotate those photos that inspire me on my studio wall, looking at them from time to time as I work. Sometimes seemingly of its own volition, a memory makes its way off the wall, scrambles itself across the paint-speckled floor and drops with gusto onto my canvas.

Like many of the techniques and processes I employ, there are no hard-and-fast rules to painting a memory, so I invite you to sit back and come along with me as I paint some of my own. This is more of a glimpse into the unfolding of my own work and process, and I hope you can use it as a spark to bring your own images and memories into your art!

Remembering the lazy, meandering walks we took during our two months in Puerto Escondido, Oaxaca, in 2008, I selected several photos from my wall of inspiration (OK, they didn't *really* jump onto my canvas by themselves!) and laid out some paints, pastels and gel pens and a sturdy piece of watercolor paper.

### What You Need

- acrylic paints
- bamboo skewer
- black acrylic ink
- memorable moment photos
- paintbrush
- scratch foam board
- variety of mark-making tools
- watercolor paper
- white gel pen

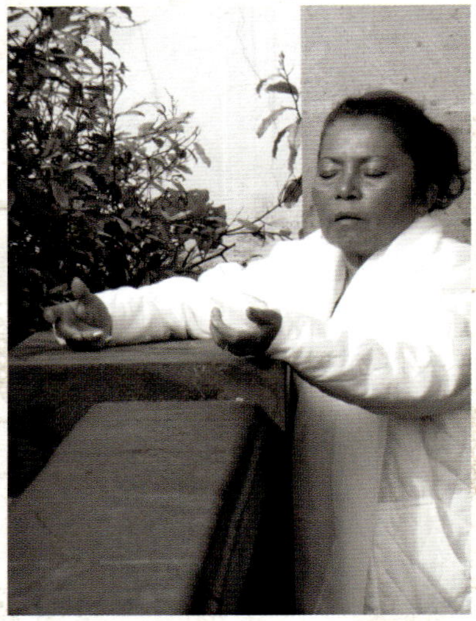

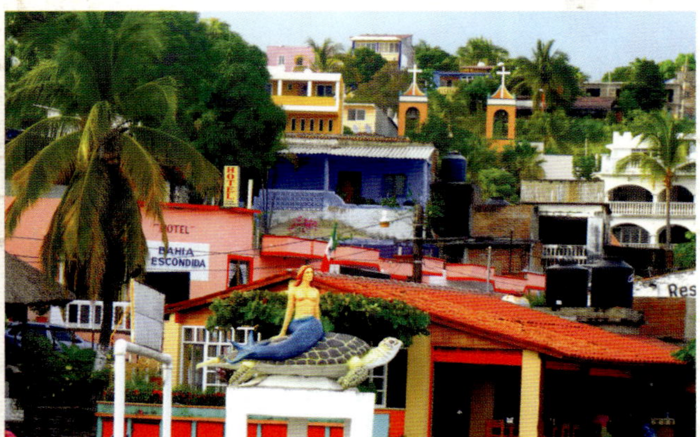

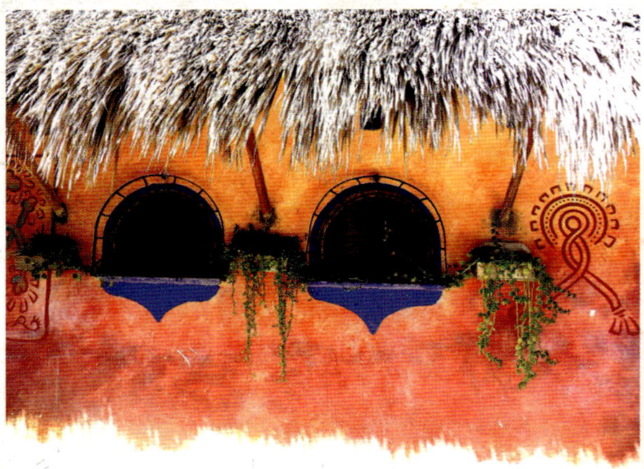

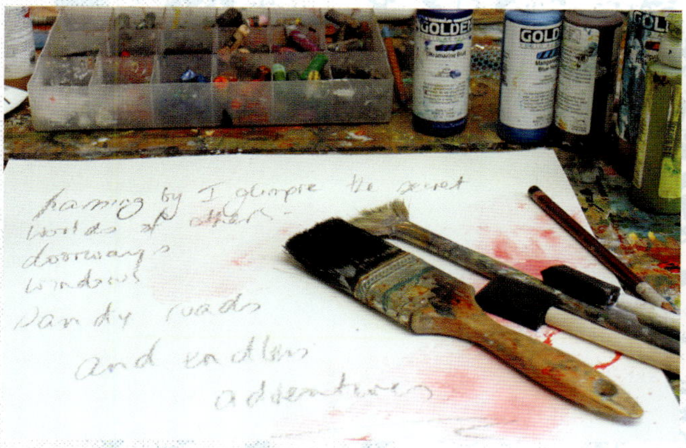

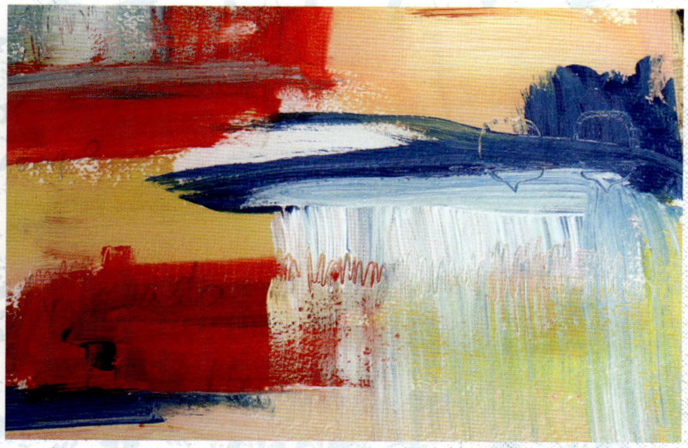

**1** Looking at your own photos, begin to think about the types of things you love that made you take these pics in the first place.

Here, I saw how much I love small glimpses into windows and doorways, imagining the lives of those who live there, the things we might have in common and the ways in which our lives might be very different. Jot down some of the feelings that come up in words right there on your paper.

**2** Choose a palette of colors based on those that are strongest in your photos and brush them across the paper quickly in thick, lavish strokes, varying directions and overlapping some colors.

Here, I used a bamboo skewer to scratch through some of the layers of paint, using elements of the photos and the memories that flow on as my inspiration: a design underneath a window, the memory of the waves crashing, the texture of the thatched roofs on the houses and palapas.

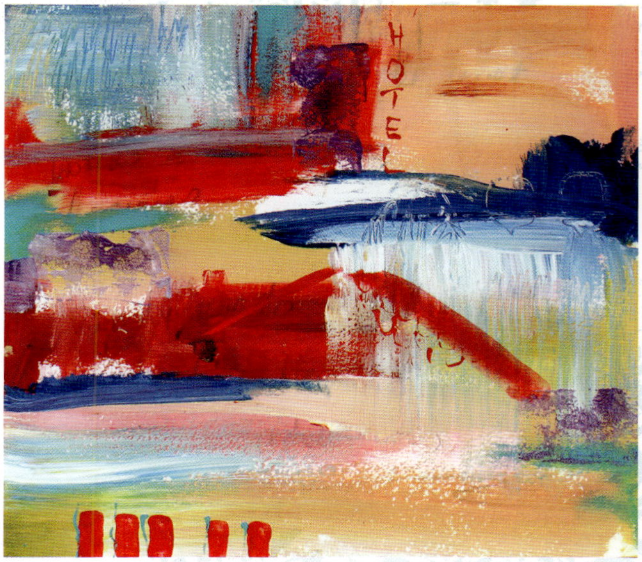


**3** Continue looking at your photos and see what speaks to you. I am drawn to load my brush with intense red, and intuitively I select a few more elements to add to my work in progress: a hotel sign, part of a red-tiled roof, some strong vertical blocks of red from the doors at the bottom of one of the pics with a touch of the turquoise that nudges the red.

Add these additional elements without thinking hard about it.

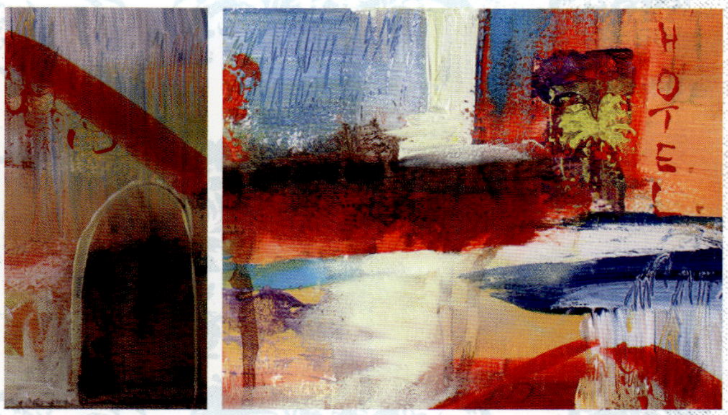


**4** Consider adding in some darker areas to add contrast to the work. Maybe add a border to an element with the shape of an arched window, or etch a design from one of the photos into foam to create a stamp. I added stamps to the work in several places, and the colors continue to build visual interest. The scraffitied area above the roof evokes the memory of tropical downpours.

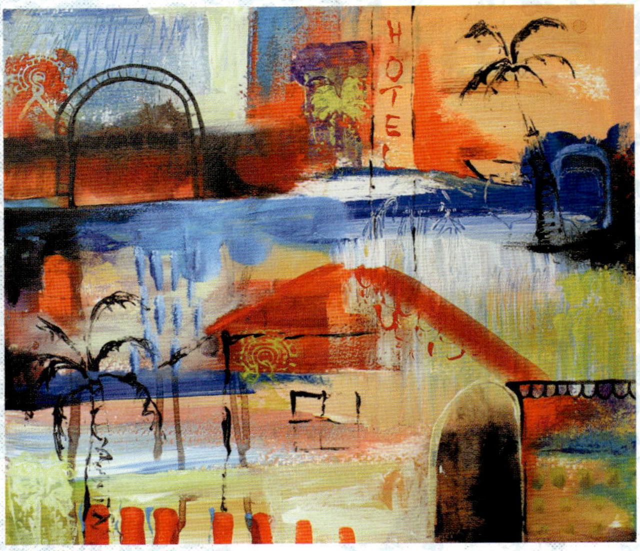

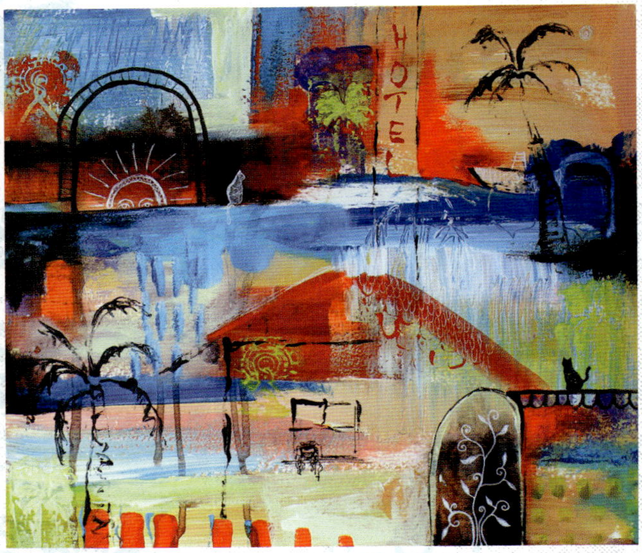

**5** Continue to play with paint, making various marks to unify areas. Here, I added some details with black ink and a bamboo skewer—some palm trees, a boat, another archway—as more memories of our adventures in Puerto Escondido drifted through my mind. I grounded some of these images by loosely scumbling the ink over the colors beneath.

**6** You can fine-tune some of your details using a white gel pen. I added more details as I thought about the sunsets we watched over the ocean each night, the kitties who nuzzled around our feet at our favorite restaurant, waiting for scraps of fish and prawns, the fishing boats lined up on the beach, and everywhere lush green tropical foliage.

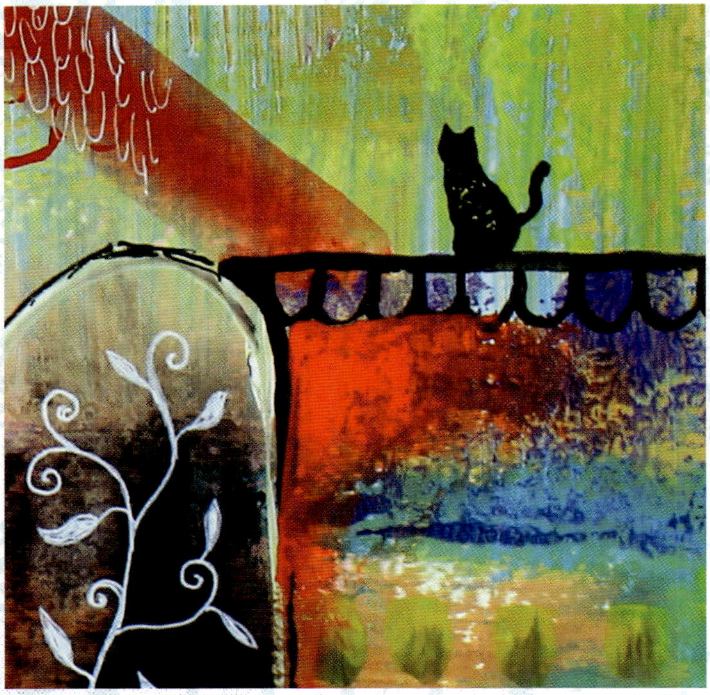

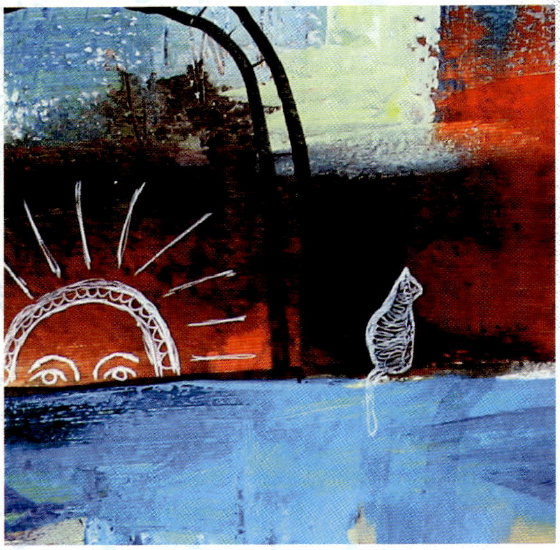

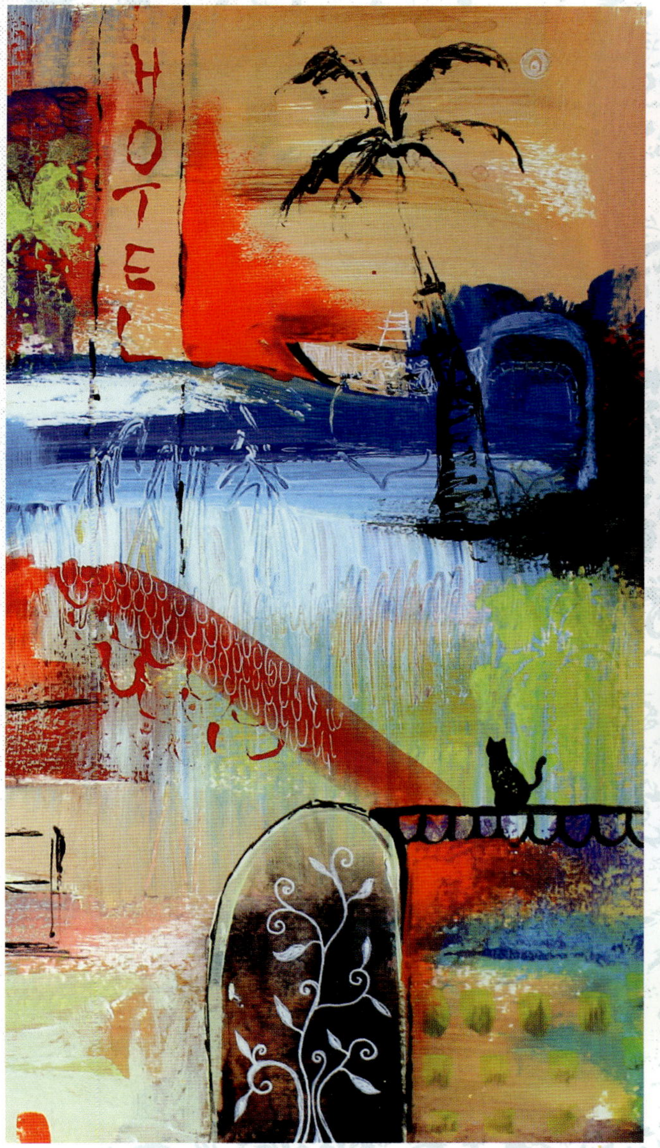


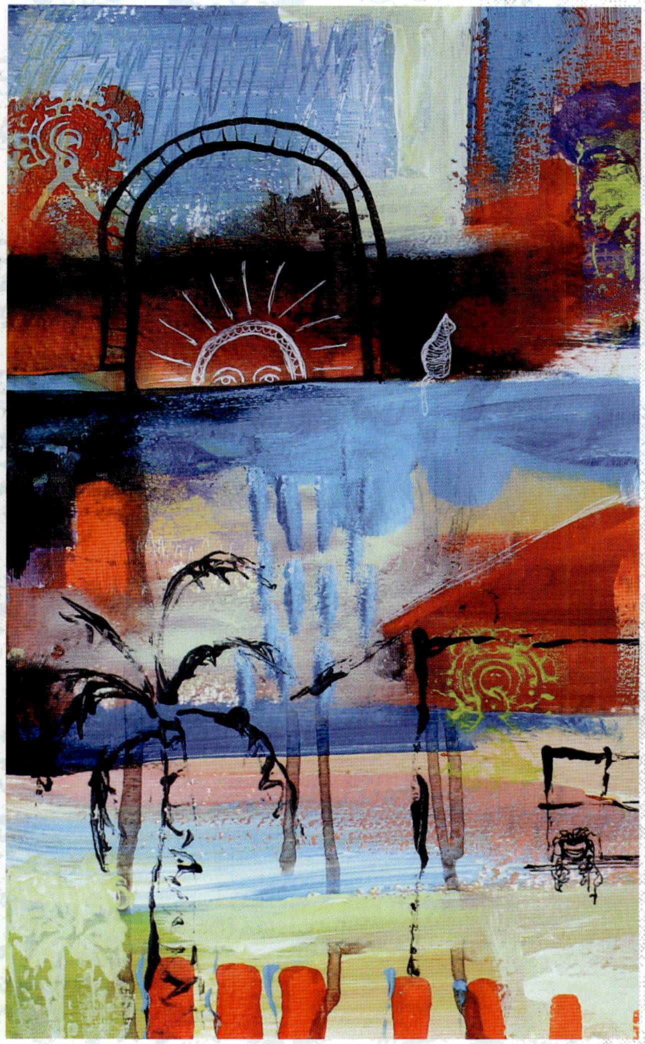

**Possibilities**

After I finished this painting I played around with a viewfinder and realized that it spoke to me more as two separate works—rich, evocative representations of a very special time in our lives.

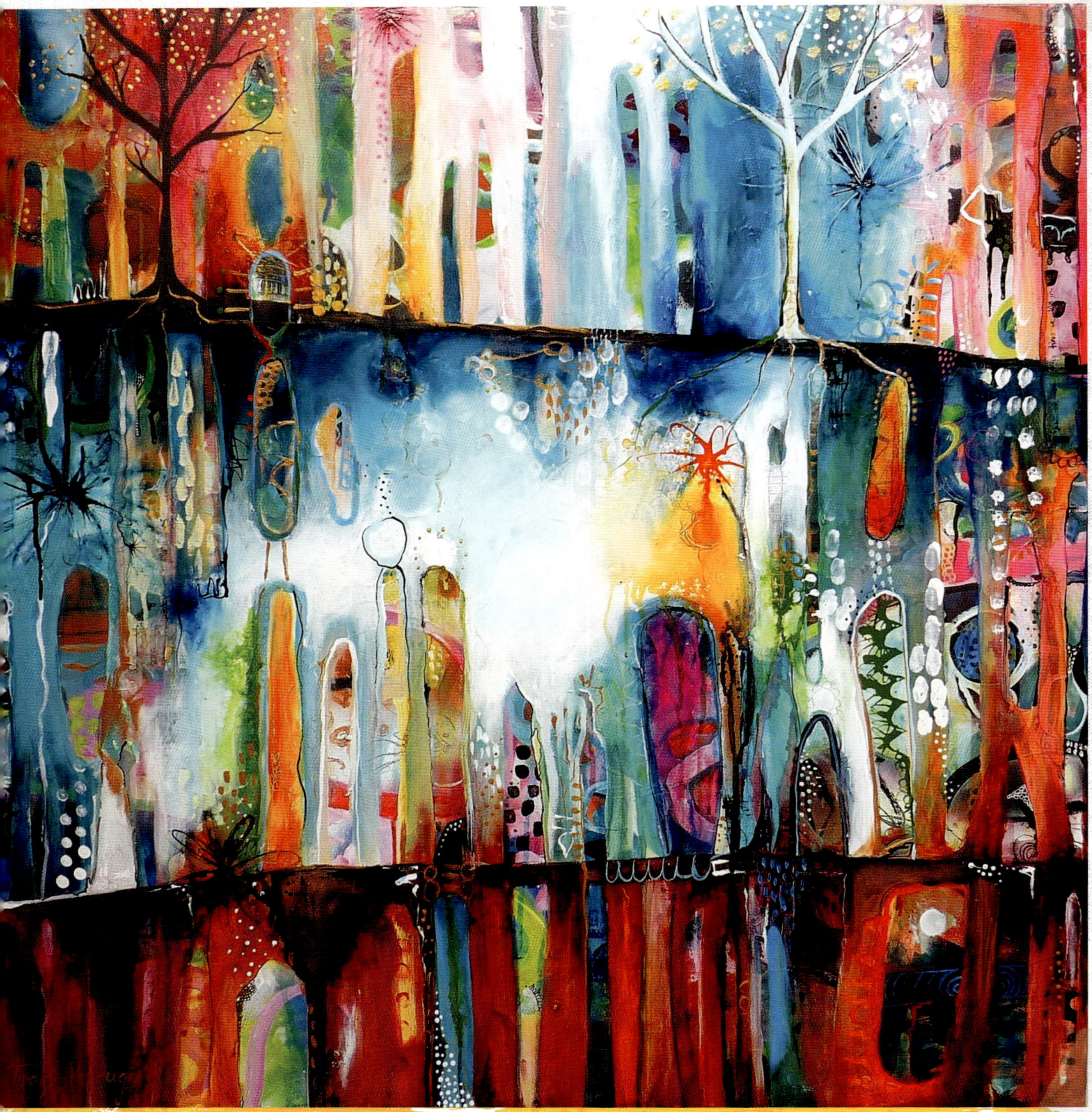

# chapter five: inspiration all around

## Seeing with fresh eyes and an open heart

Close your eyes. Wherever you are. Take a deep breath. Empty your mind. Now open them wide and look around as if you are seeing your surroundings for the first time, and begin to describe what you see, tiny piece by tiny piece. There is inspiration everywhere.

I am sitting here in my bedroom, my favorite afternoon spot in the house during winter. It is warm and filled with light. I open my eyes, and looking down, I see the notepad I am writing on—messy scribbled thoughts, uncertain ramblings—trying to find clarity amongst the scrawl of text and haphazard margin notes of my first draft.

The notepad rests on a patchwork, embroidered Indian cushion, which is centered on my lap. The cushion evokes my senses with its riot of fuchsia, teal and orange, and here and there a vibrant red thread zigzags with dramatic flair, striking notes of discord and harmony, each with their own beauty. Some of the patches are faded and bits of thread have worn away. I am transported to a Rajasthani marketplace, and although I have not yet visited India, I can almost smell the spices wafting through the air. I run my fingers across the textured surface and begin to imagine, creating stories in my mind, seeing other, earlier hands painstakingly sewing these patches together, wondering about their stories, seeing their hands in my mind, the color of nutmeg and cinnamon, lined with a lifetime of manual work.

I wonder what other mother embroidered this sage green flower with its hot pink center. I want to submerge myself in this color, these imaginings, sketch these ancient symbols and find out what they mean.

Ah, I am inspired …

*And above all, watch with glittering eyes the whole world around you because the greatest secrets are always hidden in the most unlikely places. Those who don't believe in magic will never find it.*
—Roald Dahl

Looking farther, beyond the cushion, I see my white-socked feet, casually crossed, at the end of my outstretched legs. I am wearing black yoga pants, and the black and white provide a stark contrast against the heavily patterned quilt cover in tones of aubergine, cherry, chocolate and coffee. A realization! My quilt cover is a concoction of delicious colors. I want to eat it! Suddenly I am dreaming of making stuffed eggplant with walnuts and zucchini and a rich tomato sauce followed by a slice of Black Forest cake laced with espresso.

Ah, I am inspired …

To the left a shaft of sunlight falls against the adobe wall in the perfect shape of a rhombus. Its straight geometric lines are softened by the niche built into the rough-textured surface. Serendipitously it is centered exactly in the illuminated rhombus. Inside the niche, a memory lies—a rock in the shape of a love heart, one of many we have collected over the years. This one carried 12,000 km (7,500 miles) from La Mission in Northern Baja, Mexico, where we spent our twenty-fifth wedding anniversary in 2012. I am flooded with memories: checking into our Airbnb apartment on the beach and finding the bedroom filled with silver helium balloons, fresh-baked cookies and fruit platters in the kitchen, a kind and generous offering by a caring host to celebrate our milestone. I am instantly back in Puerto Nuevo eating *langosta* and drinking margaritas as the late afternoon sun warms our faces and mariachis sing *Besame Mucho*. Later back at the apartment we drink too many cocktails while watching multiple episodes of Stephen Hawkings's *Into the Universe* and pondering the big questions . . . drunk on love, life and el Jimador tequila. The next day we walk the rock-strewn beach together, savoring the short five days until I return to my teaching tour.

The heart rock is illuminated by the beam of light, nestled in the small diamond-shaped alcove, against a background of patterned glass. The glass blocks we picked up for a song—discarded, unwanted remnants of another person's pre-renovation demolition, prized additions to our newly built bedroom. One man's junk, another's treasure. Each block is stamped with a grid pattern several times horizontally, vertically and diagonally, catching the light and defracting and diffusing it into a kaleidoscopic offering of rainbow prisms, green foliage and blue sky. Bringing the outside in like tiny jewels.

I want to put my pen down and run to my studio to capture the beauty, the memory, the feeling.

Without even moving from my bed, just by opening my eyes and taking time to be still and reflect.

Ah, I am inspired …

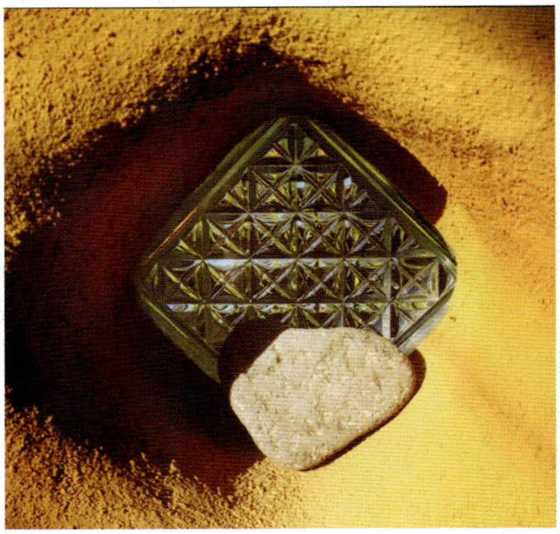

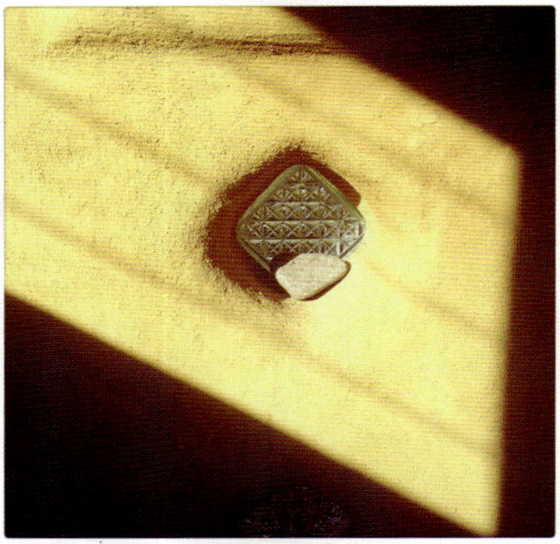

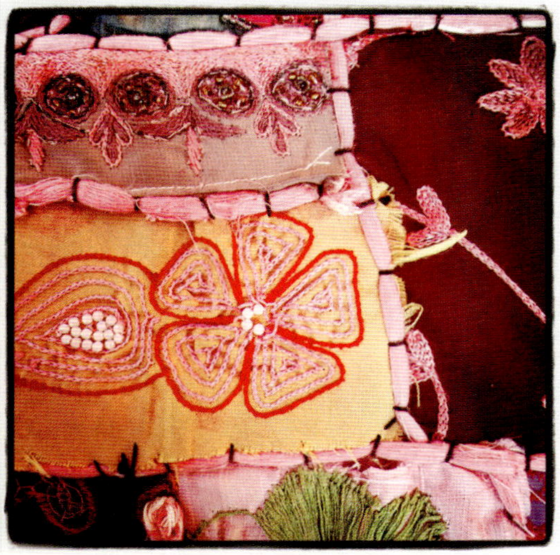

# seeing beauty in all things

**by e'Layne Koenigsberg**

Confucius said, "Everything has beauty, but not everyone sees it." Why then do some people see beauty in every person and in every situation and others don't? "Seeing" beauty is not just a matter of using our eyes. It's also a practice of living with our hearts wide open. It is my belief that what we look for in life is exactly what we see. For example, if we go into the kitchen and someone left dishes piled high, we might get frustrated the kitchen isn't clean. We can choose in that moment to be frustrated, or we can change our focus and be grateful for the beautiful meal that was created resulting in a pile of dishes. Our judgments, opinions and frustrations can get in our way of seeing beauty in the world.

There is a little game I play that enables me to shift my perception of any circumstance at any moment. I pretend I'm looking through a kaleidoscope.

I take a few deep breaths and in my mind's eye I turn the kaleidoscope just one degree and guess what . . . the world takes on an entirely new picture. So, if I'm ever feeling annoyed, fearful or just plain bored, I bring my breath deep into my belly, which brings me into the present moment, and then I mindfully find beauty in all that surrounds me.

So what other things get in the way of our ability to see beauty in all things? Simple enough: We usually get in our own way, which is wonderful news because only we can change ourselves. One big obstacle obstructing beauty is that we move too quickly through life. Days mushroom into weeks and weeks snowball into years. We rush from one commitment to the next, and at day's end have no energy left for self-care. Constantly feeling overwhelmed by my endless to-do list, I finally had a profound realization. My list was never going to be finished . . . and that's a good thing; it means I'm still alive; I'm still interested in fully living life. And I found a solution to my dilemma of feeling overwhelmed. Instead of a to-do list I create a must-do list. When my must-do tasks are complete, I'm done for the day. This is a fantastic way to feel accomplished and also provides the time to slow down enough to do the things in life that nurture our souls.

We must continually ask ourselves, do we take time to savor laughter, to find our internal rhythm, to see our own inner beauty, to explore the activities that arouse passion in our bellies? Do we develop the art of relaxation, gaze in amazement at light refracting off a raindrop on an autumn leaf and make waves when we have a strong conviction? Do we seek out interesting people, cultivate deep, meaningful relationships and dare to dream big? We can take a look around our home and look at the friends we have and see in this mirror the life we have created. Do our environment and our friends support our dreams and passions? We can use beauty as our barometer for measuring a rich, happy life—keep only what we love, the items that are uplifting and make our hearts sing, and keep friends who support us and also manifest beauty and goodness in their lives.

To see beauty we must wake up the senses and cultivate a receptive attitude to appreciate that which is simple. Simplicity is a state of mind. If we're all up in our minds, we miss the subtle nuances in life: the moisture in the air before a storm, the illuminated palm trees' reflection in the pool and people's facial expressions speaking volumes their words do not express. It is through the language of the heart, not the chatter of the mind, that we become attuned to life's profound moments and the infinite beauty surrounding us.

# the infinite possibilities of failure

I'm not sure that I've ever thrown away or gessoed over an artwork. I've shoved them away in a corner to gather dust, tucked them into folios and folders and then finally, sometimes years later, pulled them out for a rework when inspiration struck. I've cut them up into interesting pieces for collage or to work into mixed-media pieces or create handmade cards. I've turned them into gratitude flags, folded them into concertina books, scrawled poetry across them and made bookmarks for gifts and giveaways.

I no longer regard any piece as a failure, but instead I see each one as a vehicle for infinite possibilities! What can we learn from our explorations? Not everything you create will be amazing. In fact, for a while, as you are starting out, it's possible nothing will. Its OK; it's all part of the adventure.

There is an extraordinary freedom in allowing yourself to play and experiment *without attachment to outcome*, without worrying whether you will have a salable piece or whether you have just wasted your time. Giving yourself the gift of time to create without expectation or fear of failure will enhance your creative life in so many ways. I promise you.

Here are a few things I like to do to find inspiration when my creative play (more times than not) doesn't lead to a masterpiece.

- Take a piece that you are not in love with and spend some time trying out new compositions by taking photos of cropped areas that work. Think about balancing lights and darks, larger areas of color with more delicate marks, focusing in on areas of the work that tell a different story when they are isolated.
- Crop into several different areas of the painting and let your imagination run free. Perhaps your ponderings will become the spark of a new work or a whole new series.
- Crop in even further to find simple shapes and more abstract elements will begin to appear.
- Import your photos into a simple editor like Picasa and play with the settings. Invert the colors and see what happens. Not only will you be exposed to a whole new palette that you might fall in love with, but you will also have an instant lesson on the color wheel and complementary colors!
- Play with your photo editor again, inverting and enhancing colors and trying out different effects. Save each image you like as a separate file for future reference. Whenever you are stuck for inspiration, go into these files for an instant boost!

Think about different ways you could utilize these idea sparkers. An image you isolate might make a great personal stamp, a fabulous beginning for a series of landscape linocuts, or it could be the inspiration for a giant abstract painting around the concept of journeys!

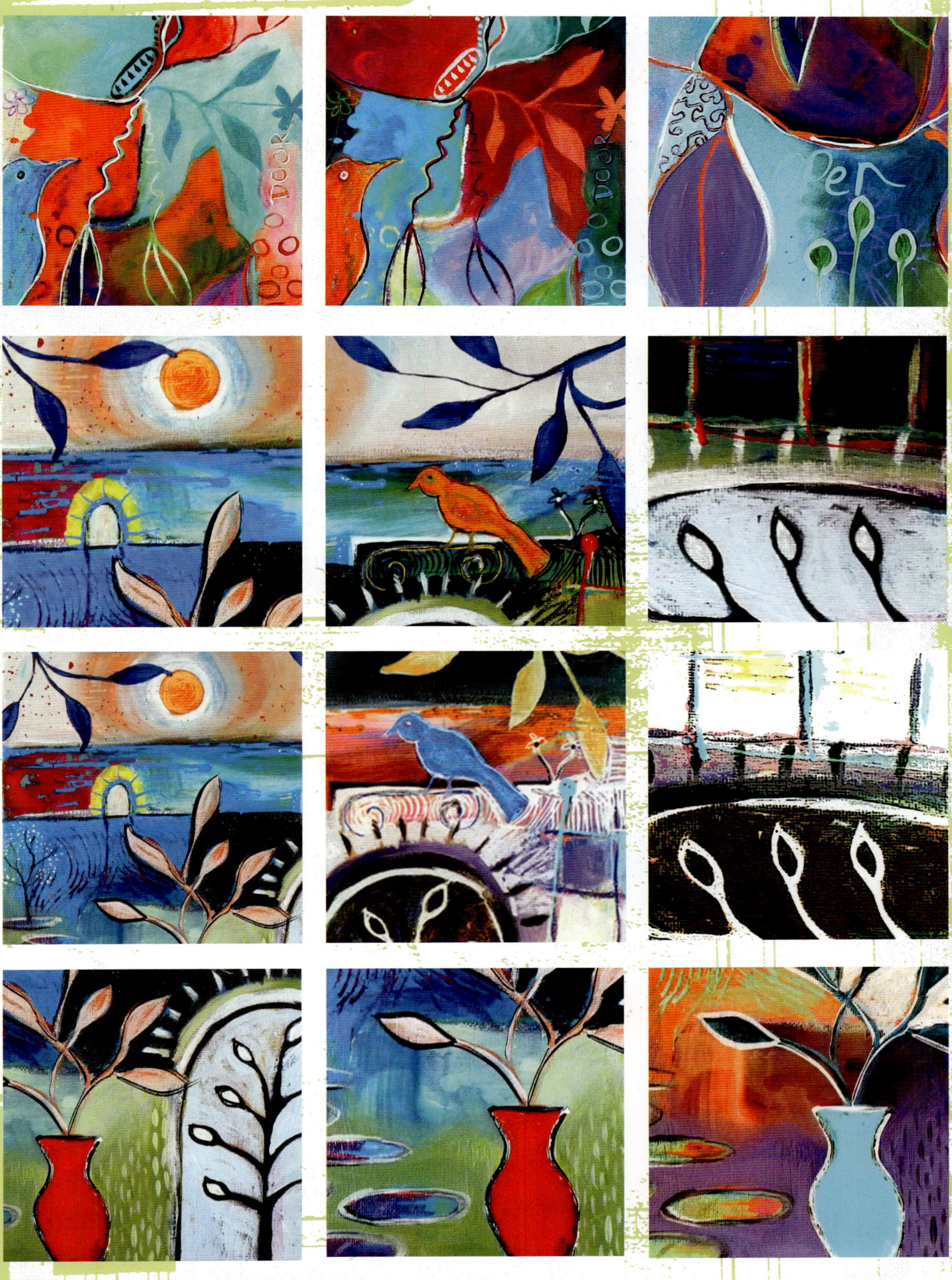
DOOR
DOOR

# inspiration as you

**by Erin Faith Allen (Photography by Lucy Sharpe)**

You know what you look like in photographs, but in this lesson we are going to take a self-portrait photo and embellish it to express beyond how you look. We are going to express how you feel, in your soul, using a few different mixed-media techniques.

Is your soul a stream-of-consciousness word parade that flows across your surface? Does it swoosh in gentle abstract harmony or blaze its way vibrantly across the page? Have you ever created a piece of art with direct connection and intention to express this pure and unique essence of self?

The clarity of self-image will assist greatly in manifesting your dreams, desires and circumstances that are your heart's desire. To hold a self-created image of who you are is a talisman for growth, a gift that keeps on giving for years to come!

In this lesson you will be given tools of self-awareness that can be utilized in your studio and career to unleash your potential through this creative process at any time you need to connect with yourself for answers, guidance or fun.

**What You Need**

- acrylic markers
- acrylic paint
- gesso
- paintbrushes
- palette knife
- patterned paper
- pencil
- self-portrait photo

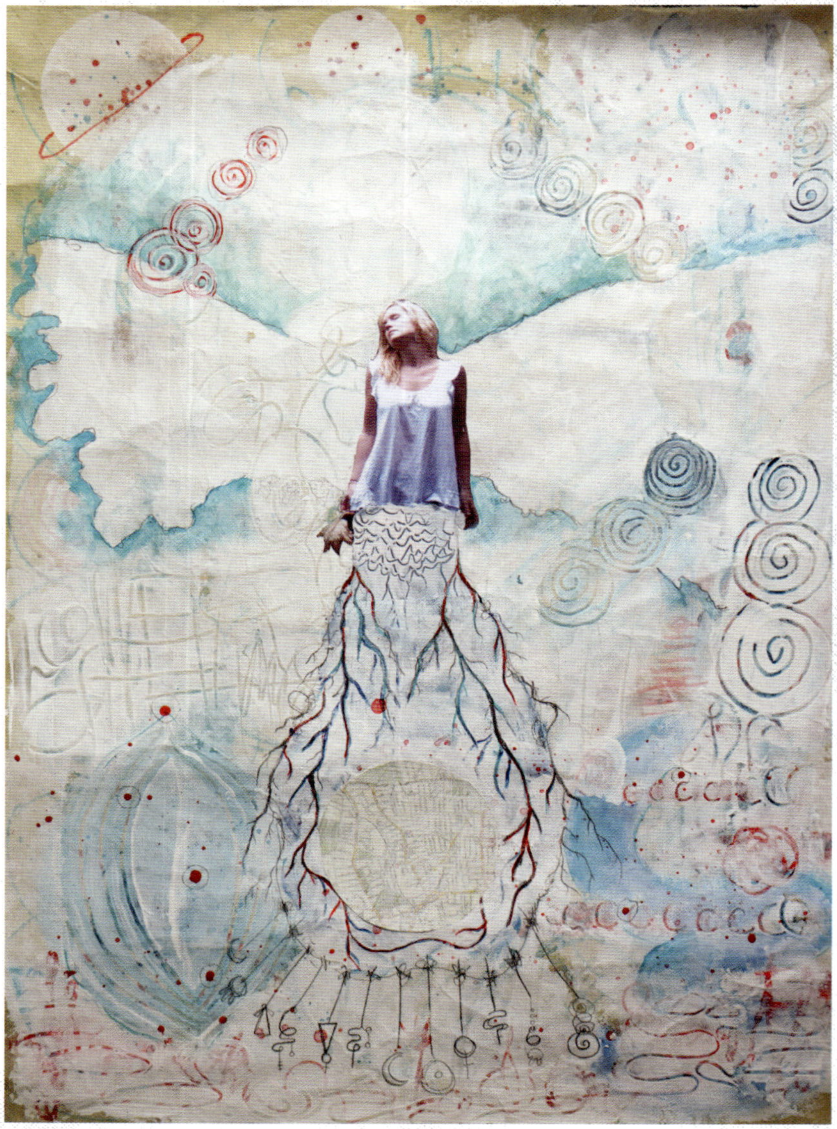

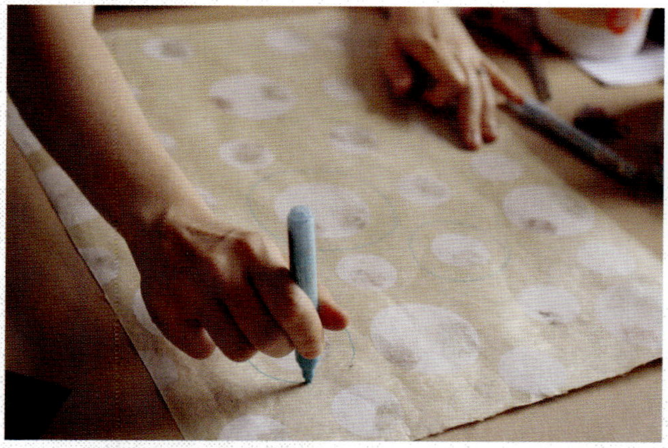

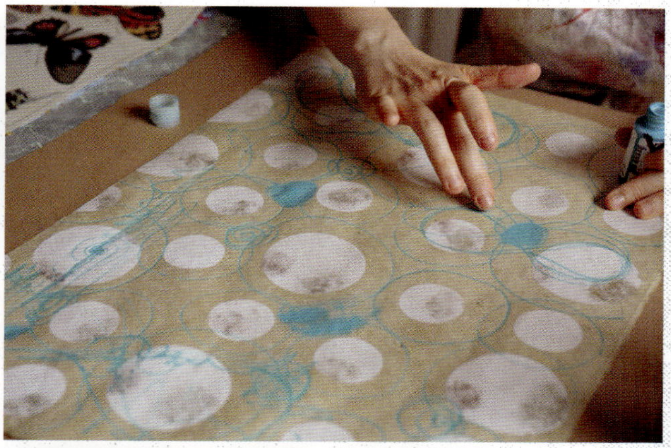

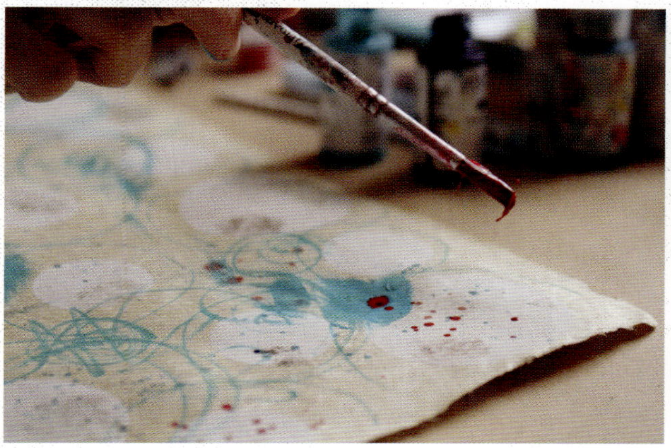

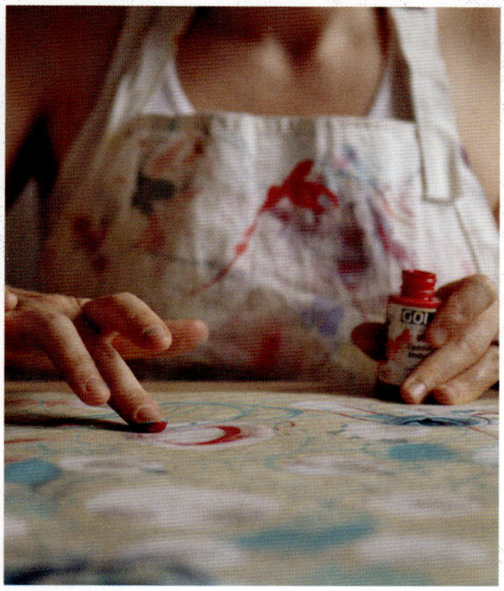

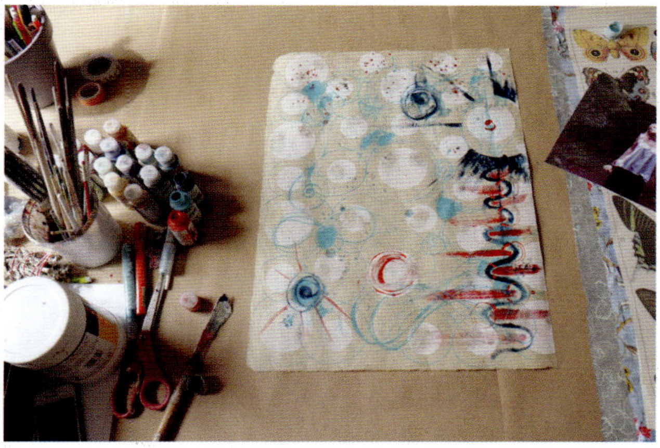

1 Begin by making marks on your paper with an acrylic marker. (Because the paper I've chosen has circles on it, I am going to build my mark-making off that pattern, by drawing more circles.) Use this time of mark-making to really begin to settle into your creative imagination, allowing the actions of marking to open up your creativity and forget about the real world.

I let my arm and spirit talk to me, and move the marker anywhere and everywhere in an intuitive and free way. The more freely I let my hand move around making marks, the more freedom I am giving to my self-expression.

2 Next, select acrylic paint that you would like to use for more mark-making, and, as above, begin to spread the paint freely. Though I often use my fingers, use your brushes if you'd like.

3 Spatter paint using a paintbrush to make random marks in selected areas on the surface.

Working with my fingers and paints often connects me to a more primal space than a paintbrush does. I think the reason for this is that it puts me straight into contact with my surface, without any tools other than ME. Since we are trying to access a space of pure creative expression without a thought process, painting from a primal place is perfect for this lesson.

4 Continue to work with paints and markers until you have a pattern that you feel connected to. Remember this is about intuitive working, following where you feel your creativity taking you. (On a technical note, one important thing to remember is to let your paints dry before you try to use a marker over the top of them, or the wet paint will ruin your marker.)

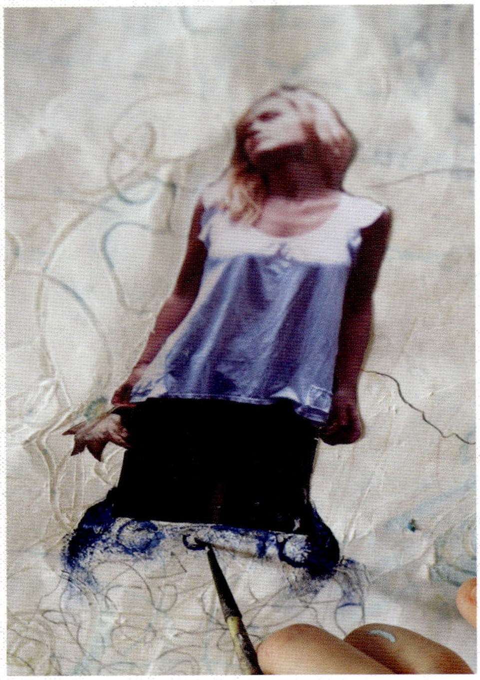

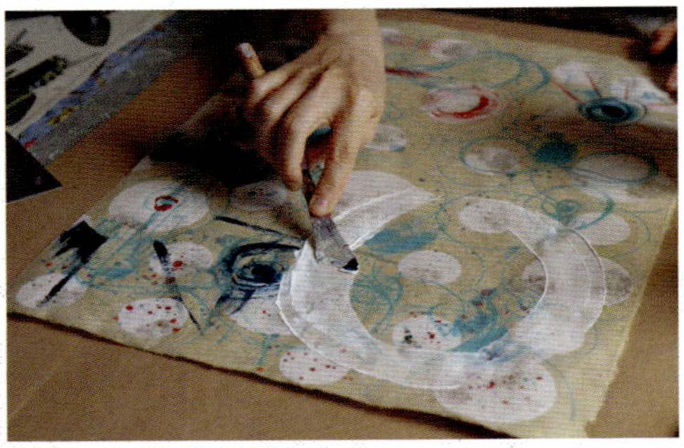

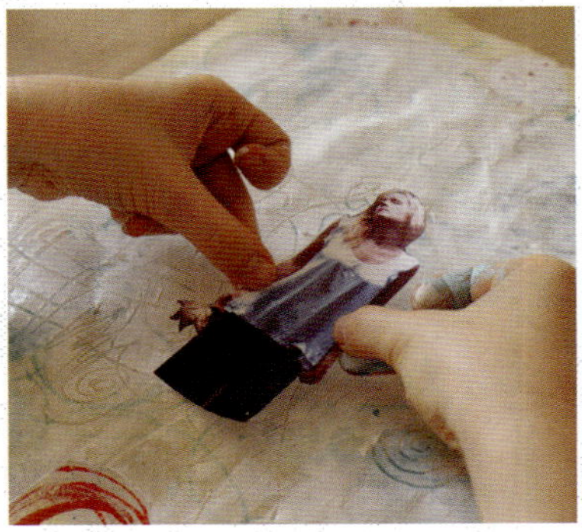

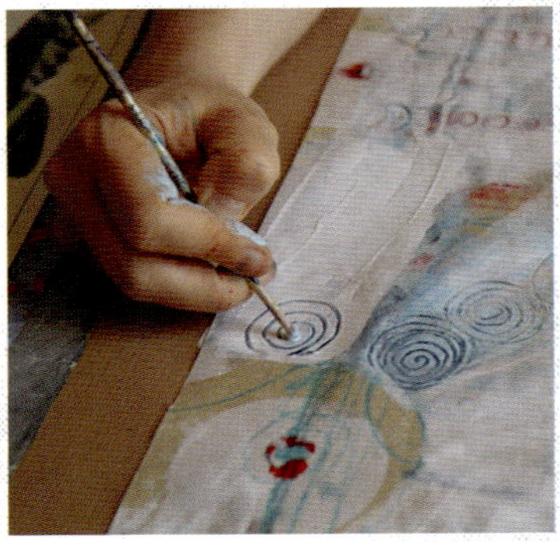

5 Get out your gesso and begin spreading it with a palette knife. Apply it in random patches or in a shape like I have done here. Again, just follow what your gut tells you, and here is where the fun lies: You can apply it in thin layers that will still allow some subtleties of your mark-making to show through like soft, muted, colorful texture, or you can apply it a bit thicker.

Where the gesso is a bit thicker, take the hard end of your paintbrush and begin to draw into the gesso. You can use this technique to show the underlayer of color and mark-making, to draw in shapes or text that you love, or to outline a shape you want to fill in with other colors. I like to apply it both ways—thin in some places, thicker in others—and I love putting symbols into my work this way. It creates amazing texture and energy.

6 Take your self-portrait photo and let it tell you where it wants to be attached onto the surface. (You might want to cut it out of the background, so you don't have to worry about blending the hard edges of a square photograph into your work.) Once you've placed your self-portrait onto the paper, amplify the power of your imagination and let yourself "see" what is not there. Usually, the first thing I see is what I begin to build on the surface.

Take a step back, and see and feel other areas that you would like to fill with symbols and do so using the previous techniques of fingerpainting and drawing into wet paint with the hard end of your paintbrush. When the paint is dry, use a pencil to shade some areas so they stand out and to draw symbols. This is a gentle peering into what your imagination wants to tell you. It is not forced, contrived or in any way planned ahead. It is a soft gaze, built on your intuition and what imagery may appear in your imagination.

When I gazed gently at my self-portrait, I saw wings and root-like veins, so I began to allow for those pieces to be added into my piece. I began to blend the cutoff edge of the photograph into a matching color palette with white gesso and texture created with the end of my paintbrush. Applying the gesso slightly thick, I used the hard end of my paintbrush to draw root-like veins over the area where my legs should be. I drew a very quick outline of wings using my pencil and shaded the outline of the wings with turquoise acrylic paint to separate them from the background and give the illusion that the figure is rising off the surface.

In most of my work I use photographs and then draw in what isn't there. I don't worry about perfection and a drawing that looks realistic. I like intuitive, simple, quick lines that convey an energy. I like simple and quick because they don't leave time for self-judgment.

Finally, I cut a circle from a map and placed it onto the lower body of my image. Fingerpainting gesso over it helps it blend into the surface. Ta-da! A collaged self-portrait that expresses how I *feel* in my *soul*. I hope *you* have fun exploring *your* soul!

# traveling inspiration

**Laurie Mika**

I have found that travel provides one of the greatest sources of inspiration for me. Experiencing new cultures provides the catalyst to create a new piece of art the minute I return home! Exploring flea markets and finding little treasures to embed in clay also helps to provide a visual reminder of the places I have been.

One small object can often spark a whole mosaic as was the case with my most recent trip to Morelia, Mexico and the butterfly wings I collected there. Morelia is home to the famed monarch butterfly migration. The monarchs begin their long annual journey in Canada and migrate to Mexico and then return to Canada. The length of the migration exceeds the normal lifespan of the monarch so it takes many generations of butterflies to complete the migration. In Mexico, it was believed that the monarchs represented the souls of the departed, especially since their arrival in Mexico in November coincided with *Dia de los Muertos*, or Day of the Dead.

All along the forest path leading up to where the millions of butterflies cluster in the trees, one can see butterfly wings lining the paths like orange and black jewels. Inspiration abounds in a majestic setting like this, and seeing the contrast of life and death in the forest around me started my mind reeling with the possibilities of these butterfly wings. I knew when I got home that I wanted to try to embed the butterfly wings into polymer clay. I also knew that I wanted to do a figurative piece as a takeoff on the word *monarch*, which is essentially a head of state, king or queen. How perfect for someone like me who has been hung up on crowns and royal imagery for many years now!

Upon my return home (like the next day!), I began a series of pieces related to the monarch migration.

The world is one gigantic panorama of possibility. One need not look far or wide, for inspiration abounds if we open our eyes and our hearts to all this planet has to offer. Really taking the time to look and to grab onto that which speaks to your core and fills you with wonder is at the heart of inspiration.

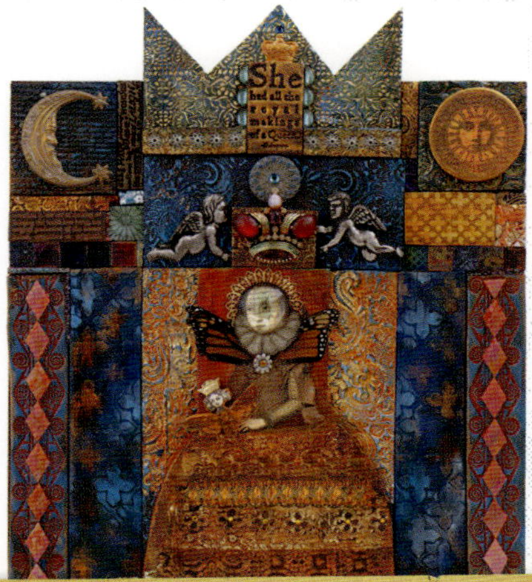


*This piece,* Monarch Queen, *depicts my monarch butterfly queen being coronated by angels. This representation combines European medieval and Mexican folk art traditions.*

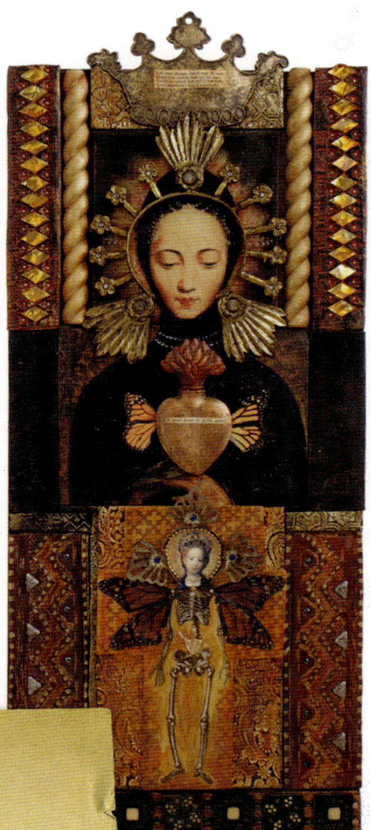

*For* Circle of Life, *I began with a skeleton body with the queen's head and butterfly wings that ended up on the assemblage. This refers to the life cycle of both butterflies and humans and also refers to metamorphosis and how "Nothing endures but change."*

exercise

# palette prints

I often use pieces of plywood as palettes, building up interesting textures and color layers and then later using the old palette as the beginning of a painting. A twist on this (and a great way not to waste precious paint) is to press some cartridge or watercolor paper down onto your palette at the end of a painting session to pick up any leftover paint and create a monoprint on the paper. I store all of these palette-printed papers in an inspiration stash and pull them out from time to time to see what I can find!

**What You Need**

- acrylic paints (including white)
- bamboo skewer
- fine brush
- gold or silver gel pen
- used palette (either on paper or board)
- watercolor pencils

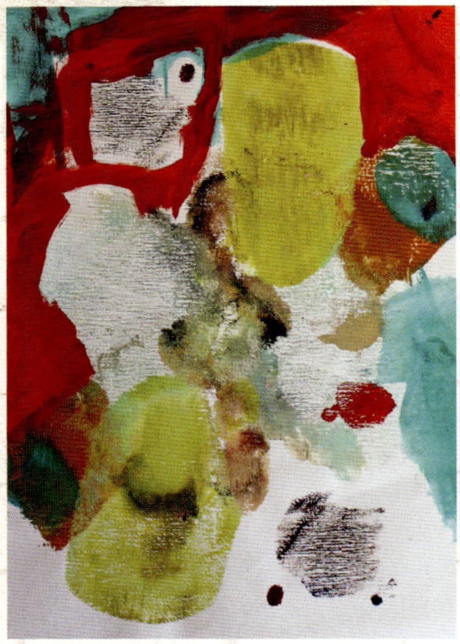

**1** Begin creating palette prints and save them for a day you're feeling dry on inspiration. On this sheet I had printed the leftover paint from my palette and wiped off all the excess red paint from the brush I was using last. As soon as I picked this palette up, I noticed the two black dots in the center and saw the potential little elephant peeking out at me!

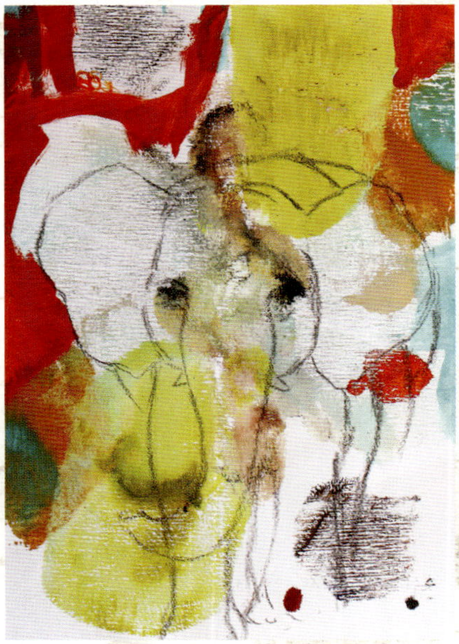

**2** After finding inspiration in your print, gather any resources you might need to begin such as reference photos. (I used two here.) Then begin sketching what it is you'd like to create. I lightly sketched an elephant with a Derwent watercolor pencil. Any dark color will do but in this case I used Bark.

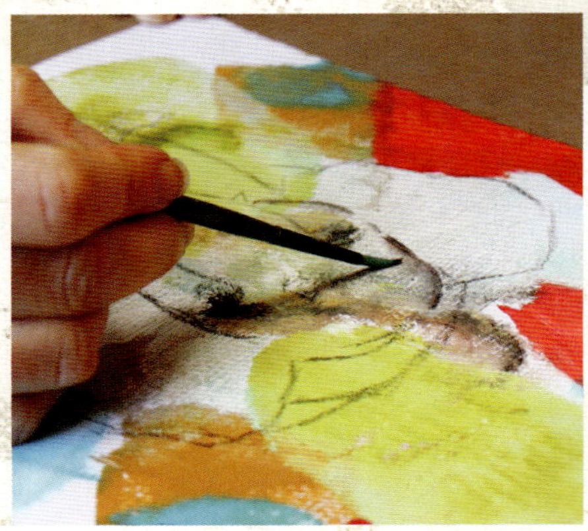

**3** With a fine wet brush, pull out some of the color from your sketched lines to begin to introduce some tonal variation.

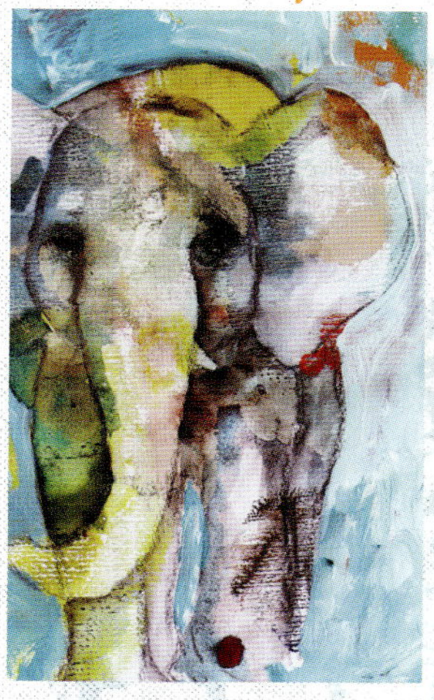

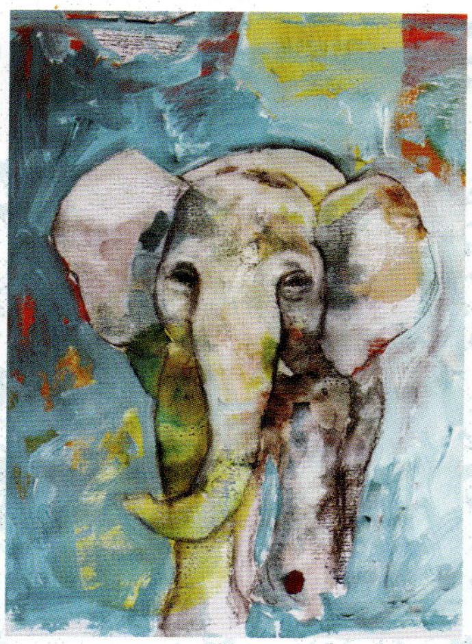

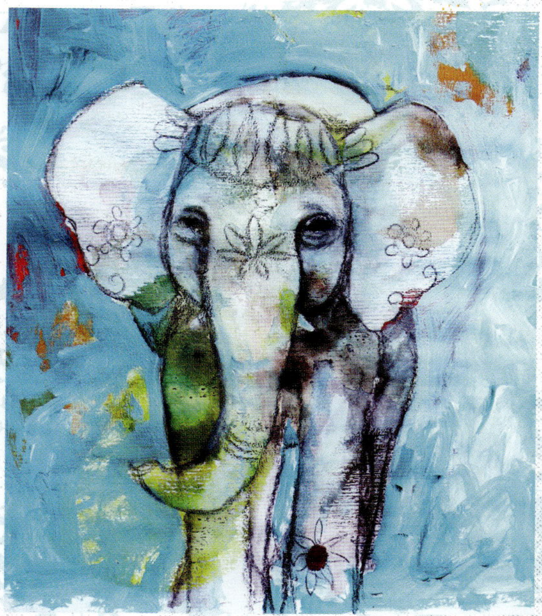

**4** Lightly and loosely, paint around the sketched shape with a solid color, such as the Cobalt Teal I used here. Leaving small glimpses of the colors underneath will add visual interest and keep your painting cohesive. (I also used a tiny amount of Turquoise Phthalo, wetting several areas around the ears and top of the legs and dropping the turquoise into shadowed parts of the body of the elephant.)

**5** Have fun adding some finer details with watercolor pencils. Inspired by the painted Indian elephants, I began to add some decorative patterns.

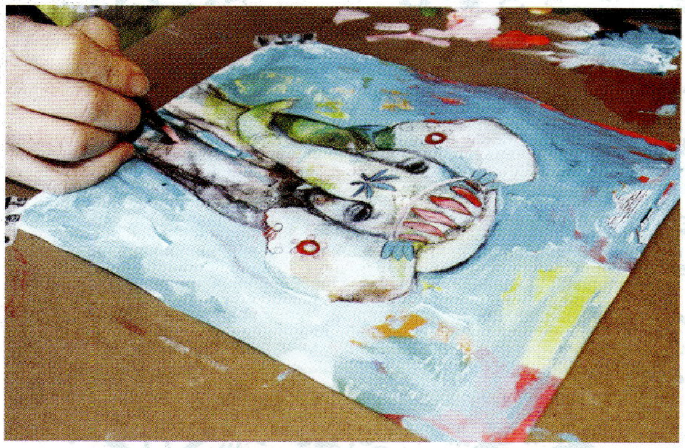

**6** Choose a few bright colors and some white, and paint the decorative elements. Vary the tones of the colors by adding more or less white and repeat colors across the designs.

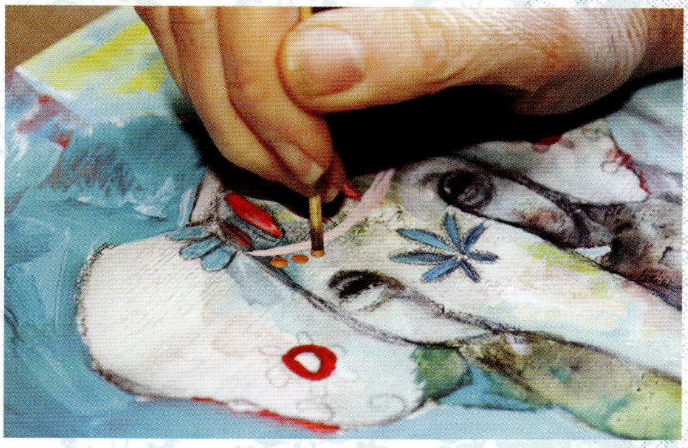

**7** Using a bamboo skewer, add some dotty accents in gold or silver, using paint or a gel pen.

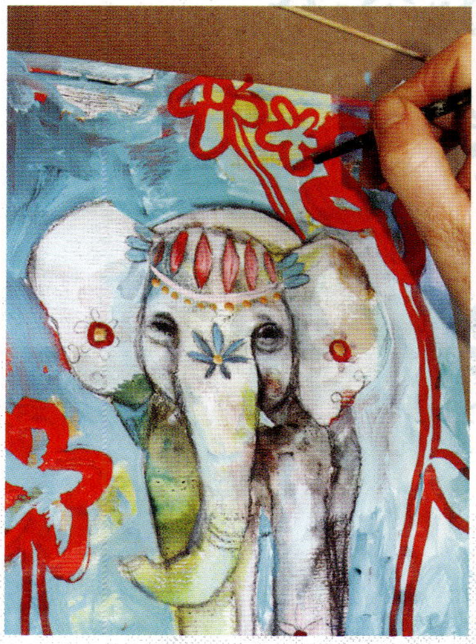

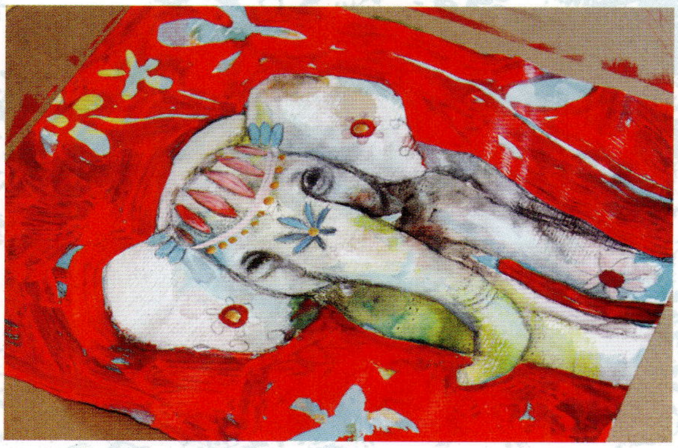

**8** Choose a color that is a contrast of your background color. (I used Pyrrole Red.) Paint over the initial background color leaving little flowers or peek holes.

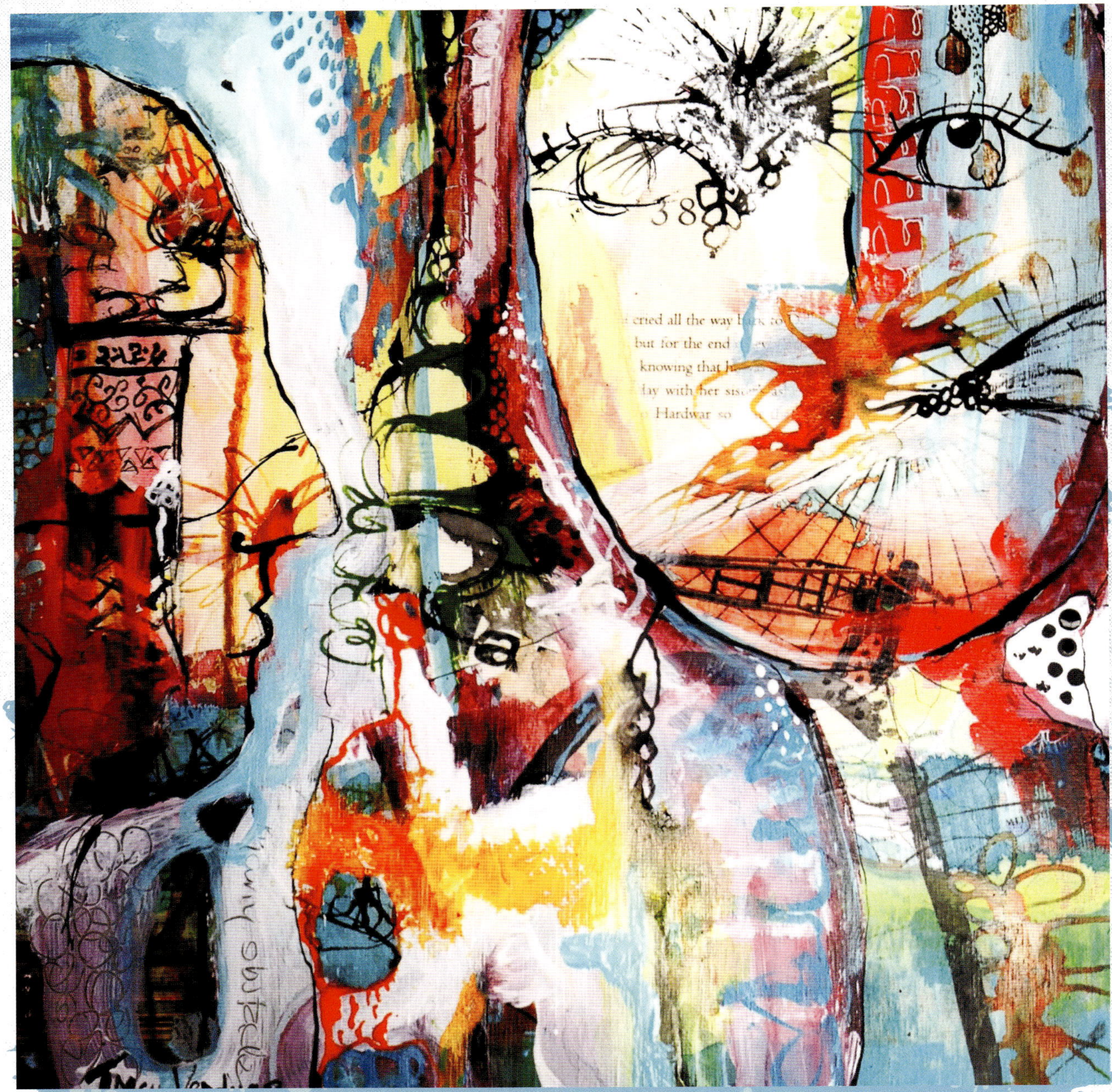
cried all the way
but for the end
knowing that
Hardwar so

# chapter six:
# your garden of possibility

### Cultivating the life of your dreams

### Holding the Key

Somewhere . . . way down deep inside of you there is a gem
which holds all the wisdom you have ever or will ever need.

It may be dusty and it may take some time to shine it,
but its essence is untainted.

Open your senses and you will start to see a glimmer
from the corner of your eye.

Slow it down and you will open up the breathing space that births a dream.

Cradle your imperfection and wonder at the miracle of each moment.

You are at the center of that miraculous NOW.

Pay attention to the whispers that linger in the sacred silence.
Grasp them with a determined fist; give them wings through loving action,
and then gently open your hand to let them fly.

Each one of us has access to a field of infinite possibilities,
and each of us holds the key to allowing.

No need to wait until you know everything; each day is a day to learn anew.

Will you open the window wide to leap . . .
or choose to stay in a prison of your own making?

*And the day came when the risk to remain tight in a bud was more painful than the risk it took to blossom.*
—Anaïs Nin

For a very long time I had this kind of ambivalent attitude toward creating the life of my dreams. Let's just say it's difficult to do when your dreams are not at all clear or defined. I also harbored dubious feelings toward the very idea that we are in charge of creating our own reality. For a long time I thought that meant that if bad stuff happened I would be to blame.

It is a huge responsibility to *create* your own reality, and it still does my head in . . . sometimes . . . but mostly I am at peace with it, and at the core of my being there is a deep knowing that we do, indeed, shape the fabric of our own personal universe by the thoughts that loop through our minds day after day.

As a child I wanted desperately to be seen.

I would pirouette around the room, spinning and leaping, imagining myself dancing in *Swan Lake*, or coming up with wild improvisational dance moves inspired by whatever music was playing on the record player. My grandfather would laugh and try to trip me up, calling my performance The Dance of the Dying Duck.

In the car on long Sunday drives to look at display homes or picnic at Warragamba Dam, I would sing at the top of my lungs wondering if I sounded more like Olivia Newton-John or Dolly Parton. Dad would counter by winking and cringing and turning the radio way up loud to drown out my voice.

The tall poppy syndrome was well and truly alive in Australia in the seventies and, not surprisingly, I learned to tone it down, play it smaller and not be boastful in letting my talents shine.

My parents had shown us the ethic of working hard, had achieved (after many years) the Australian dream of a house on the water on the Gold Coast, only to lose it all in a financial crisis—the house, the business and their marriage by the time I was seventeen.

It's no coincidence that the soundtrack of thoughts that looped through my mind in my twenties went something like this: Gotta work very, very hard to get anywhere; don't take big risks; nothing is certain; money doesn't grow on trees; people with money make more money; things can change for the worse in a second and don't get too big for your britches.

Alongside all of these thoughts, my shiny, adventurous, creative self was screaming to be heard, but was almost completely drowned out by the chorus of woeful negative repetition!

In my thirties (after the surprise revelation that my aunt was really my biological mother who had given me up for adoption at eighteen months to her older sister) I added into the mix: Don't trust; I am unwanted and I don't belong. Phew . . . what a hefty soundtrack to carry around, and in the words of Dr. Phil: "How was that working for me?"

I was working my butt off, nickel-and-diming it in every business venture I started. I was disorganized, unconfident and always, eventually, heading for failure. I had years of struggling with money, health, emotions and relationships. Struggle felt like my default position.

I wish I could tell you, sweet seeker of happiness, that the change was revelatory, sudden, an epiphany from Heaven. And maybe for some, it happens like that. For me, however, it happened little by little, small paradigm shifts, punctuating years of treading water and sometimes even a feeling of slipping backward.

Through it all, however, I was planting seeds and those seeds were beginning to grow. Sometimes they would do nothing more than germinate, lift their struggling heads to the sun for a brief moment and keel over dead, but each time my parameters of possibility shifted just that little bit more, and over time my garden of possibility began to flourish and bloom in every color of the rainbow.

It began, this subtle change in defining a clear, purposeful and intentional life, with becoming aware, with beginning to tap into that deep, listening stillness and learning to watch my thoughts as a silent observer—practicing detachment as they raced around my monkey mind.

The detachment was the hardest part, and for many years I watched these crazy thoughts, fully aware of how little they served me, knowing how much they harmed me and the beating up on myself for having them. I also began to become aware of the things that *lit me up*, making lists that included making things (I hadn't yet begun to paint), cooking, travel, libraries and helping kids feel good about themselves. As I put my attention on these things in my life, I found that more opportunities to expand upon them began to appear.

I dabbled in paint when Santana was a baby, invited people into our home for Mexican cooking classes and, with Marco, began a business importing beautiful handcrafted folk art from Mexico and Guatemala into Australia.

In 1999, I came across an article in the local newspaper about a weekly art class for beginners and the biggest seed ever was planted!

There was also heartache and pain during this time. Very few of us get through life without it, and there is a gift in the strength, empathy and wisdom that come out of it. In the darkest of these times; in the midst of relationship crisis, panic, depression and loss, I had a dream one night; it was clear and bright and carried with it an overwhelming sense of hope and joy.

Our humble home had undergone a magical transformation. It was filled with love, laughter and light and Marco was in the beautifully renovated kitchen cooking up a storm with our daughters who looked to be in their early- to mid-twenties. Their partners were also with them, and everyone was having a wonderful time. In the living room, surrounded by greenery and with light streaming through the skylights overhead, I saw myself, older, early fifties, in a business suit with two other women I did not recognize. There was warmth and joy and excitement amongst us, and I caught snippets of the conversation: retreats, women, creativity, travel . . . our flourishing business!

I woke up with a start and knew, without any doubt, that eventually everything would be OK.

I am still a few years away from becoming that woman, Marco does not cook very often but tells me that one day he would like to learn, and after twenty-seven years, we have worked through our struggles, are still together, happily in love, and the renovation that he completed on our home in 2008 is even better

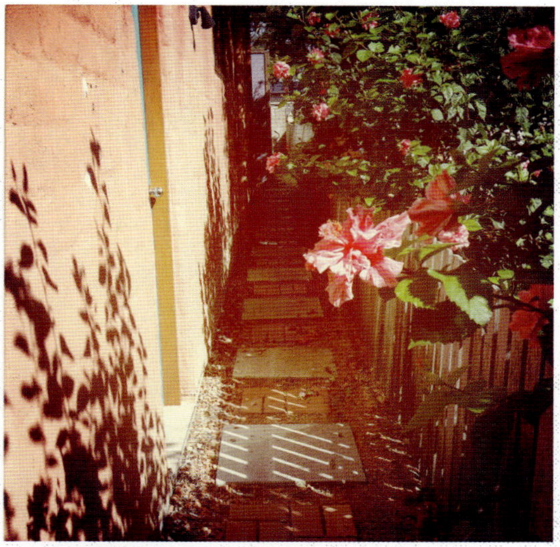

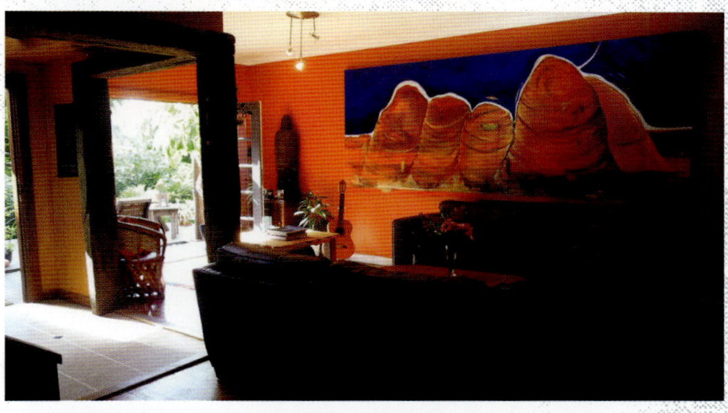

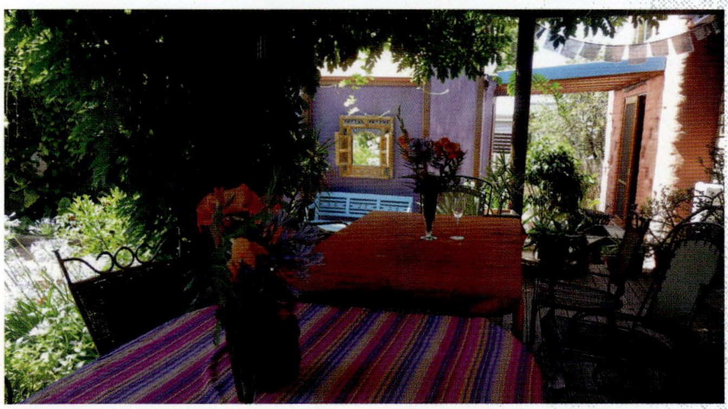

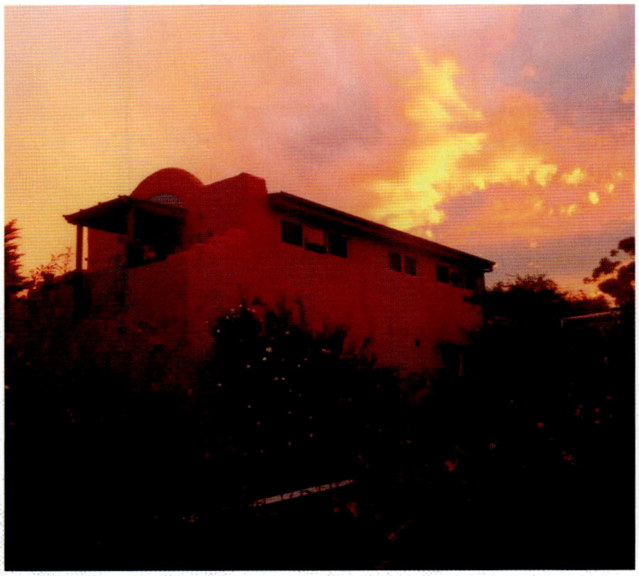

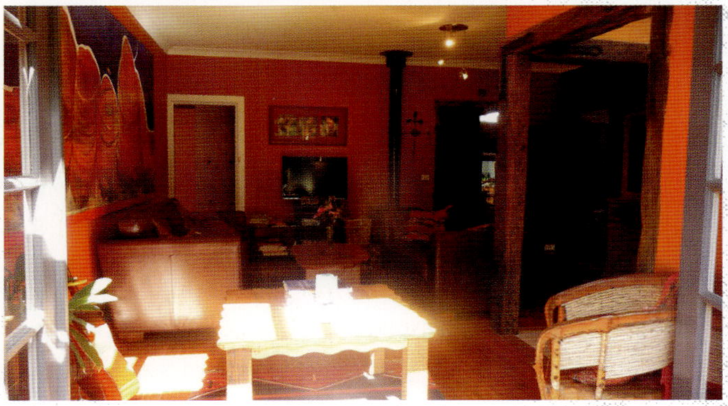

than the one in my dream! Sometimes I search the faces of the beautiful creative women I now call my creative tribe and wonder if I have yet met the women in my dream.

### Listening to Whispers and Honing Your Dream

Somewhere around this time I purchased my first art book by Portland artist Dory Kanter. While the title of *Art Escapes* intrigued me and the exercises inside were fun and informative, I was even more blown away by the discovery that there was, in this world, a job that involved traveling to beautiful locations around the world with other creative people and helping them along on their creative paths.

I remember so clearly thinking, *Sign me up!* and running inside to Marco, bug-eyed, pointing at the book and yelling "This is what I'm going to do!"

I then remember turning the book over to see who the publisher was. I saw the words North Light for the first time and heard the whisper inside: "One day you could write a book for North Light Books …"

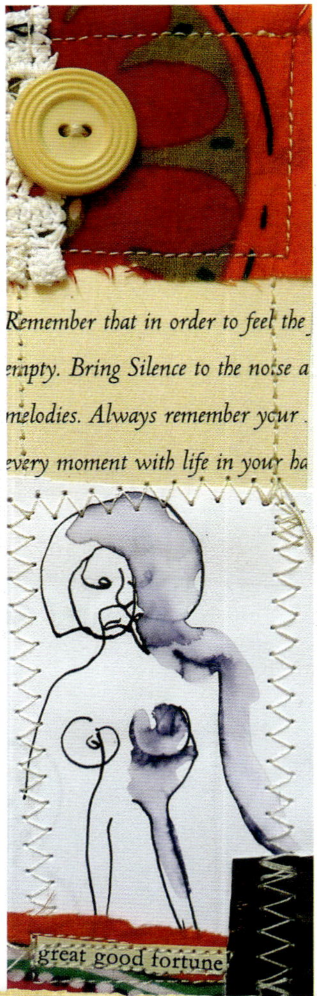


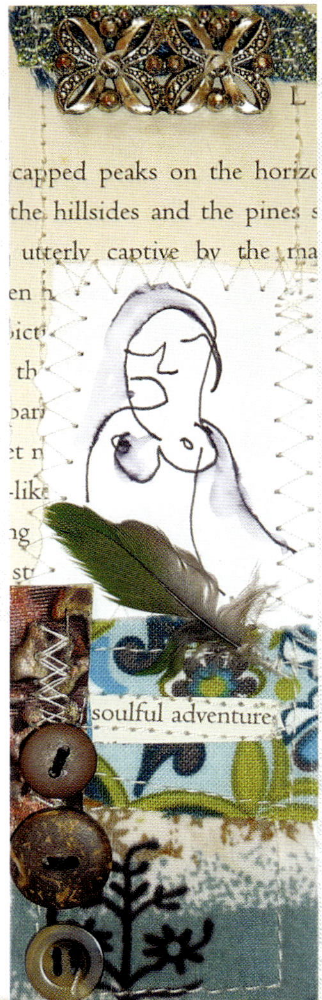


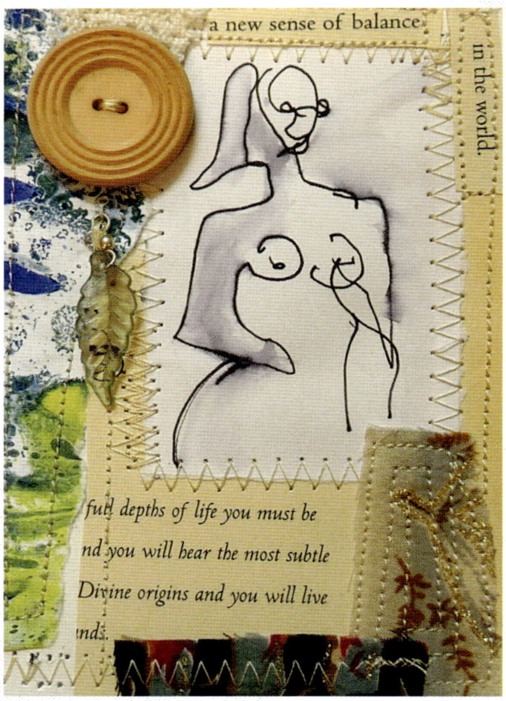


*These small mixed-media pieces were created intuitively, holding my highest, shiniest self in mind while drawing the naked self with my eyes closed. Using a variety of stitched and glued elements, I created a whole series of these divine women, adding text from an old book that seemed to serendipitously help me find clarity around many aspects of not only my journey but the journey of my women friends.*

# planting your seeds

- Begin cultivating an inner stillness and awareness. Pay attention to your thoughts and begin to focus on the things you are grateful for and the things that light you up.
- Do more of the things that light you up and allow yourself to design a dream life, which would encompass your passions. Own the fact that you are worthy of this dream.
- Search out those who are living their biggest dreams and read their stories. Make contact on their blogs or by e-mail. Say hello and you will find out they are real people just like you and me. Begin to understand that if it is possible for them, it is possible for you.
- Begin to align yourself with others who believe in possibility, who believe in their own greatness and will help you believe in yours. Spend less time with people who want to keep you small.
- Take small, steady steps toward your dream but don't wait to be perfect at what you do. You will be waiting a long time.

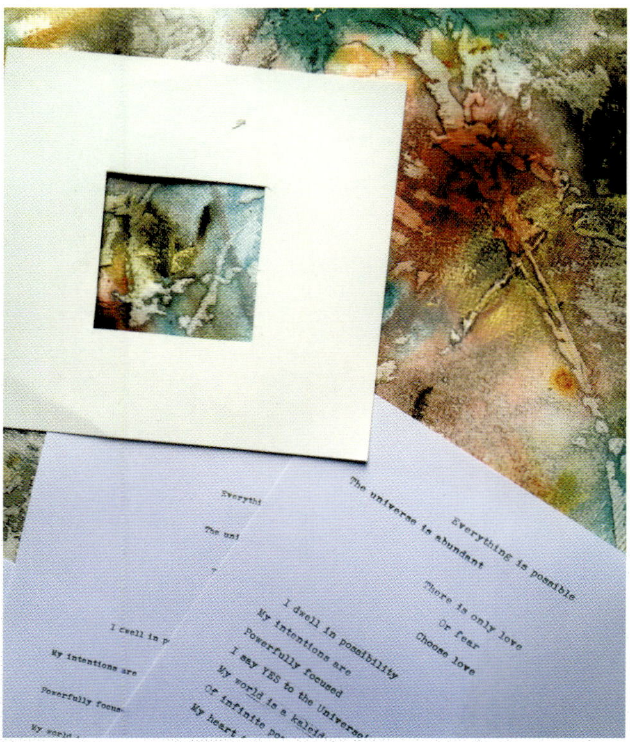


- Test the waters along the way. Jump in! Try out some different strokes, a few different bathing suits. Not everything will work out. You will learn along the way how not to drown and which swimmers work for you.
- Write a letter to your "now" self from your "future" self. Date it one year or five years from now, whatever feels right for you. Tell yourself all about the exciting things you are doing! Here's a little glimpse of mine: *Sailing in the Riviera with a client who has just commissioned me to provide paintings for his new hotel chain, financing a wonderful creative school in an impoverished* colonia *in Tijuana, teaching all over Europe for a year, celebrating my fiftieth birthday there and writing a best-selling memoir about it to inspire other women about the power of possibility and the diminishing myth of middle age.*

Dream big! Write down your wildest creative dreams!

- Above all, remember to be gentle with yourself and treat yourself as you would a beloved child or dear friend. You will fall. You will make mistakes. You will learn from them. We all do. The sooner you can get out of your own way, the sooner you will find the clarity to fulfill your vision.

*You have brains in your head and feet in your shoes. You can steer yourself any direction you choose. You're on your own and you know what you know. And you are the one who'll decide where to go.*
—Dr. Seuss

# unfolding dreams

by Seth Apter

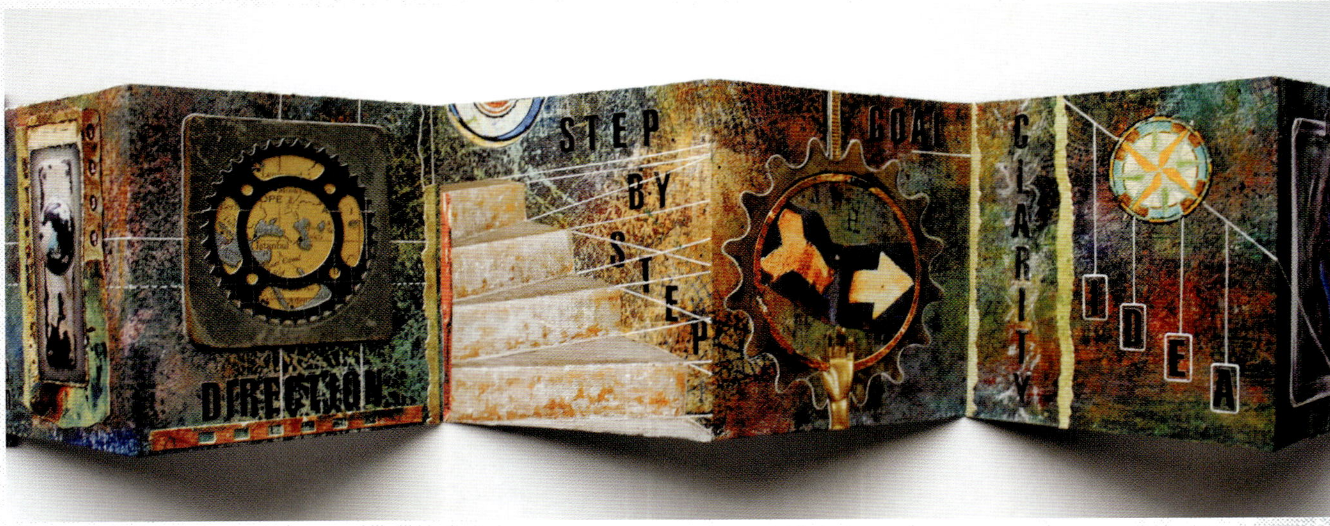


A book is the perfect container through which to create, capture and live your dreams. It serves as a metaphor and a physical representation of all the possibilities. Books traditionally tell a story and, in this case, this book tells the story of my hopes, my goals and my dreams. Like every book, it has a beginning, a middle and an end. In my story, this time line reflects the development of, the effort toward and the realization of my dreams. I can close the book when I am feeling too vulnerable, and more importantly, I can open it at the point when I am ready to experience the possibilities. As I turn the pages and unfold the book, one by one, each step I need to take to realize my dream unfolds in front of me, serving as a reminder and a guide. It is my story, my muse and my dream come true.

**What You Need**

- 90-lb (190gsm) watercolor paper
- acrylic glazing liquid
- book board
- brayer
- collage material, ephemera, photographs, die cuts
- fluid acrylics
- gesso
- heat gun (optional)
- letter stickers
- markers, pens
- masking tape (optional)
- paintbrushes
- PVA or other adhesive
- rub-ons
- scissors
- textured materials

**1** Cut a sheet of 90-lb watercolor paper into a 40" × 5" (102cm × 13cm) strip. (If necessary, use masking tape to connect a series of smaller pieces.) This will become your inside pages. In addition, cut 90-lb watercolor paper into two pieces sized 7¾" × 7⅜" (20cm × 19cm). These will serve as covers.

Using acrylics, paint both sides of the watercolor paper strip and one side of both of your covers. Use as many or as few colors as you like, applying the paint in any pattern you choose.

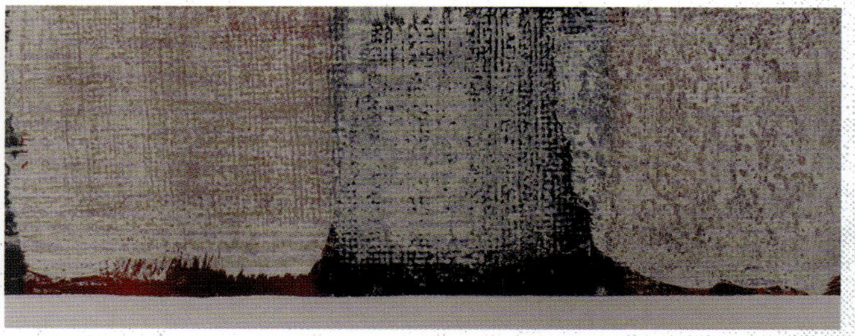

**2** In small sections, brush white gesso over all painted surfaces, being careful to leave some sections of the underlying colors showing. Place your choice of textured material (e.g., bubble wrap, embossed paper, fabric) on top of the wet gesso, roll a brayer over the surface, and pull off the textured material. Repeat this process until you have covered all of the painted watercolor paper.

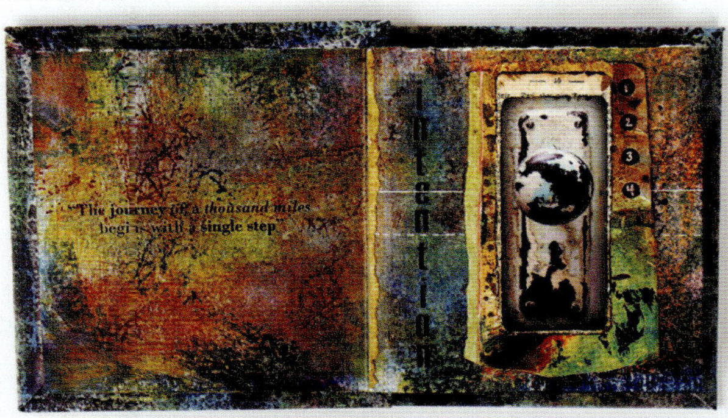


**3** Layer a series of acrylic glazes over all the gessoed surfaces in a random fashion. The glazes can be made by mixing fluid acrylic paint with acrylic glazing liquid. Allow each layer to completely dry (by air or heat gun) before adding the next layer. Repeat until you are happy with the results.

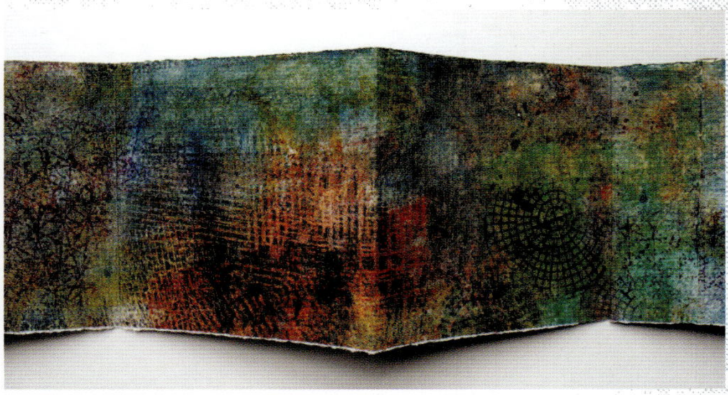

**4** Fold the paper accordion-style. Each page should now be approximately 4¾" × 5" (12cm × 13cm).

**5** Create your covers by cutting book board into two pieces, 5¾" × 5⅜" (15cm × 14cm) each.

Glue your two book board pieces to the center of the unpainted side of your watercolor paper covers.

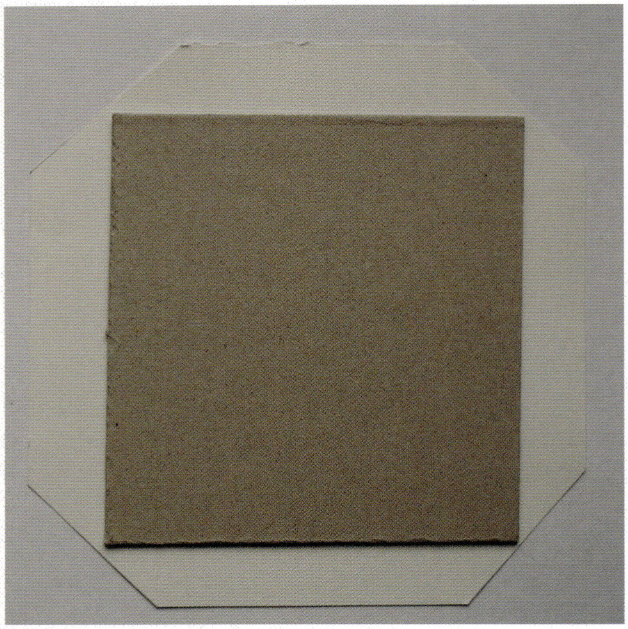

**6** Miter the edges of your paper covers.

**7** Fold over the edges and glue them to the backside of the book board.

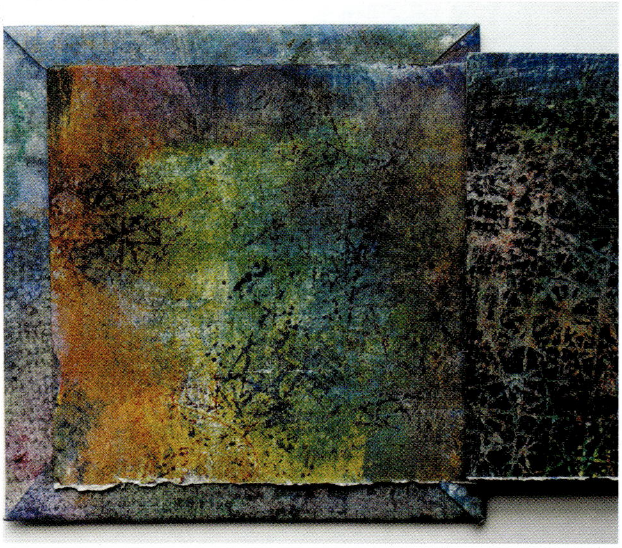

**8** Glue the inside pages to the covers by adhering the page at the end of each side of the folded watercolor paper strip to the underside of the covers.

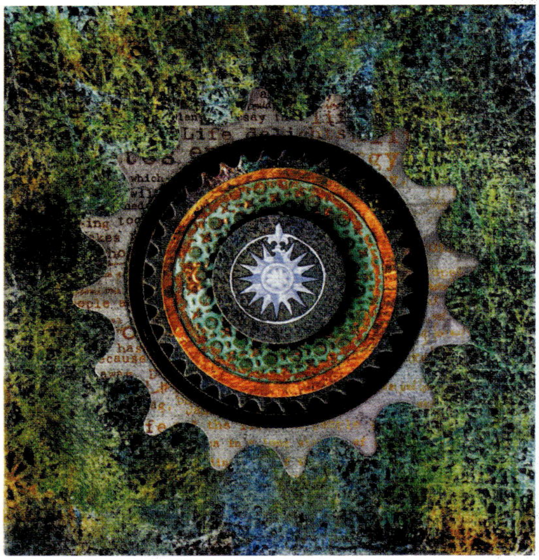

**9** Design each page by choosing materials based on your book theme. You can collage, add altered photos, write, draw and make marks using pens and markers that work on acrylic paint, and add rub-on and sticker letters.

Design your cover using the same materials. You can also create dimension by using embellishments and/or found objects.

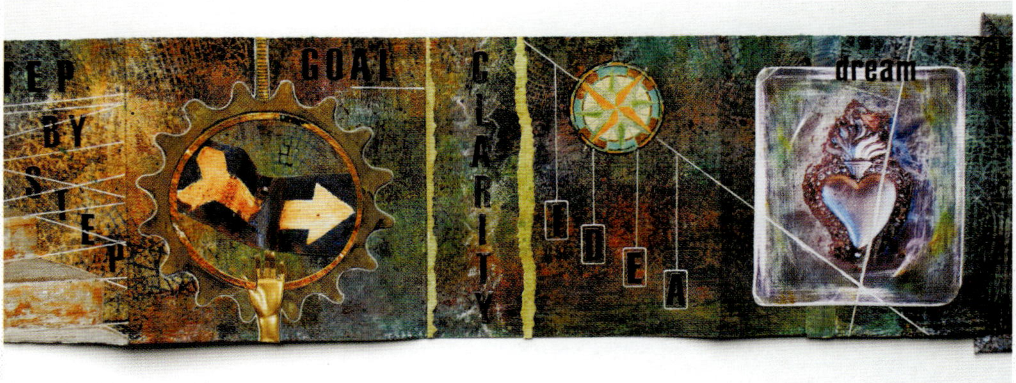
BY
GOAL
CLARITY
IDEA
dream

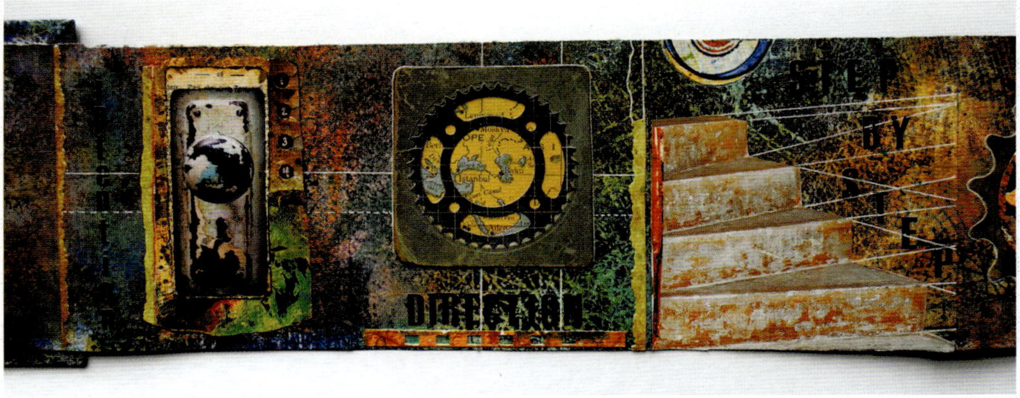
BY

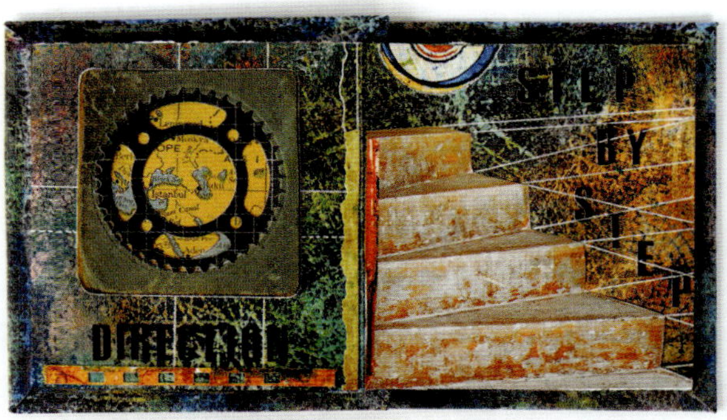
BY

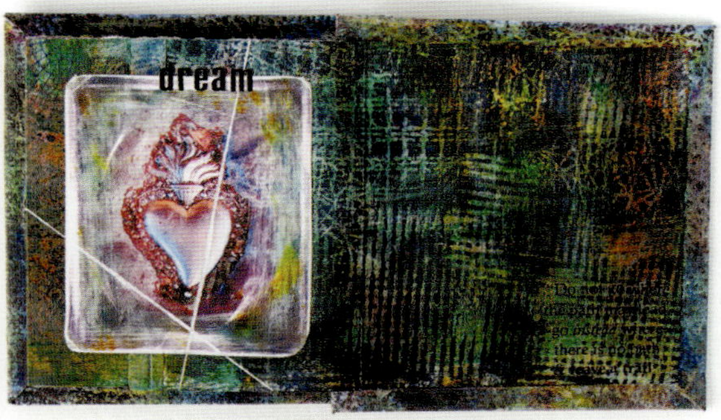
dream

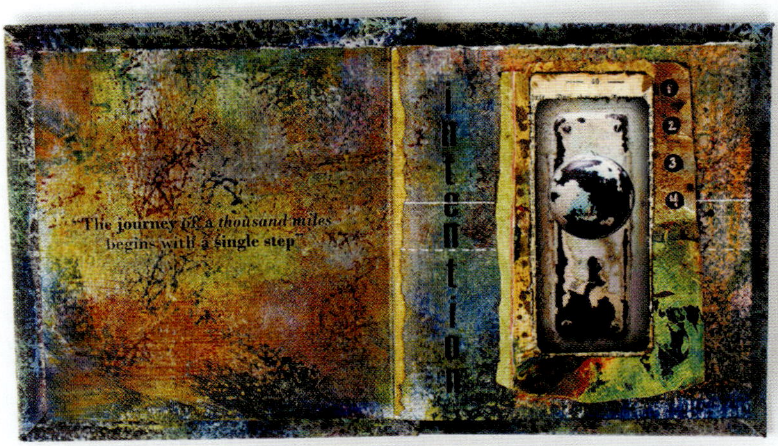
"The journey of a thousand miles
begins with a single step"
intention

exercise

# Little Book of Dreams

One of my earliest childhood memories is of a huge old book that I would haul down off the shelf, time after time, titled *People of the World*. I would stare at those black-and-white photos of exotic people with bones through their noses and incredible headdresses, and something deep inside me would stir: wanderlust, even though it would be many years before I would begin to travel.

As a teenager my grandmother gave me an ancient atlas (as I look at it now I realize it's about as old as I am), and I would spend hours poring over maps, writing detailed lists of the places I would go and the things I would see.

Before I ever discovered my passion for creativity, my dream job was to be a travel writer or travel show host, so it was quite natural as I began my art journey that I began to look for ways that art and travel could interlink.

In 2006 our family created a huge vision/dream board to help clarify our intention to take a seven-month family holiday, camping our way up the West Coast of the United States for the summer and then heading down to southern Mexico for several wonderful months living in a tropical village on the beach in Oaxaca. Together we cut and glued and talked and dreamed and a couple of years later found ourselves on the road, living the dream that we had envisioned together. It would take another book to tell you all the stories leading up to the trip and the miracles that occurred while we were on it, but for now, let me say I strongly believe in the power of intention to manifest your dreams, and creating a dream board is a powerful way to declare your intentions!

In this project we will create a dream board and then turn it into several smaller books of dreams to place in areas in your home as reminders of the life you are creating. My project here will be based around my travel dreams, but you may want to focus on your art, your family, health, abundance or all of it! Whatever it is you would like to see more of in your life.

While you work on your dreams, try to also hold in your heart all that you are grateful for. Gratitude and desire are two sides of the same coin.

**What You Need**

- ephemera
- gel medium
- gluing brush
- large sheets of paper
- patterned paper
- scissors
- small stack of magazines you don't mind tearing up
- white cardboard or posterboard

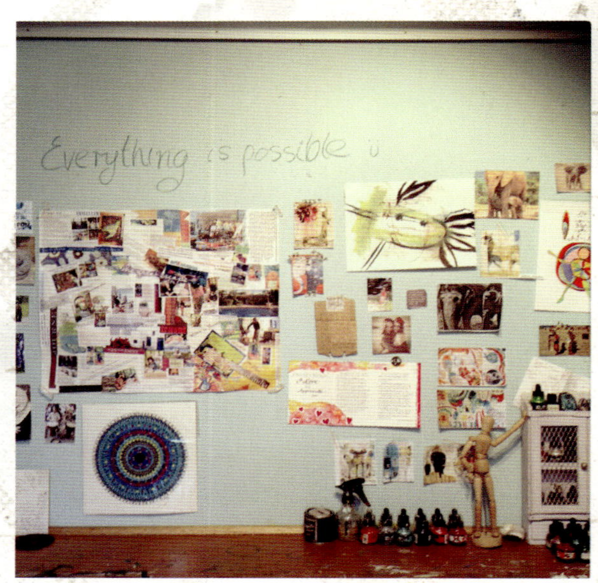

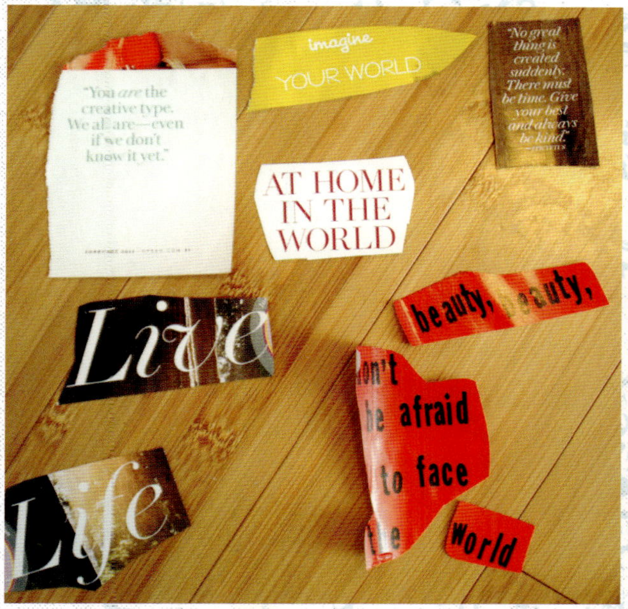


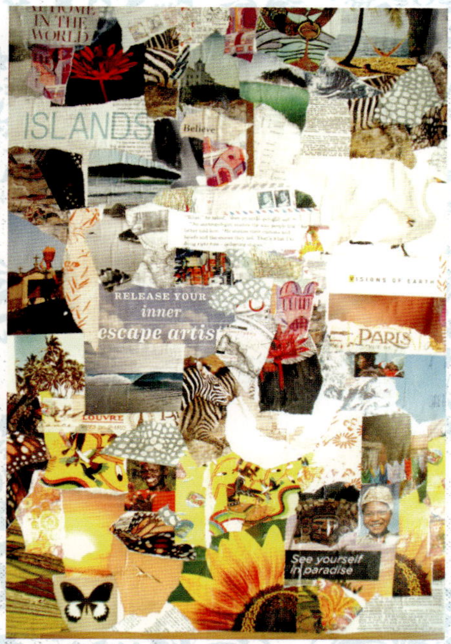


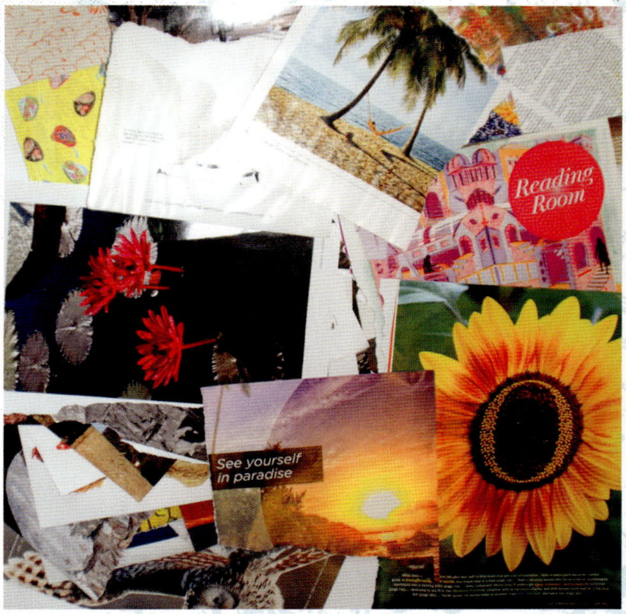


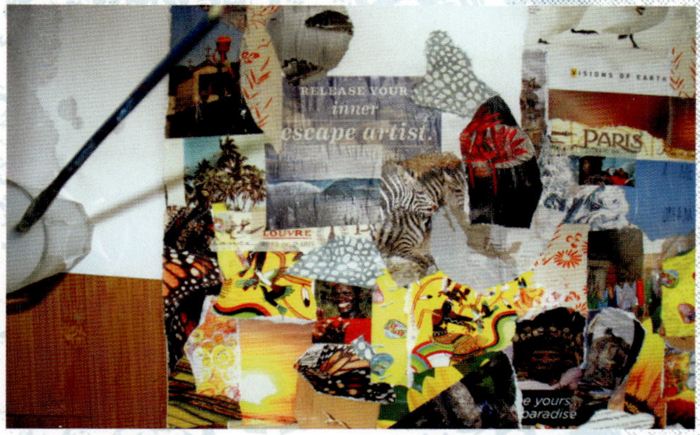


**1** Take a trip to your local thrift store. (In Australia we call them "op shops"—short for opportunity shop. Don't you love that?) Grab a bunch of old magazines and books that might offer pictures and words on the theme of your dreams.

Find some quiet time and thumb through your stash of books and magazines, holding your dreams in mind, tearing out images and words that appeal. Don't think too hard and try not to get distracted. Add in some patterned papers and ephemera that you love.

Spread your collage goodies out and loosely separate them into smaller groups with similar color themes.

**2** On a large sheet of white cardboard or posterboard (I used 24" × 26" [61cm × 61cm]), starting from the bottom edge, begin to glue down images, using gel medium. Try using scissors only for the pieces on the edge and tearing the other pieces. Place images and words intuitively, overlapping edges and linking by color palette. Repeat elements as you go. (Monarch butterfly wings were collaged in several different areas on my collage.)

As you begin to fill the board, look at the shapes you are tearing and look for empty spaces that will work for these shapes. Trust that something magic will unfold when you are focusing on your dreams. As you work, remember to think about the things you have in your life that you are grateful for. It is much easier to manifest your dreams when you are coming from a place of abundance and gratitude than a place of lack.

Allow your dream board to dry.

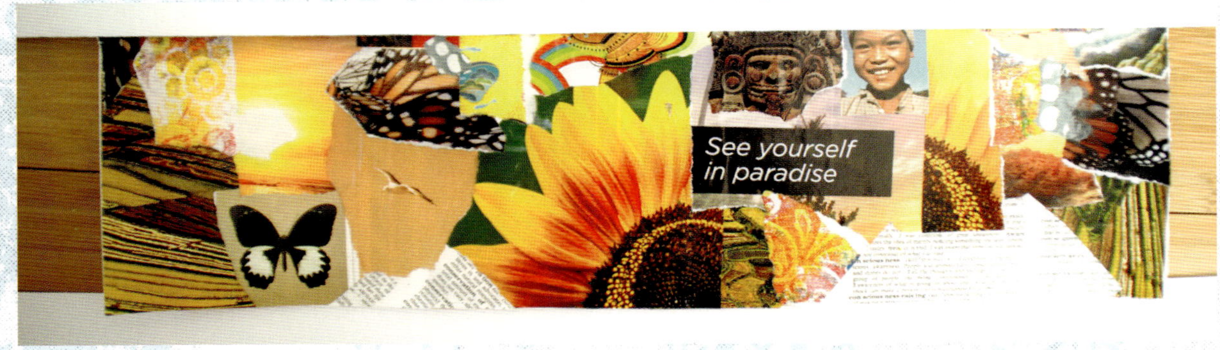


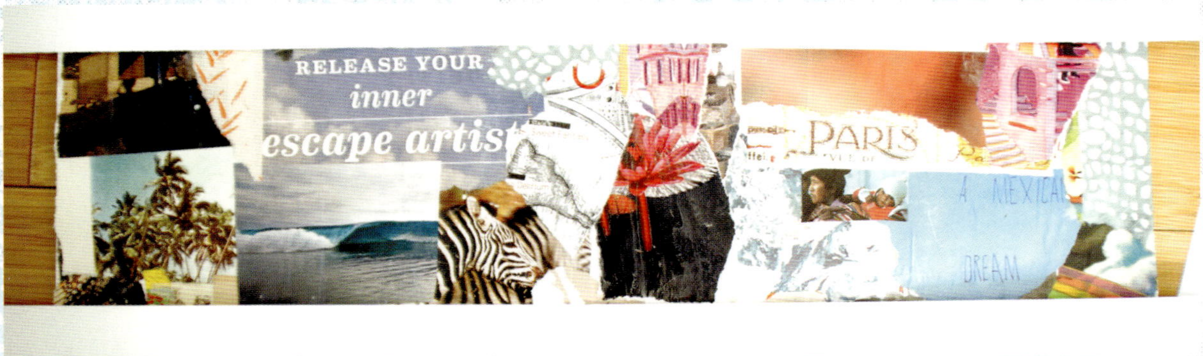


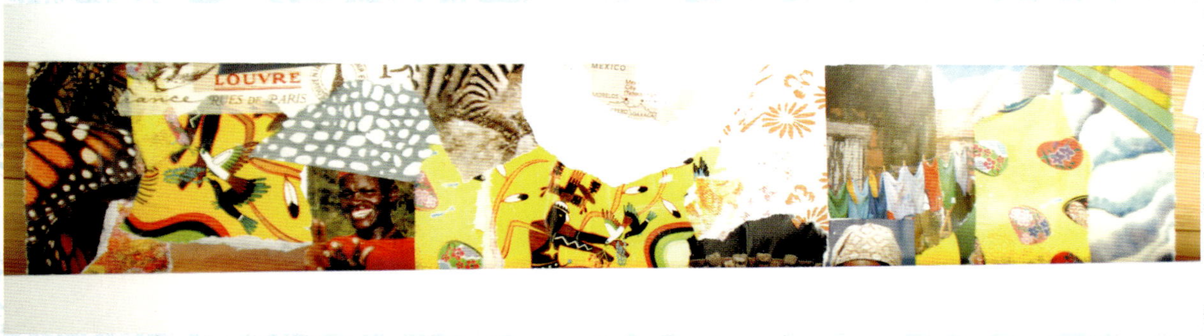


**3** Using two large sheets of paper to crop out sections of your dream board, find the best places to crop your full piece into several smaller strips. This is going to allow you to create multiple little dream books. The strips need not be equal in size to one another.

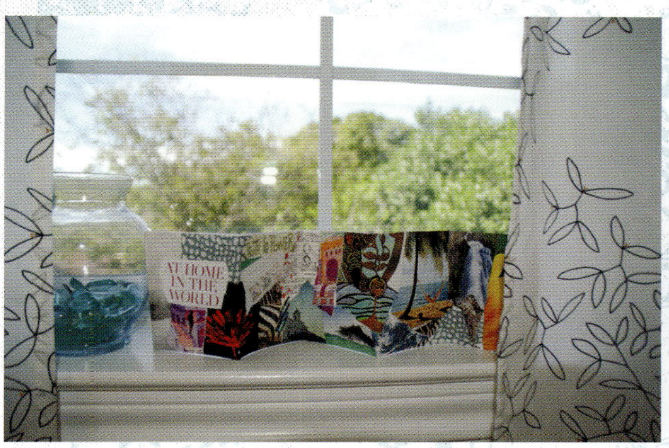


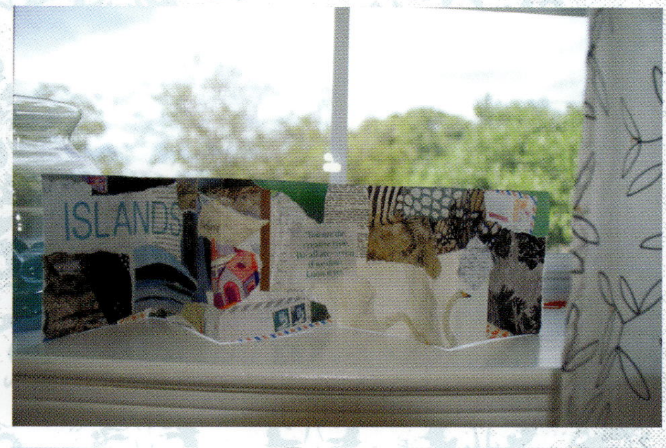


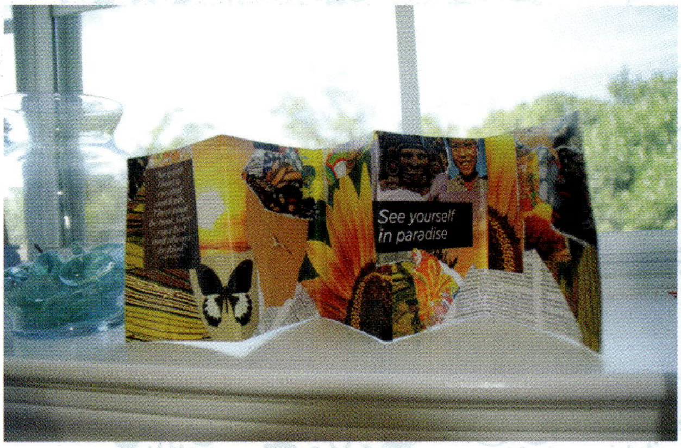


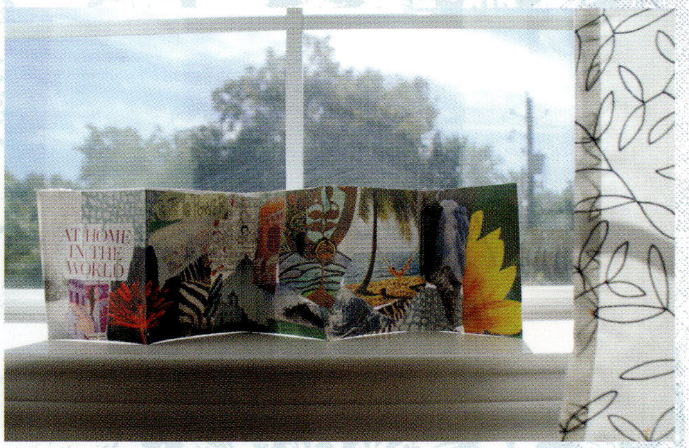


4 Using a simple accordion fold, create your little dream books! You will probably find plenty of serendipity in how each book comes out. Many will have a central theme or message. I love it when this happens!

Place your dream books in several places around your home to remind you of the dreams you are calling into your life, and don't forget to take a little action each day toward making them a reality.

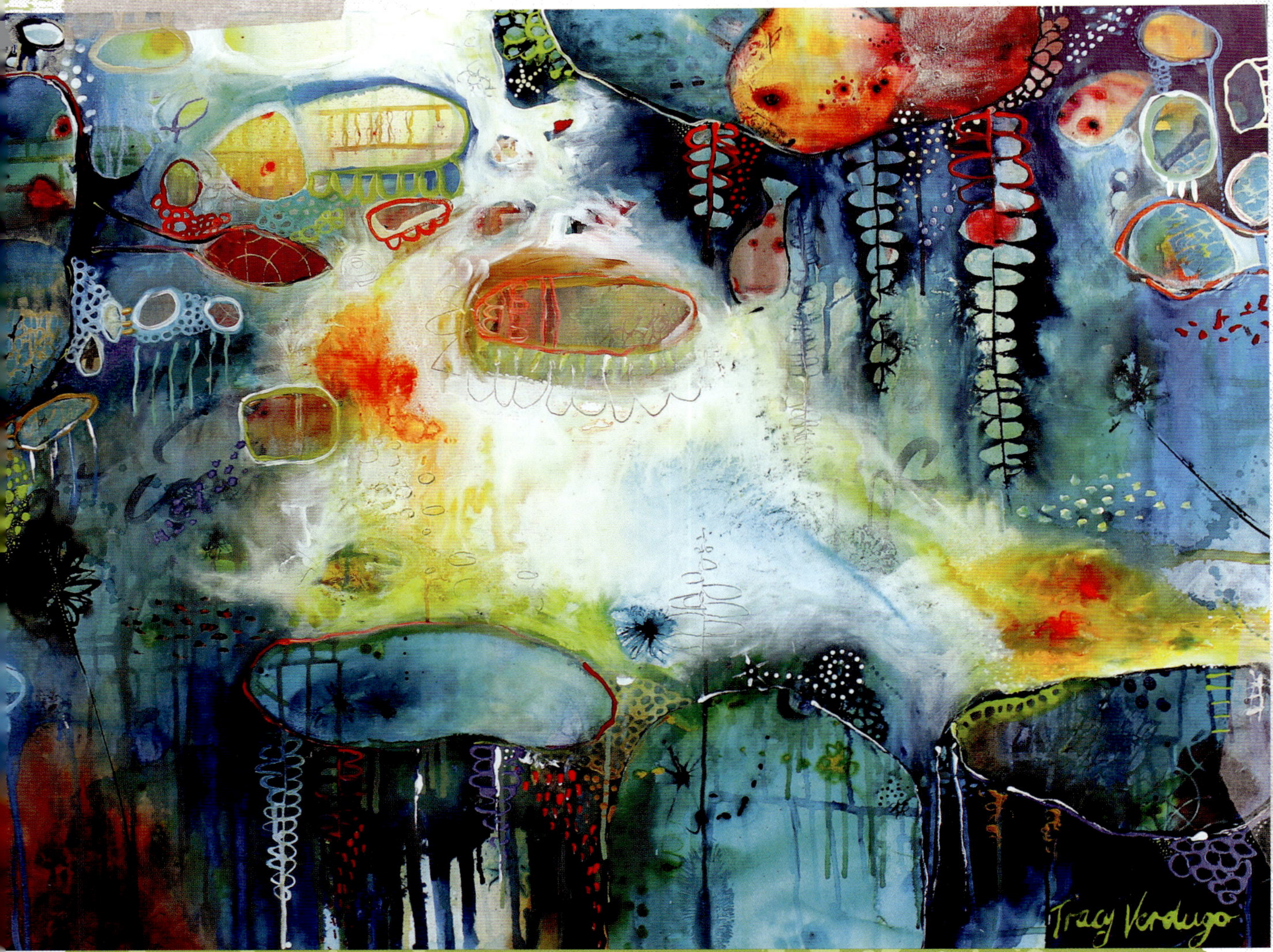


*This painting,* Night Dive, *was inspired by the one and only time I have ever (despite staying up the entire night before terrified at the thought) sunk beneath the black depths of the ocean with a scuba tank on my back.*

# chapter seven: creative wanderlust

## Being open to the artistic possibilities of the journey

**cre·a·tive wan·der·lust**
krē-ā-tiv/ wän-dər-ləst/

1. the insatiable urge to make cool things, see new stuff and imagine and experience new possibilities
2. the act of living a joyful life
3. the experience of being open to the creative possibilities of the journey.

Okay, I made all that up! But its true, don't you think?

There is nothing quite like the thrill of a new place, an unknown culture, the excitement of being in a place you have never been before where the mundane becomes magical.

The sky, a different blue; the trees, a different shape; the people sitting at the bus stop somehow more intriguing, more interesting than the ones in the park back home.

Traveling allows us to see with fresh eyes, to approach our new surroundings with curiosity and wonder, to revel in the differences and connect with the similarities.

Travel allows us in many ways to drop our masks, to relate to others outside the parameters of religion, race, profession and income status.

And guess what? Allowing ourselves space and time to create brings us exactly the same gifts …

*Twenty years from now you will be more disappointed by the things you didn't do than by the ones you did do. So throw off the bowlines, sail away from the safe harbor. Catch the trade winds in your sails. Explore. Dream. Discover.*
—Mark Twain

Creativity is a perfect partner for wanderlust, and the journeys we take can be large or small, years in the world or a moment under a microscope, each equally valid for the possible worlds that open up for us.

A trip around the world can offer a multitude of new perspectives, but so can a trip around our neighborhood if we are willing to open our eyes to see what is there.

Over thirteen years of teaching kids' classes in my little backyard studio, I have learned to read the barometer of unbridled energy that accompanies my gorgeous students as they tumble into the room all effervescent and wild after six hours of holding themselves in check at school. I offer them a place to explore where there is no right and wrong, where we learn from and inspire each other as we fearlessly create. Many of the things I bring into my adult workshops I have learned from these cherished kids.

Sometimes their energy cannot be contained in such a small space and so out into the world we go, seeking new perspectives, viewing the world from high up on the tree platform, leaning back against the peeling bark of the beautiful melaleuca tree, lying next to the seaside daisies, up close and personal, sketching a buzzing bee collecting pollen.

Sometimes we leave the confines of our property and set off on an impromptu journey to the beach to make sand sculptures or sketch, "accidentally" falling into the water on hot, steamy days.

On one such day we gather our sketchbooks and pencils (no erasers because there are no mistakes) and head south toward Moona Moona Creek. I have devised a game and our only prop, besides our sketching tools, is a small container filled with torn bits of paper. On each piece of paper I have jotted down a random number—7, 52, 18, 165. Before we leave I pull out a scrap of paper. Collectively we walk—big, deliberate, hilarious steps—counting out the number and stopping when we reach our counted destination. At this point, pencils ready, we draw the first thing our eyes land on. Some kids sketch their shoe, with tangled laces resting on spiky grass. Another captures the traffic sign across the road, sharply outlined against a loose backdrop of eucalyptus trees. The neighbor's letterbox is featured, as is a piece of crumpled garbage in the gutter.

We pull another number and move on, continuing this way for almost an hour, down the dirt bush track beside the creek, past the mangrove mudflats and into the forest before heading home, when the mosquitoes become too fierce, and we are spending more time slapping our legs than sketching. Sometimes a low number is pulled and at first the kids complain, "We've hardly moved! There's nothing new to draw here! It's exactly the same as the last spot!"

"Look around. Draw what you see," I tell them. They do and fifteen new, inspired sketches emerge from fifteen small, intent and busy hands.

How many times have you stopped on your journey today to really see where you are standing?

How many fresh perspectives can you muster as you travel through the world today—inner, outer, large or small?

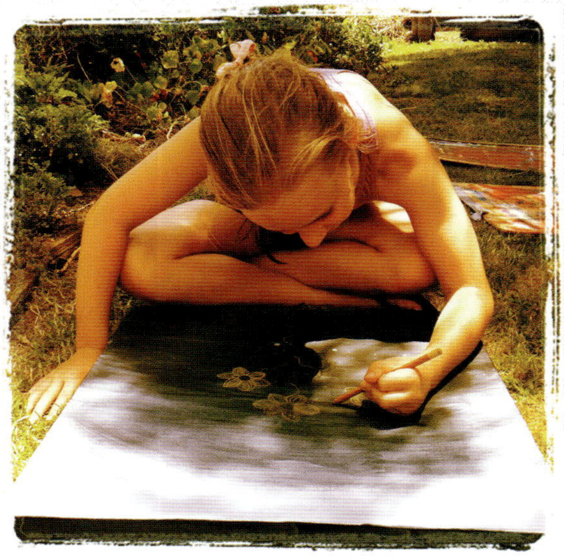

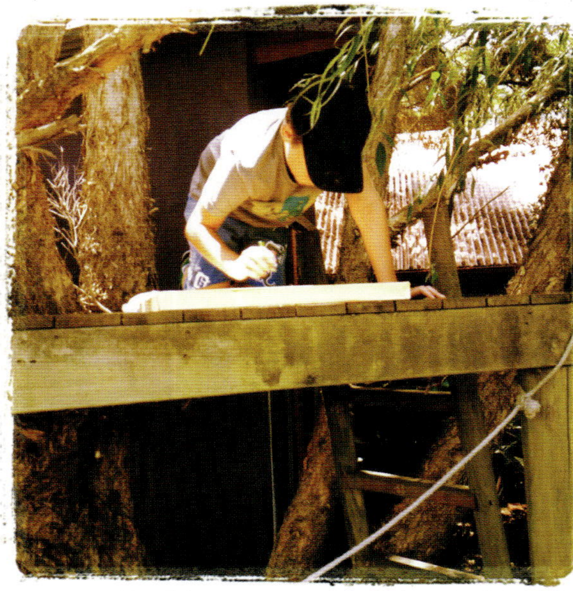

# the wandering dress

Santana springs into the lounge room, face alight with excitement.

"I just got an e-mail from Oh Deer! They picked me!"

"Awesome!" I say, "Sounds wonderful! What's Oh Deer?"

"It's an online vintage boutique!" she exclaims. "They have this collaborative thing they are doing called The Wandering Dress, and they asked for submissions so I sent them some of my photos and they picked me! They only picked twenty photographers from the whole country and I'm one of them!"

She is flippin'-the-moon, happy-pants excited, as my sweet friend Kelli would say. I am überproud and excited for her, too. Happy that she has taken the risk of putting her work out there and overjoyed that she has received validation for her beautiful photographs.

The concept is fabulous. The first of the twenty photographers will receive a simple vintage dress in the mail and will have five days to capture an interpretation of the dress using their creative vision. They will then choose their favorite shot and submit it to the boutique to be featured on their website. The exposure will be great and it is a win-win situation for everyone involved.

Without even having seen the dress, Santana begins to dream up storyboards and locations for her photo shoot with her gorgeous friend Erica as the model.

When the dress arrives, it is a cute little polka-dot number in coral and white. The girls head off for the day and come back with an incredible portfolio of images, rich in mood and texture, sultry shots against the white sands and sparkling water of the bay. This demure dress shows its wild side, teamed with a simple feather-adorned headband and thin leather belt, lifting its hems to show Erica's long tanned legs. This brief stop in its wandering journey brings out its carefree nature spirit.

Santana sends it along to the next photographer, and over the coming weeks the dress takes on many personalities: The addition of a lace collar on a red-locked, porcelain-skinned model, set against a trailing jasmine vine, suggests an Edwardian theme; a hula-hooping, wide-smiled girl wears the dress with joyful abandon while another sits cross-legged on the grass in bobby socks. Each photographer's carefully constructed vision tells a new story, adding layers of interest to the simple dress.

The dress is a willing participant, open to new surroundings, willing to play dress-up with new accessories, blooming and growing with each new experience, swept along by its fabulous creative journey, becoming ever more expansive as it steps more fully into the possibilities of its own potential.

What if we allow ourselves to be like that wandering dress? Immersing ourselves in our lives wholeheartedly, open to exploring new things, expressing the myriad of emotions that make us human, fully accepting our wildness and our vulnerabilities, our hesitations and our strengths. Open to wearing our tutus and tiaras and equally as comfortable makeup-less and lounging in our pj's. And what if each of us has our own visionary photographic director by our side gently guiding us through the events and circumstances on journeys that will lead us to our highest growth?

How will you celebrate your journey today? Will you allow creativity to be your constant companion?

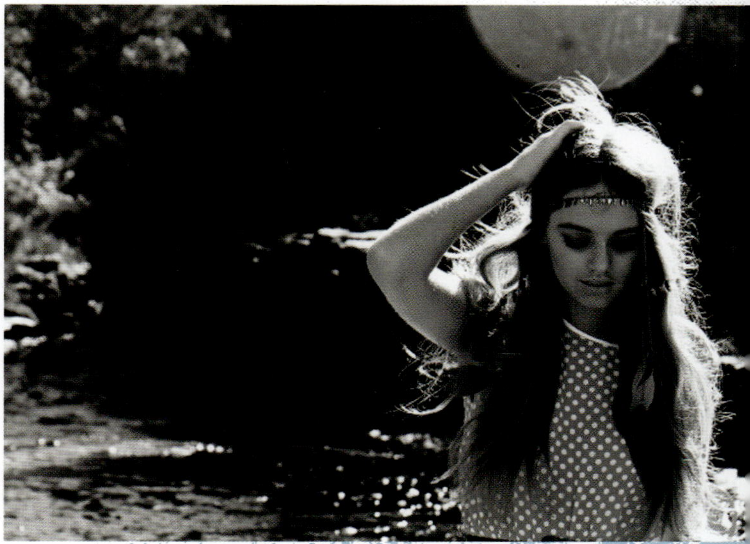

# exploration fuels the muse

**by Kecia Deveney**

In my early days of becoming an artist, I would just sort of putz around in my little nook making gifts for the holidays. I had a lot of fun just playing, and the enjoyment came out of the giving part. Then someone suggested that I start selling at shows, which seemed like a great idea. However, there was a part of me that doubted my work because I felt like I wasn't really following any rules; I was just doing my own thing. I think I had a misconception that to make real art, you had to go to art school and you had to follow rules (naïve thinking!).

At one of the shows, a girl mentioned "altered art" to me, a category I hadn't heard of before. She suggested I check out some magazines at the bookstore, which I did. I couldn't believe that there were other people doing what I was doing. It was so strange because all my life I've been called "weird" for things I like to do or find enjoyable. But here were all these other people doing the same thing. It was like finding a tribe!

As my career progressed, I was published and then got into teaching.

Somewhere along the way, I realized that art came from the heart and followed no rules. It seems now the only rules are ones we impose on ourselves.

Self-criticism is the biggest joy killer in creating art. When doubt begins to creep in, it's hard to continue on. Luckily, I don't have too many moments any more of self-doubt. I've learned to proceed with projects by taking my time and evaluating.

If I don't like something, I think about why. But I don't take any drastic measures on anything until I've thought about it. If I have to let a painting sit for a few weeks, I will. When I am stuck on something, though, I find getting out into the world helps. As an artist and full-time caregiver for my son, I am isolated and spend a great deal of time at home, which can be very claustrophobic and cagey.

My sensors begin feeling confined. So for me, leaving the house on a beautiful day and hitting a flea market or antique store (my favorite pastime), is a big boost to creativity. Same with traveling; it's the newness of an area—never been experienced before—that sends a signal to my inner core and reignites the passion I have for my work and how I see the world. I always return inspired by things I have seen or purchased. I also take lots of photos wherever I go and those photos are reminders of colors or juxtaposition that appeals to me. Those things come in handy later when trying to make my art come together.

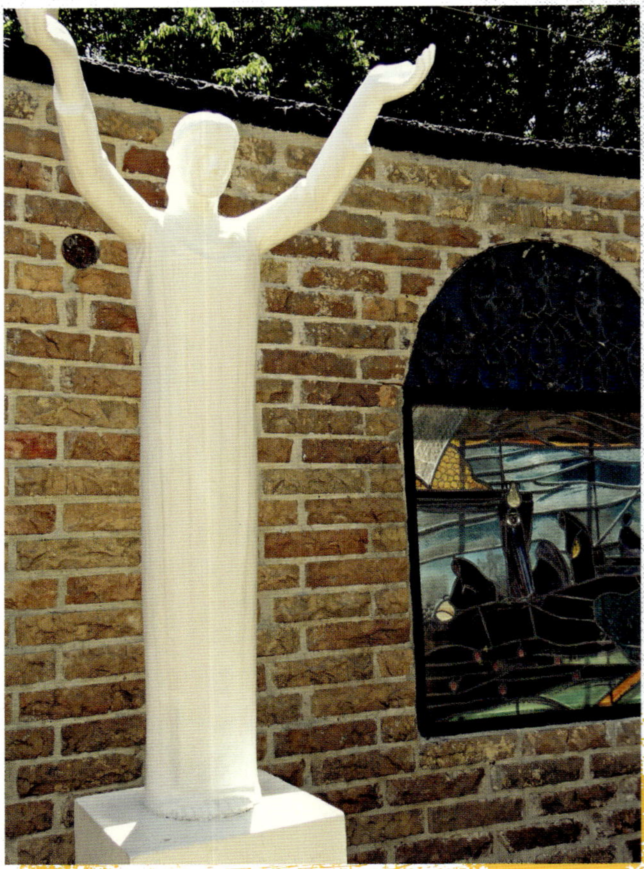

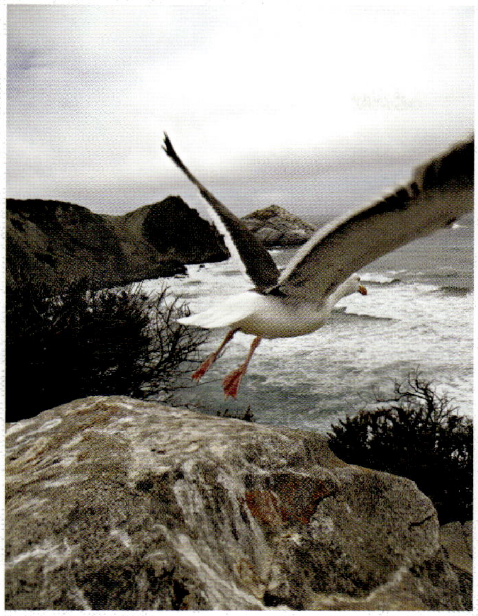

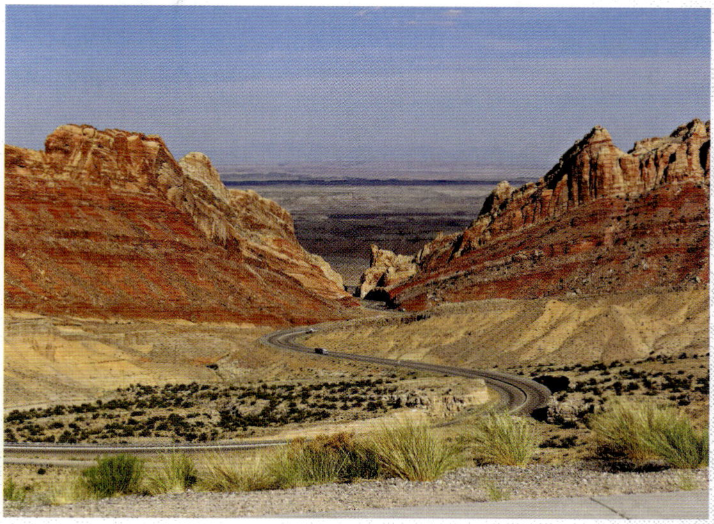

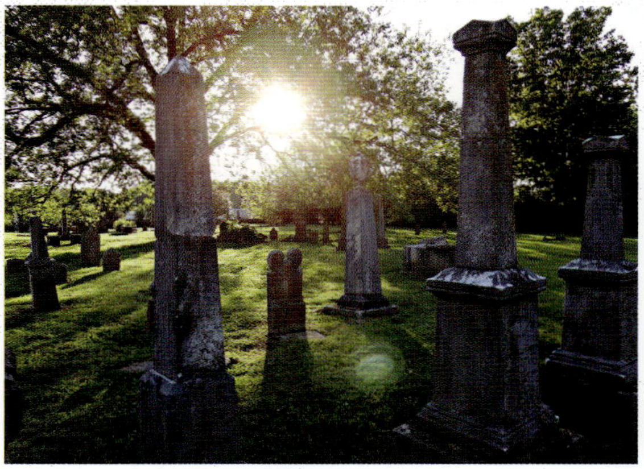

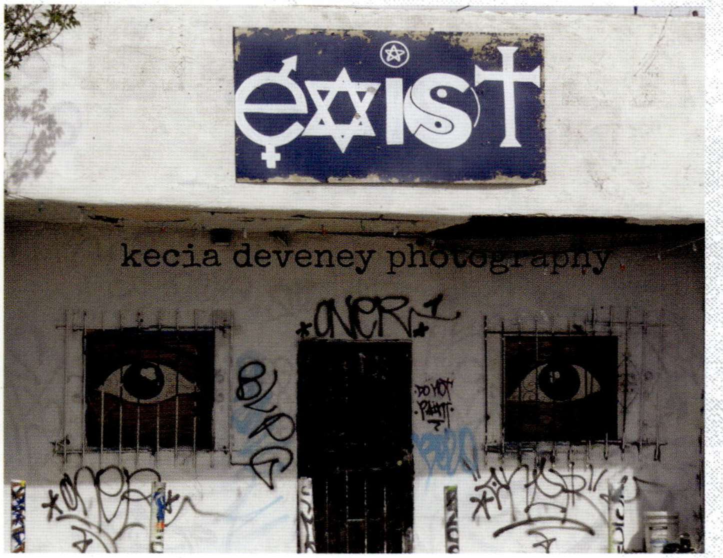
kecia deveney photography

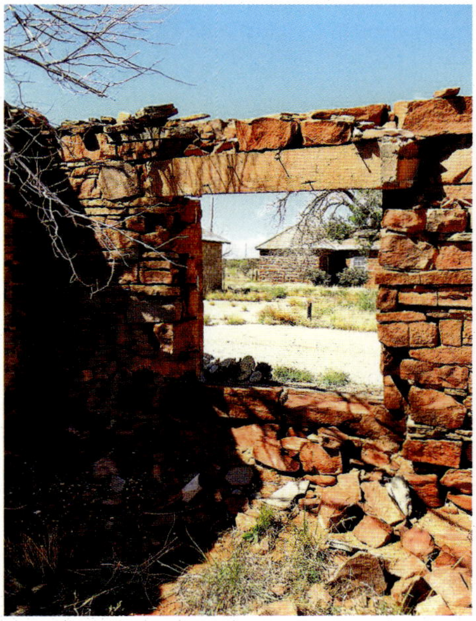

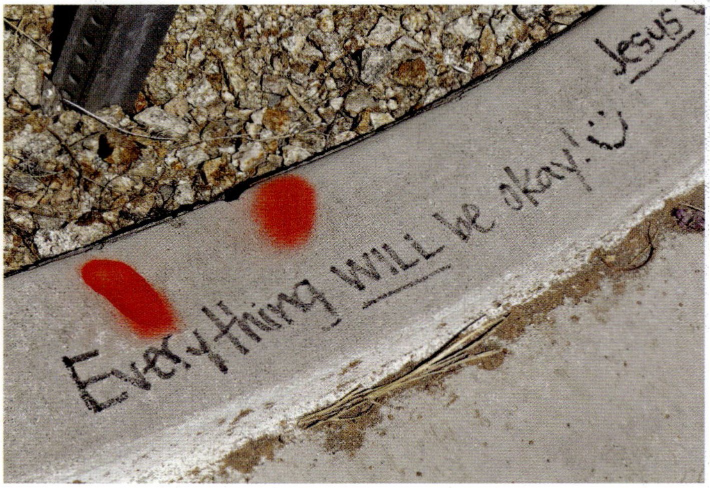
Everything WILL be okay! :)
Jesus

# wanderlust is inspiration

**by Erin Faith Allen**

Wanderlust is a rather potent thing, creatively speaking. Travel evokes something primal, ethereal, cerebral and emotional in me. The newness of location swirls around me and scintillates my senses; I am left reeling in the most delightful ways.

My senses go on overload taking in the amazing sights, smells, sounds and feelings that are soaked in the new atmosphere. Invigorated to begin the process of wrapping my head around—and absorbing—the newness of culture and its insidious ways of being in everything, I feel surrounded by a blanket of visceral stimulation that piques my curiosity.

Whenever I travel, I carry my camera loaded up with memory cards and a couple trusty lenses. I shoot absolutely everything I see. I also bring my diary and let words tumble out of me that contain the experience that is underway.

Being a constant seeker of new information and knowledge, and always challenging myself to evolve, means that I am eager to learn how the things I am experiencing in traveling to foreign countries rub up against my edges. New cultures inevitably ask me to open, expand and bend in order to learn from the people and land that surround me in this new destination.

Inevitably there are emotional experiences to match the sensory, and I save them together in a precious creative cocoon of diary meets camera. Here they incubate in wait for full and complete expression in times to come.

I am an intuitive artist, writer and photographer, meaning I don't contrive or preconceive anything; I simply open and express what is present and wants to

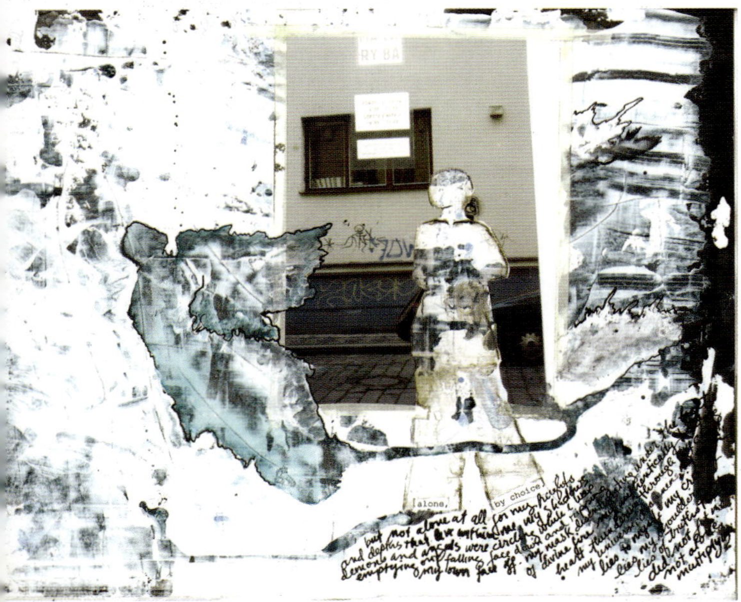


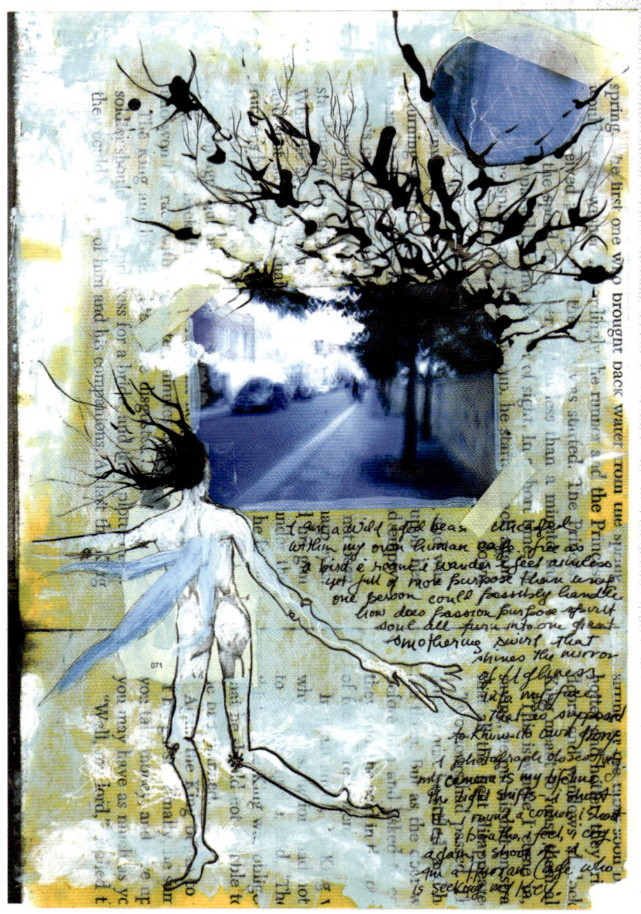

be known. Ultimately I trust in my creative instincts and have faith that what my impulses ask me to capture will unfold in a creative process some time later.

In my journal I write what I feel, uninhibited. In the same way I capture what I feel using the camera as my tool so I can hold on to precious and transitory snapshots of time that have never happened before and will never happen again.

Upon returning from my travels, I begin to comb through my photos and instinctively choose a number of them to print out through listening to the surge of feelings any particular image evokes in me. If I have a gush of feeling, I know this photograph packs a powerful punch that will surely inspire me in my studio.

Once the photos are printed and lying in a tantalizing stack on my studio table, I begin to call back the energy. And it always comes back, the memories and impressions of the foreign land I walked and engaged with all my senses. Photographs that I take are very powerful when I revisit them; it is as if they are magical portals back in time. They explode in a symphony of sensory memory that otherwise lies dormant somewhere in my body.

One by one, I place my photographs amongst textures, text, imagery and paper and a full range of my favorite trusted mixed-media techniques.

What this creates for me is a full circle of experience, from out in the beautiful wide world, into my camera lens and journals, and onto a surface in my studio.

I live for the anticipation innate in wanderlust itself, the experience of my senses in a foreign land, the overflowing (and sometimes breaking) of my heart as I witness and feel my new surroundings, and the expression of my discoveries and adventures of my travel upon return to my studio.

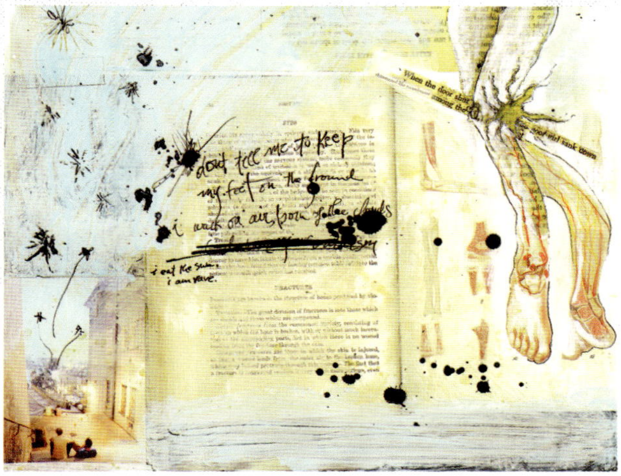


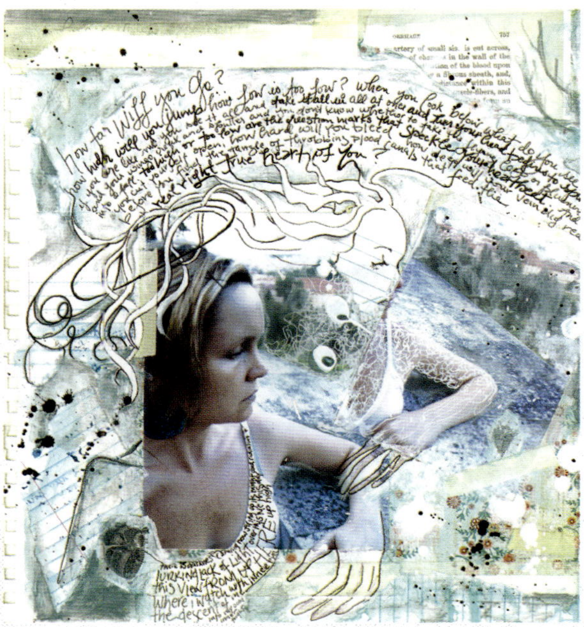


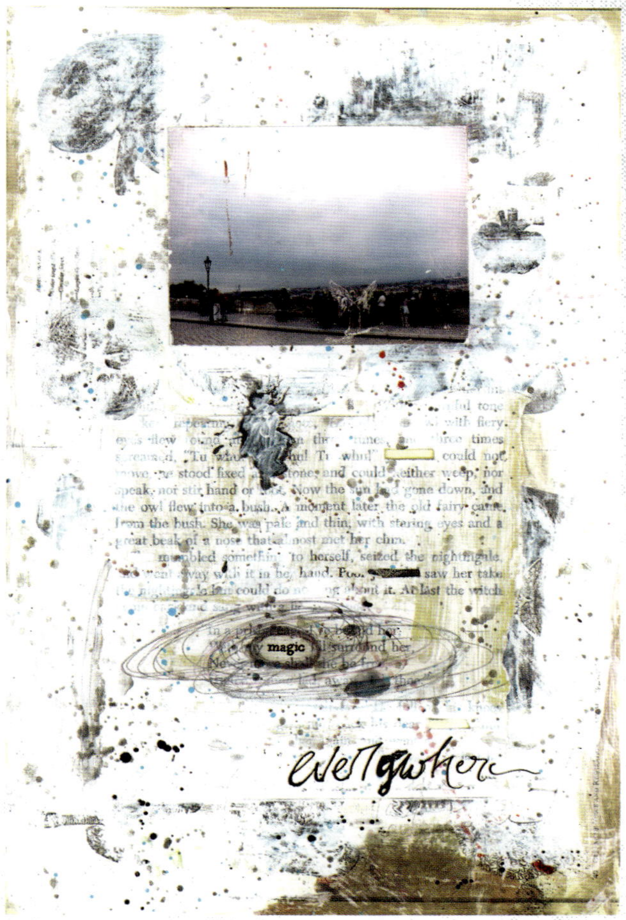

# recipe for artful travel

by Lisa Sonora Beam

Travel and art making are my twin passions, so I always make travel journals wherever I go. When people see my travel journals, they are surprised to learn that I travel very light, with just a small backpack, which includes all of my art supplies.

Traveling light allows me to experience life and new foreign lands more authentically. This is an example of a travel journal I made in Mexico, using many found supplies and carrying only a few of my favorite basics.

First I'll share tips on how to travel light with art supplies and experience life more like the locals do. Then I'll walk you through how I made this page and what materials I used.

## Travel Art Journal Tips

- Pack just a very few essentials in your carry-on, things that are hard to find elsewhere.
- Find a small zipper bag that fits in your day pack or purse, and limit your art supplies to this one small bag. I like to use cosmetic bags and plastic zippered pencil pouches (the kind made for children's school supplies) for my travel art supplies.
- Bring the smallest sketchbook or notebook that you can work in. The more portable your book, the more you will use it.
- Plan to find your supplies on the go as you travel. Shopping for nontouristy things when you travel puts you where the locals do their shopping. Places to look for art supplies: school supply stores, drug and department stores (check the stationery and children's sections for inexpensive art supplies), office supply stores.

Supplies to look for: date stamp, small scissors, glue stick, markers, stickers, envelopes, crayons, alphabet stencils.

Visit creative places you like to go at home, except do this when you travel. Here are some of the creative places I make a point to visit when I travel, and the supplies I look for:

- Used bookshops: A hardcover book with nice thick paper makes a great sketchbook. Simply whitewash the pages with cheap craft paint, or collage the pages on black paper. Used bookstores also often have old maps, postcards, guidebooks and foreign language dictionaries. Clippings from books make great ephemera to add to your travel journal.
- Sewing and fabric stores: Look for trim, ribbon, glue, glitter, buttons. Many fabric shops also sell paint and art supplies.
- The local post office or newsstand: Postage stamps and postcards are great to use in your travel journal. Use the postcards for pages and the stamps like stickers.

Now that you've explored your travel destination like a local and found some new supplies to add to your travel journal, it's time to face the blank page.

Find a place to play in your travel journal. I like to work in cafés. The bonus of working in public is that you often meet like-minded people who are interested in art and artists who are sketching or writing.

### My Travel Art Supply Bag Includes

alphabet rubber stamps or lettering stencils

permanent ink pad - black

permanent marker - black

a few black ink pens, a pencil

a few tiny bottles of cheap craft paint in my favorite neutral colors: buff, light grey, white

watercolor crayons (broken into small pieces)

small roll of clear shipping tape

individually wrapped moist hand wipes (to clean hands, stamps and remove extra glue from pages)

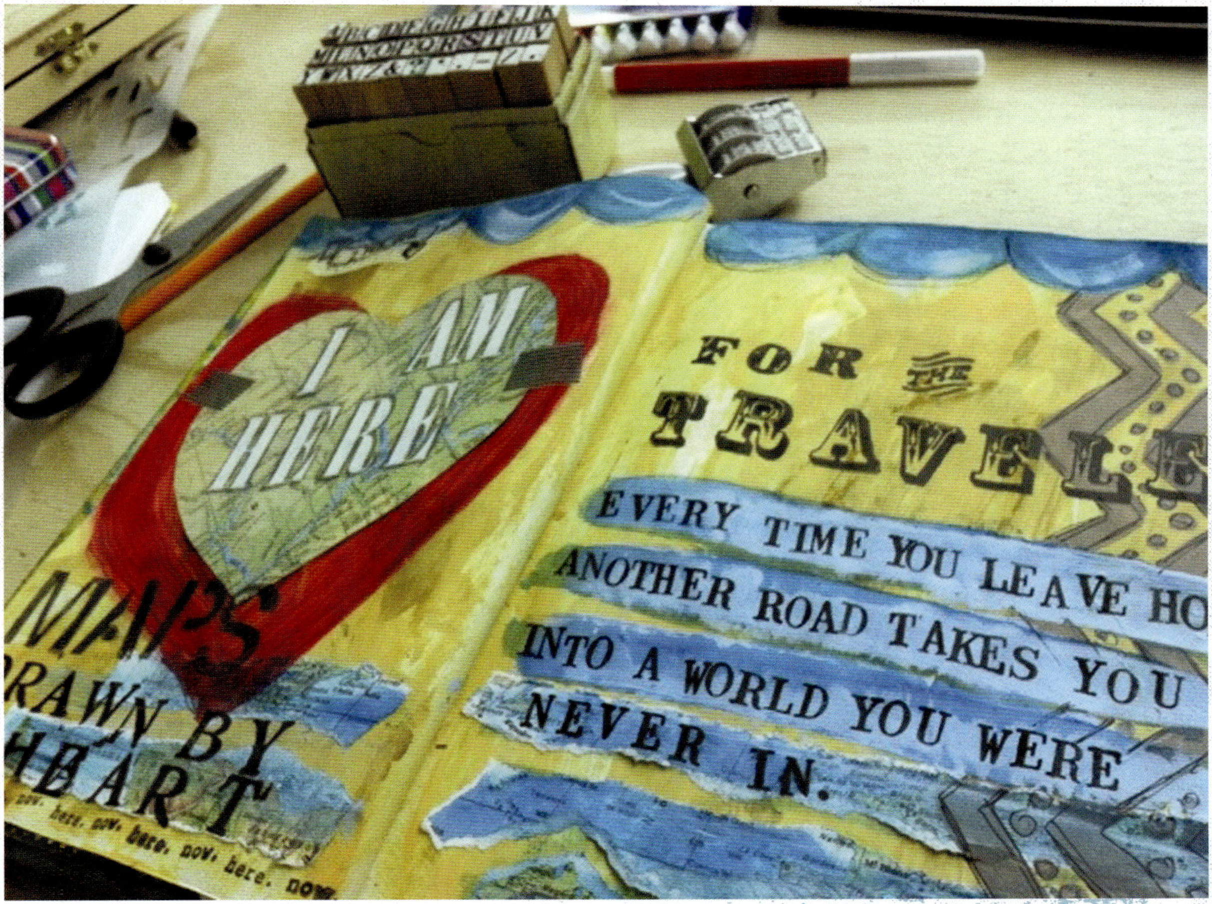


**Technique**

In Mexico, blank sketchbooks are impossible to find. So for this travel journal, I recycled an old book found in a used bookshop.

1 Whitewash the pages with a watered-down layer of light-colored acrylic craft paint: white, cream, buff or light gray are my go-to colors.

2 After the base coat of whitewash dries, add color with a bit of water-soluble wax crayon, watercolor pencils or watercolor paint.

3 Now you've loosened up. Sip your coffee and observe your surroundings. What details do you notice? Use your pencil to sketch in a few details. On this page I made some cloud-like designs because the Mexican sky is so beautiful. I also sketched a pattern I saw on a textile.

4 Think about your experience. What do you want to remember right now? It doesn't have to be about travel adventures necessarily, but whatever you are experiencing in the moment. Here, I was thinking about my great love of travel and of art making. So I cut out a heart-shaped map and used a rubber stamp to capture my feelings.

5 Add painted lines to emphasize phrases or a snippet of poetry or dialogue you hear. I also cut blue pieces of paper from the map and used the colored paper to "paint" with. Use rubber alphabet stamps or lettering stencils or even your own handwriting to write on top of the painted lines.Consider adding the date to your page, in pencil or using a date stamp.

# meditation walk and nature mandala

**by Louise Gale**

Taking ourselves on a meditation walk can be an inspiring part of the day and essential for our creative souls.

Our world is constantly filled with inspiration and when we slow down on a meditation walk, we start to notice layers of detail to fuel our creative intuition. Whether you are in an exotic location by the ocean, a weekend away in the country or in your own neighborhood, creative wanderlust can always be found.

The world is your art studio and nature your materials.

In the following exercise we are going to take some time out to slow down, ground ourselves in the natural world and use materials we find along the way to create a nature mandala. *Mandala* means circle in Sanskrit, an ancient Indo-Aryan language, and is used to create sacred space for meditation. We will be creating our own mandala with found objects and use our creation to relax, ground ourselves and connect.

Our nature mandala will also be a gift we will leave behind for others to find, practicing the art of letting go. Meditation walking, finding inspiration in nature and tapping into our creative energies will enable us to spread beauty wherever we may roam.

### What You Need

- an open mind to help you clear your thoughts and connect to the present moment
- camera
- comfortable shoes
- pencils and/or pen
- sketchbook or journal
- tote bag or small bag to collect items in
- water (and snacks)

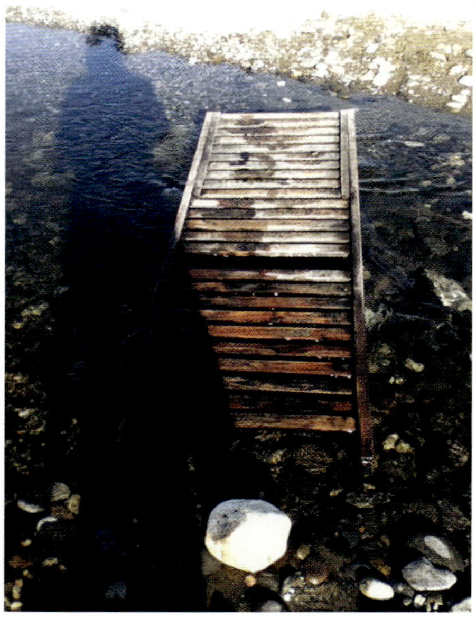

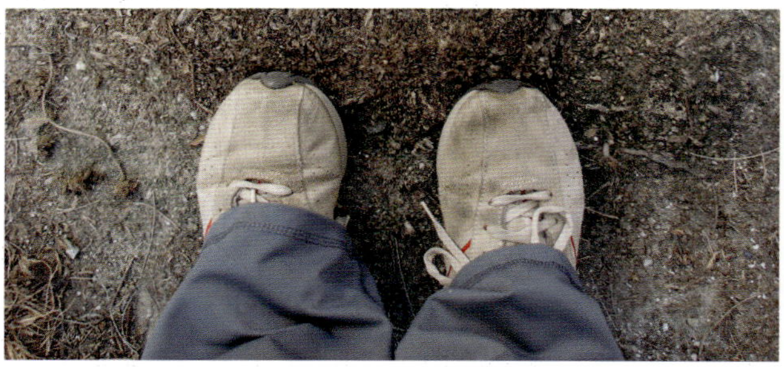

**1** Begin your journey. Stand still and close your eyes. Take three deep breaths, breathing slowly in and then slowly out. Breathing deeply slows the mind and helps us focus on the now. Let your breath flow freely and let your body relax. Notice how tension may start to leave your shoulders and neck. Open your eyes and start to walk slowly, not thinking too much about your destination, but instead giving yourself permission to just wander and let your intuition guide you.

**2** Consciously take notice. As you wander slowly, take notice of everything around you—your steps on the ground and the sounds in the air.

What colors do you see? How many petals are on each flower, what patterns do you discover in the leaves, what shapes are in the trees, the buildings or the ground you are walking along?

Maybe your walk will take you to a park, the countryside, a beach or a pond, or through an open door you wouldn't normally walk through.

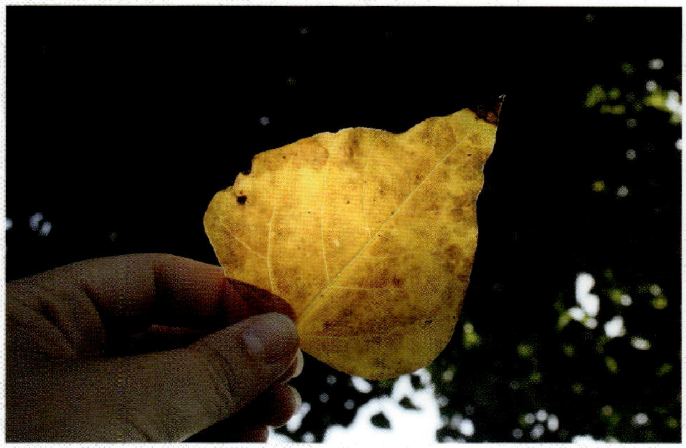

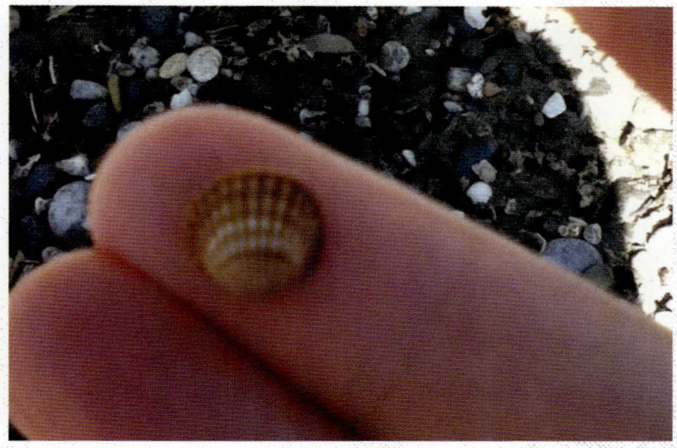

3 Live in the moment. Look around you; notice every teeny tiny little detail. Use your camera to photograph the beauty you discover as you travel, slowing down your pace or stopping to make a sketch and admiring the detail. Really take note of how you feel in this moment.

4 Gather. What found objects are around for you to collect? Leaves fallen from plants or trees? Flowers that have fallen to the ground, twigs, stones, shells or bark? Gather anything you are drawn to.

Only collect items that have fallen or are loose on the ground and pop them into your bag. If you can find items where there are four to eight of them, even better, as they will create a symmetrical mandala.

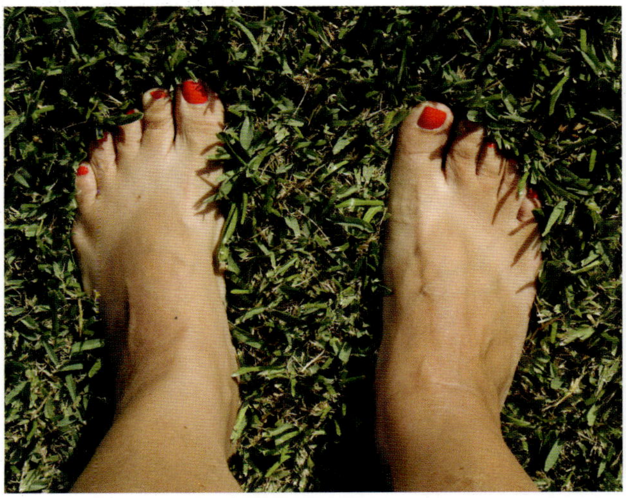

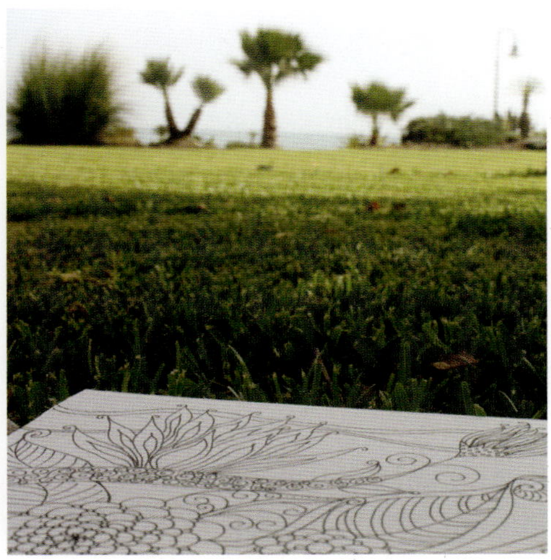

5 Ground yourself. After some time, find yourself a place to relax. If you feel comfortable to do so, take off your shoes and stand barefoot on the ground. This will help you connect with the energy of Mother Earth and is a simple way to ground yourself to be completely in the moment. Allow yourself to connect to the energy of the earth. (This is also something you can do on a daily basis in your own backyard.)

How does this make you feel?

6 Sketch the natural world around you. Take a seat and open your sketchbook/journal. Journal how you feel about your meditation walk so far and any feelings that are coming up for you. Look around you for natural objects to sketch, or select a few you have already collected.

Take some time to relax and soak up your surroundings. Drink lots of water and have a snack.

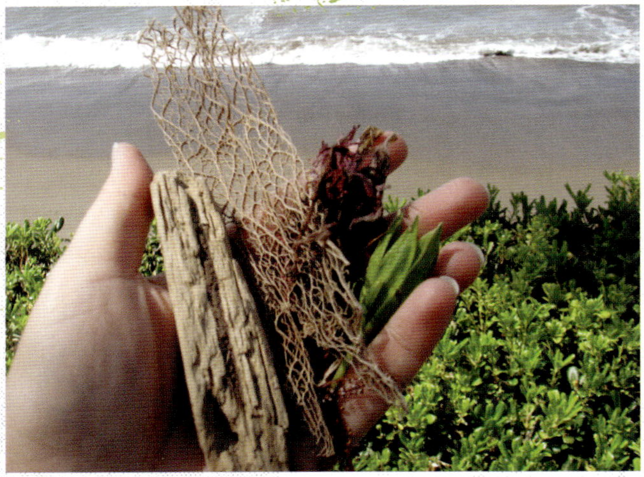

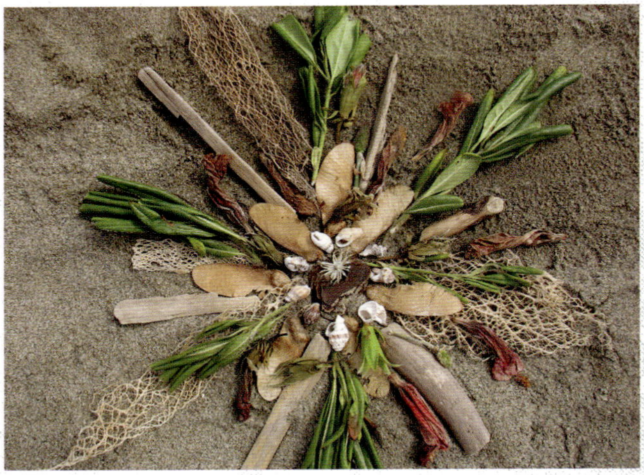

7 Prepare to create. Find yourself a place to create your mandala and gather your found objects. Place them on the ground and let your intuition guide you as to how to lay them out. You may build from the inside out or create the outer circle first with pebbles.

Think about your connection with nature as you place the objects into the circle. How do the objects feel, what colors do you have?

Consciously focus on what you are doing in this moment and simply enjoy the moment creating this offering back to the earth.

8 Create your mandala. As you lay each piece into the mandala, think about experiences, people and places you are grateful for in your life. Once you have completed your mandala, no matter how simple or detailed it is, spend some time photographing your creation, sit with it and journal any more thoughts that may arise from your meditation walk.

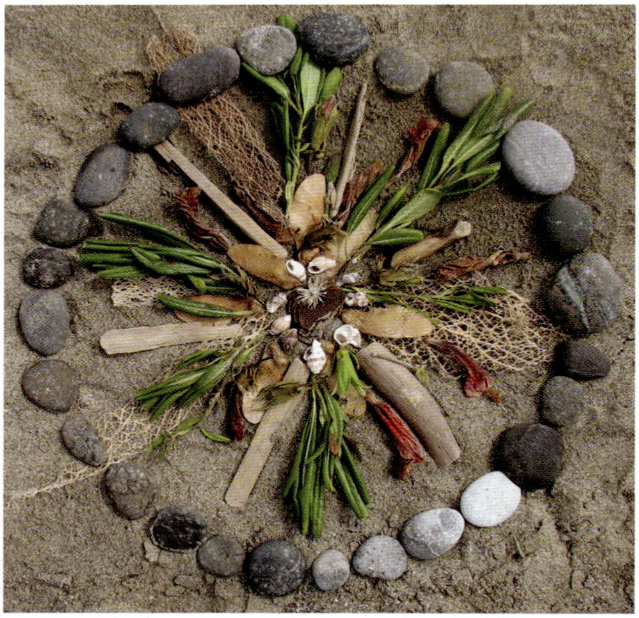

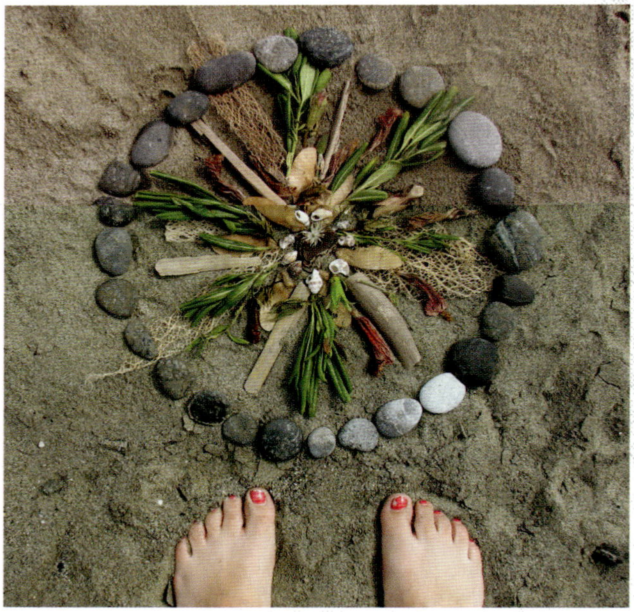

9 Let go. Thank the universe for all that you are grateful for and for enabling your creative talents to flow freely.

Thank the earth for its abundance and mindfully offer your mandala as a way of thanking every living thing. We are all connected.

You may want to leave a note for anyone who finds your creation or simply let it be in all its beauty for others to enjoy as they discover it along their own journey.

When you are ready, make your way back to where you started and complete the process by spending time with your journal, gathering your sketches, photos and thoughts.

# my ode to mexico

Mexico, sweet Mexico!

Land of vibrant colors, rich history and fiery foods. Where smells hit the senses with blunt and honest force, practicality rules and whimsical, fatalistic humor abounds.

Land of a thousand contradictions: outrageous wealth and brutal poverty, a deep-seated reverence for Spirit intertwined with stark and brutal violence.

We have traveled your potholed roads over mountains and from coast to coast by plane, by bus and in our old Chevy truck complete with our little casa on top.

We have experienced your beauty as young, childless travelers and with our children as babies, toddlers and teens. Every time you beguile me and I grew a little more into the person I was meant to become.

You have taught me the value of compassion, the beauty of difference and the wisdom of trusting in the journey.

You have filled my world with the joy of color and helped me to recognize the dormant artist within.

I have learned to welcome new friends into our home as countless *Mexicanos* have welcomed us into theirs, and through these connections and experiences I have learned that there truly are no accidents in life.

I have come to realize that faith is a wondrous thing, and that miracles and magic exist in all of our lives when we are willing to let them in.

I have learned that we don't need as much as we think we do, and that when you are generous in spirit your own world becomes far more beautiful and bounteous.

I am still learning to laugh heartily and spontaneously, and it may take many more visits before I can dance with freedom and without inhibition.

I cherish the memories and hold the future promise in my heart.

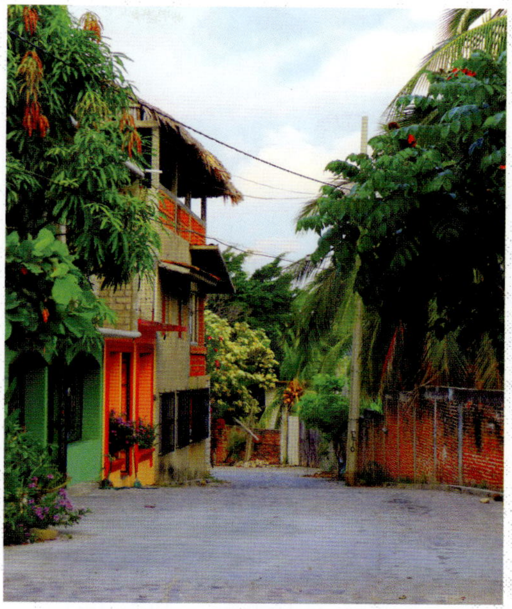

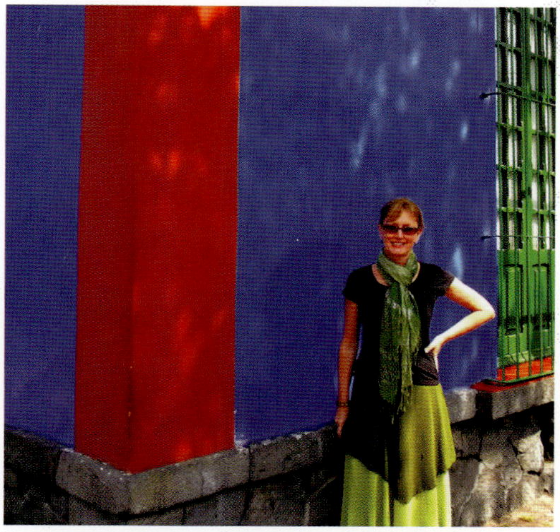

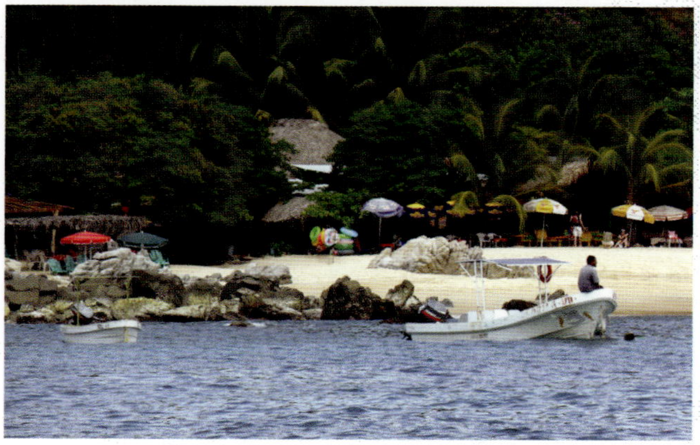

exercise

# connecting through other cultures

One of the greatest gifts I have been given while journeying through other cultures is an awareness of the expansiveness of life. In Mexico there is a knowing that life is to be celebrated and that death is just a doorway to another realm, and between the two a thin veil exists that is at its most transparent during the celebration of *Dia de los Muertos*.

In this exercise, I will share with you a fun and easy way to create your own printing block, which you could carve with a motif representing any culture with which you connect.

### What You Need

- acrylic paints
- black permanent marker
- border embellishments
- brayer
- gel pens
- paintbrushes
- pencil or pen
- piece of foam, such as from a meat tray
- small block of wood
- variety of papers

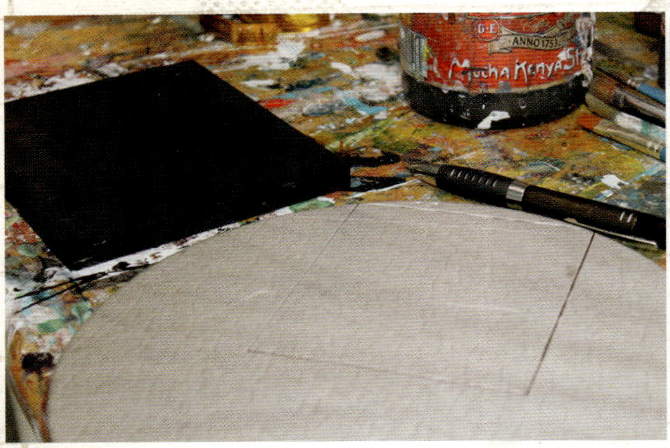

**1** Gather your supplies and paint your block of wood with black paint.

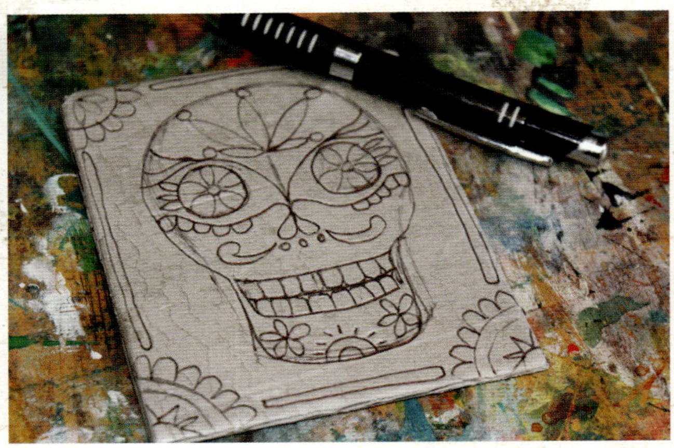

**2** Lightly draw your design onto your piece of foam.

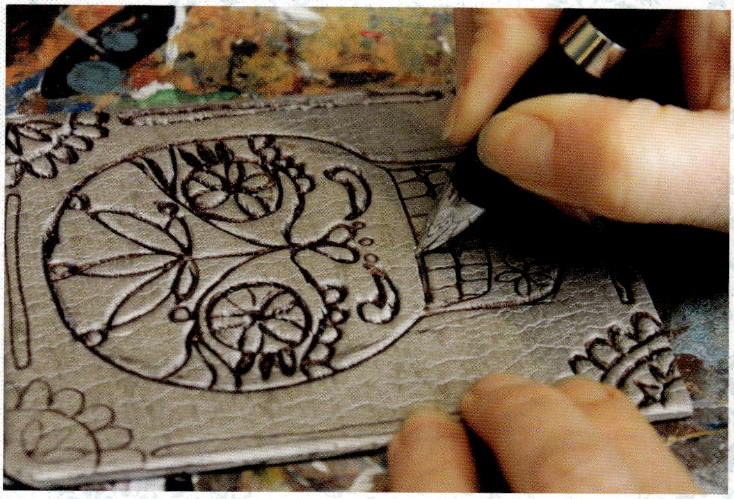

**3** Once happy with your design, press more deeply into the foam with a pen until you have made an indentation of the whole design. In this piece I created a design inspired by the Mexican tradition of *Dia de los Muertos*.

Make sure you have pressed firmly into the foam to create a stamp that works well with paint.

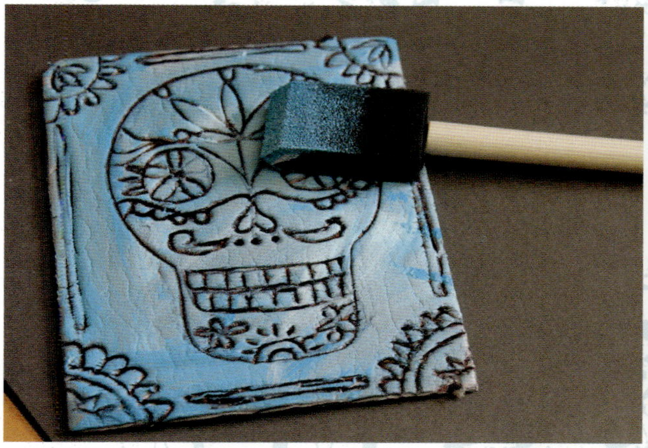

**4** Brush your favorite color of paint across your foam stamp evenly. Use a dry brush so wet paint doesn't get caught up in the lines of your design.

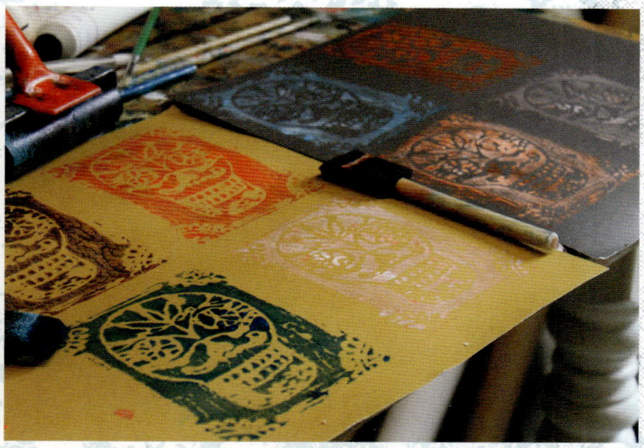

**5** Play with different colors of paint, stamped onto a variety of papers. This will allow you to play with the thickness of paint and also give you some great collage pieces for homemade cards!

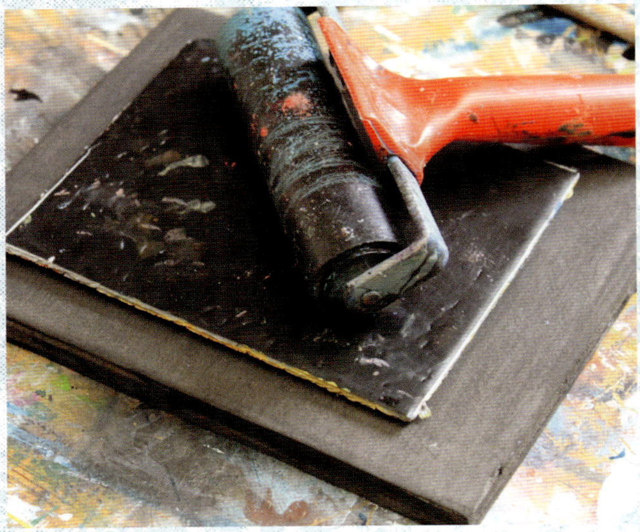

6 Choose a light color (I used Hansa Light Yellow) and coat your stamp. Then lay it facedown onto your painted block of wood, and using a brayer to transfer your painted design to the wood.

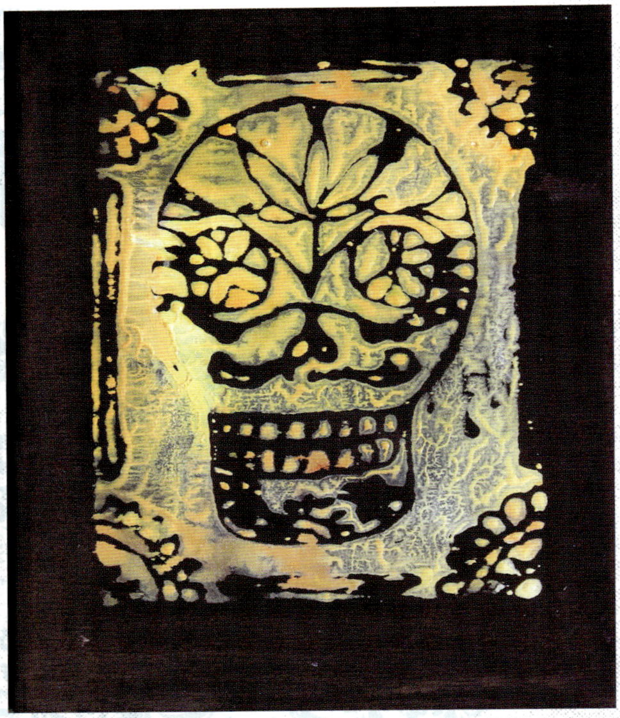

7 Be open to the possibility of an imperfect transfer. Imperfection is far more interesting than being exact for me.

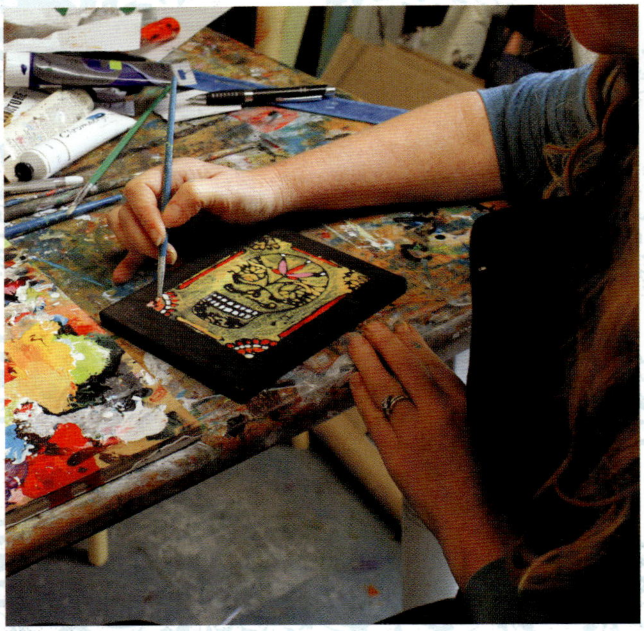

8 Using a fine brush and your favorite colors, paint in the details of your design.

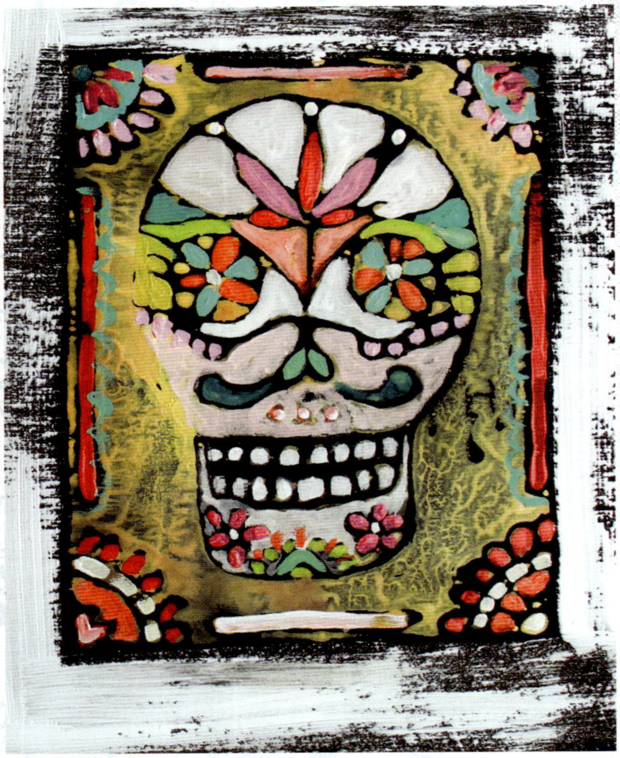

9 Using a dry brush and light pressure, paint a white border around your design.

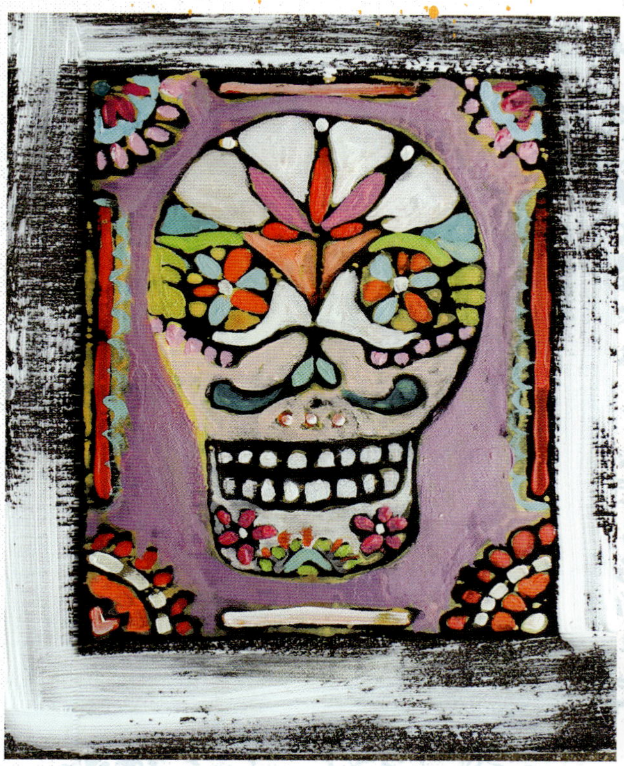

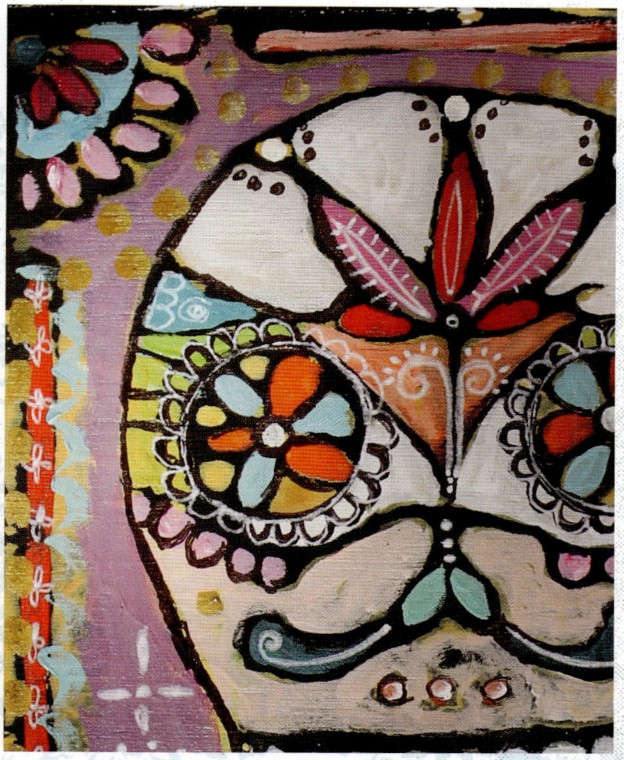

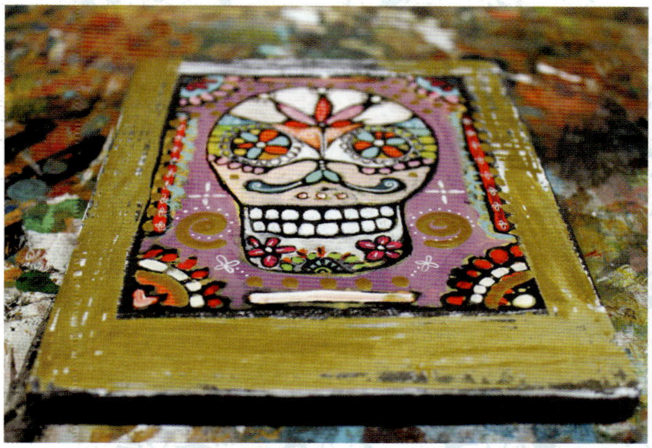

**10** Try a different color background. You can always drybrush over it, and each layer will add a new depth. Use gel pens to add in fine details and a black permanent marker to accentuate any missing transfer lines.

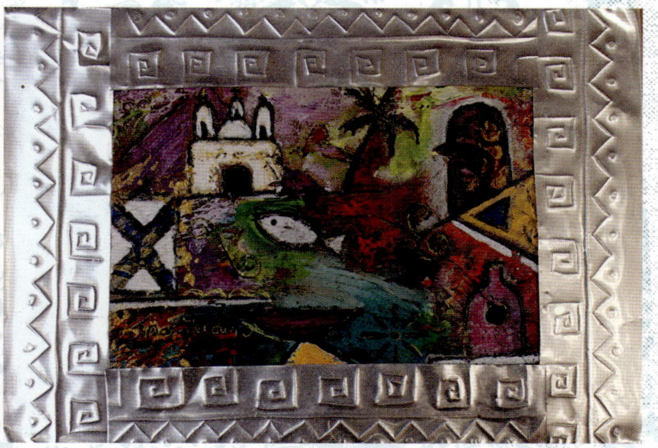

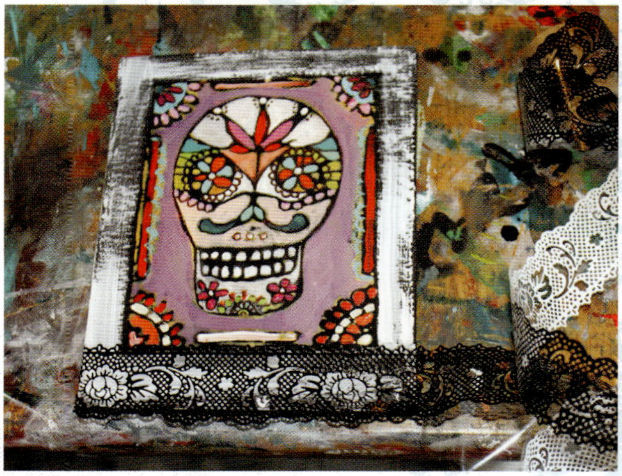

**11** Border Options:
Play with ribbon transfer stickers.

Roughly scribble with a gold paint pen and lightly rub for a distressed metallic border.

Cut border strips from aluminum foil and etch a design into them before gluing to the wood with a hot glue gun.

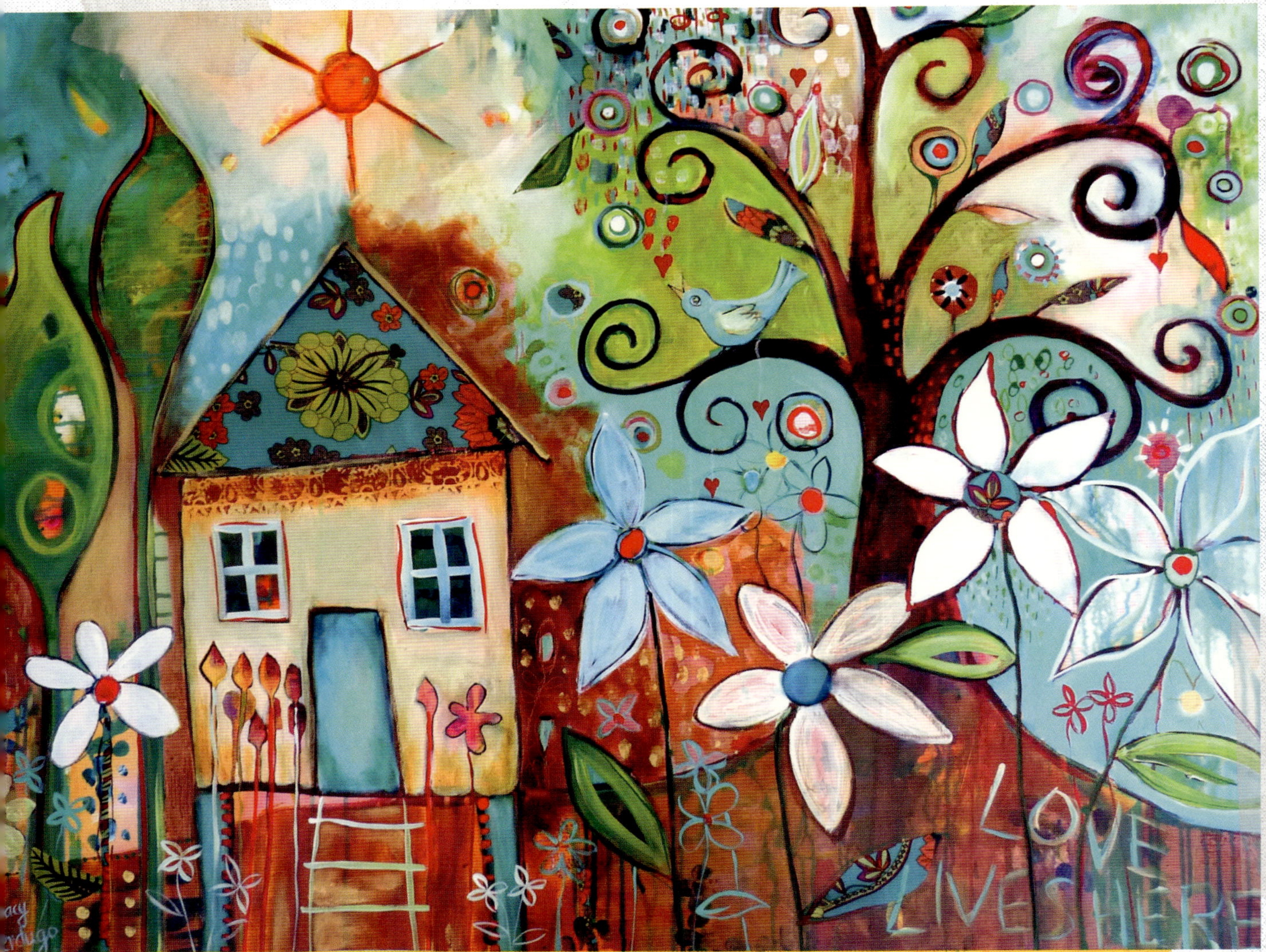
LOVE
LIVES HERE

# chapter eight: throwing out the rule book

## Finding happiness in play, faith and balance

One thing I know for sure is that when we give ourselves too many rules, we build a cage that encloses our experiences (past, present and potentially fabulous future!), imposing limitations on our world and restricting the discoveries that could be made if only we loosened up the guidelines a little. If we can open that cage door, perhaps spray a little oil on those rusty, rigid hinges, we may find ourselves heading in the general direction of a lighter state of being—our happy place!

Now I'm not talking about the rules that keep us safe in the world, the rules that keep us being kind and loving toward each other and ourselves, the rules that are necessary to hold a society together.

I'm talking more about the fear-based rules, the ones that start off with distrust, fear of not belonging, fear of failing. The ones that make us wear our hair a particular way when we're longing to experience a certain shade of magenta, the ones that tell us we're too old to try pole dancing or to wear a tutu, (thank you, Art Is You, for breaking that one!) or that it's irresponsible to take our kids out of school for seven months and embark on a family wanderlust sabbatical (I can highly recommend that one!).

You know the kind I mean.

*Tell me, what is it you plan to do with your one wild and precious life?*
—Mary Oliver

For many years I've resonated strongly with the idea that there are only two core emotions—fear and love—and that everything that happens in our lives, every decision we make, stems from one or the other. Maybe we can take it one step further.

Maybe, there is only love and we are either moving closer toward it or farther away from it with every thought, every action, like a gigantic game of spiritual warmer/cooler. Where is the love? Is it in this dark, scary cupboard? This list of things I wish I could do, if only? Getting cold, oh very cold! Is it over here in this box of beautiful dreams, this canvas swirling with color and intuition, this warm embrace from someone who loves me? Getting warmer, warmer and hot!

Take this idea for a week and play with it. Watch the thoughts that come up for you in every situation, and try to decide if they are based in love or fear. I have had many epiphanies around this concept, and they have helped me so much to release a lot of the fears I used to carry around in my life and to express myself creatively without the self-judgment that was once my steady companion.

Perhaps one of the first lightbulb moments that made me realize it was OK to throw out the rule book, happened many years ago, illuminating the night sky on a windswept deserted beach in northern Baja California. Although, in that moment, it was hard to see the light in the darkness, hindsight has a way of making important lessons very clear.

* * *

It is early January 1991 and the gray skies over Tijuana are beginning to break up enough for small glimpses of blue to peek through. We have just crossed the border after days of heavy rain that have left the drains of Southern California overflowing, unable to cope with this rare occurrence.

Behind the elegant black wrought-iron fence, the home of Marco's *abuelita* and her sister, whitewashed with turquoise trim, is a haven of foliage, flowers and memories, a refuge amongst the grey streets of the overcrowded metropolis.

We are at the beginning of *un gran viaje*! An adventure into the wilds of Mexico that will take us the better part of the year.

*Mi amor* is ready to explore the off-roads and surf the biggest waves in places no one has heard of, to sleep under the stars in swaying hammocks and discover ancient ruins in tropical overgrown jungles!

I am sitting quietly, making a list of the things I will not be doing, a list of conditions I would like him to agree upon before we begin the trip, a litany of expected dangers and ways to avoid and prevent them.

I am twenty-five, have never done anything like this before, and my head is filled with the stories from well-meaning but anxious friends and family: stories of rape and roadblocks, banditos and bribery, scorpions and landslides!

Outside the house we are ready to embark. *Abuelita* has gifted us a sum of money which, with the outrageous early nineties' exchange rate of thirty thousand pesos to one U.S. dollar, has turned us into instant millionaires. We stuff the cash inside cushions, nestle it between grains of rice in Tupperware containers, tuck it into socks and under mattresses.

The two sisters, Agripina and Toto, have lived together in this home for sixty years, both widowed young. They are fiercely independent and devoutly Catholic. Toto, in a well-worn, soft mauve dressing gown, stands beside the 1979 Chevy truck, its little camper perched on top. This will be our home for the next year. She prays intently, her olive-skinned hands passing from one rosary bead to the next as she blesses the truck, our journey and us.

Her blessing is greatly appreciated but not quite enough for me to throw out the list of rules I have been formulating, at the top of which, in bold letters, are the following two provisos:

1. Absolutely no driving after sunset!
2. No camping in isolated, unpopulated areas unless it is a known camping spot with other travelers around.

Surely not too much to ask?

We bid *adios* to the two sisters, leaving them to their afternoon *novela* and drive through the outskirts of the city toward the coast. Makeshift *colonias* cling precariously to the sides of hills, their foundations compromised by the heavy rain. A tattered blanket of cardboard, scrap metal and random bits of timber cover the landscape as far as I can see, a city built of desperate dreams.

When we round a corner, the ocean stretches out in front of us and we hit the old coast road, puckered with potholes from the recent deluge. Our mission for this first day is to get to Cuatro Casas, a prime surf destination a few hours down the coast. Marco has assured me there will be other people there, it will be completely safe, and we will arrive long before dark. Unfortunately the going is slow with the damage on the highway and by the time we reach the track that leads to the beach, it is late afternoon.

"How much longer?" I ask him, little sparks of anxiety beginning to fire in my mind. We are bouncing along the rutted track, trying to avoid the mud-filled potholes, and in the dying light I feel a sense of foreboding. We pass a group of workers leaning nonchalantly against a peeling concrete fence. They watch us with what I am sure is menacing intent.

Marco fails to swerve in time and in an instant we are bogged in a puddle of mud. My apprehension and anger heighten. By the time we extricate the Chevy, it is after sunset and although we have arrived at the beach, we are still not at the campground and have little chance of finding the right tracks in the dark.

Marco laughs off my fears and assures me, a little impatiently, that all will be OK, but I am righteously indignant that on the very first night he has broken my two most important rules!

I try to see the humoros side while cooking up some tortillas and beans in our tiny kitchen. Marco passes me a cold beer and we settle in for what will become a popular daily ritual: a healthy, albeit competitive, game of Scrabble.

Halfway through the game and almost all the way through my second Bohemia, I am sufficiently mellow to begin to allow my anxieties to subside. I head out into the night to find a patch of beach to pee, and under the immense starry sky I squat down and contemplate the enormity of this adventure we are just beginning. Closing my eyes for a brief moment I hear the waves crash and withdraw, I hear the chirping of crickets in the sand dunes, I hear . . . the unmistakable drone of a car engine. Opening my eyes I see headlights in the distance but coming closer, along the beach. I feel like a deer stunned by the headlights, with my pants around my ankles!

Hastily I pull myself together and sprint the short distance back to the truck. Heart pounding, I dissolve into panic, frantically climb the ladder up to our bed and hide behind the wall, possibly even under the blankets. "You got us into this, you can deal with it!" I yell at my bemused husband while quivering in the corner and listening to the sound of a vehicle pulling up alongside us.

In my mind's eye I see our family at the funeral service, tearfully wailing, "*Oh dios mio, que lastima!* And they had only just begun their journey. If Marco had just paid attention to the rules ..."

I hear the sound of two doors slamming shut and prick my ears waiting for the click of a trigger. Instead, a knock at the door and a voice unmistakably Californian: "Dude, is anyone home?" Marco opens the door to greet two surfers who have also lost their way and sheepishly I climb down from the bed, avoiding his I-told-you-so glare.

We invite them for a game of Scrabble and open a bottle of Kahlúa, sharing stories and much laughter, and on that night, I realized for the first time that a rule book rooted in fear was not a companion we needed on this journey or any other.

*Throw away your rule books!*

*Happiness does not live inside those pages.*

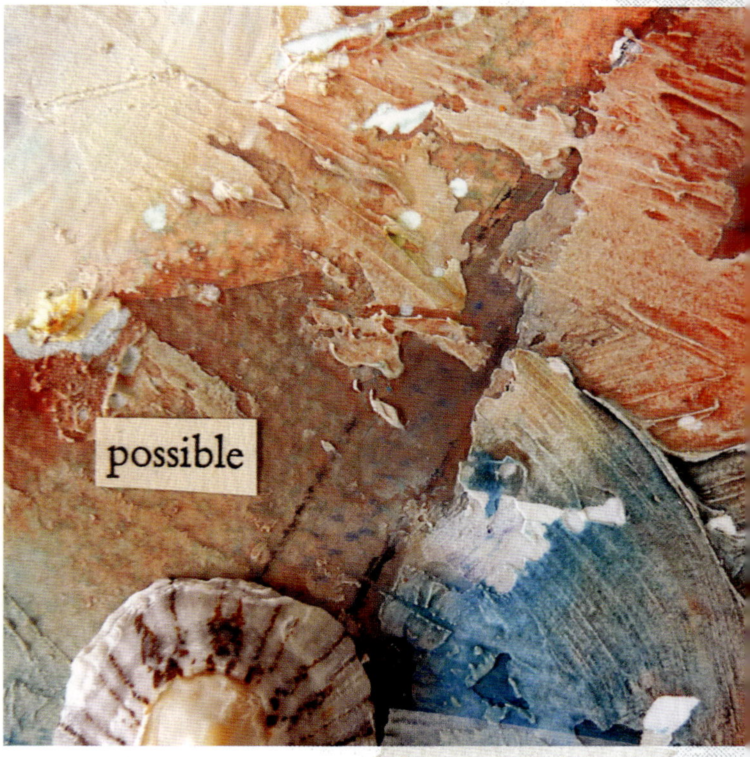

# the happy choice

**by Jessica Brogan**

One of my favorite quotes says, "The choices you make today, directly impact your opportunities tomorrow." In that vein, I'll let you in on a little secret: Happiness is not a place to arrive, it's a daily practice and a choice. The attitude you choose today, how you decide to interpret what happens to you in your life, directly affects your overall happiness tomorrow, the next day and every day in the future.

Every single person I know, both in real life and online, has had traumas and tragedy and pain in their life. No one, and this is a fact, not one person is exempt. Not the rich, not the famous, not the people whose lives look perfect on social media. The difference in how much pain and unhappiness one person experiences, versus another, lies within. It is not the amount of or the nature of the difficulties that people go through. Instead, it is the nature of the person's mind-set internally, and how she chooses to greet the issues that arise. You actually have as much control over your happiness as any other person on earth—rich, poor or seemingly perfect. Happiness is yours for the taking, but you have to choose it and go after it.

One of the most helpful practices you can use to shift your mind set into happiness mode is to develop the practice of *reframing*.

Reframing is the easiest way to change your attitude about what life throws into your path. It goes like this: You're on a long road trip, when you get a nasty flat tire. Not what you'd planned and definitely something that most people would get upset about, allowing tension and stress to infiltrate their bodies. (We often, in fact, practically wave stress in with a welcome sign.) But what if that flat tire prevented you from getting in a major car crash just a mile down the road? What if it actually saved your life? You'll never know for sure, but therein lies the key. You get to choose what you believe (and I for one want to feel good, don't you?). And that is called *reframing*.

Imagine the next time something of this nature happens, and you are sitting in the waiting room of the mechanic shop with a smile of gratitude on your face, because you have chosen how you wish to interpret the situation.

Reframing as a practice can become automatic and effortless when you practice it. It's easy to apply to small situations and hiccups in your daily life. But what about the really hard times? The deep pains and the periods of our lives that seem truly devastating? What if you came down with a disease? Or someone you know and love passes away suddenly? Or, like me, you are stricken with something you'd never even heard of before—postpartum OCD—when you're at your most emotionally fragile? How do we practice happiness in the face of *these things*?

In these times, I suggest turning to two things: art, and faith. In regards to your art-making practice, often the confused and devastated mind needs to feel a reestablished connection to the bigger picture of life, and there is no better way than through a creative practice. Anything you can do—from gardening to painting to singing—will help reestablish your connection with the greater spirit of life. You will feel less alone. You will feel healed, even if it's slight at first, each time you create. Then there is *faith*. Faith does not have to apply to the religious. Faith in life can mean that you choose to believe that good and happiness will return again. Instead of disbelief, you choose to look for the opportunities to feel happiness seeping back in. Faith is also trusting that you have the keys. If you are in turmoil, facing a great life challenge, I encourage you to listen inward. What do you hear? What do you need? Happiness can be found right there.

And finally, what about happiness in your creative pursuits? The majority of people I know have a special knack for getting cranky about their creative work! We

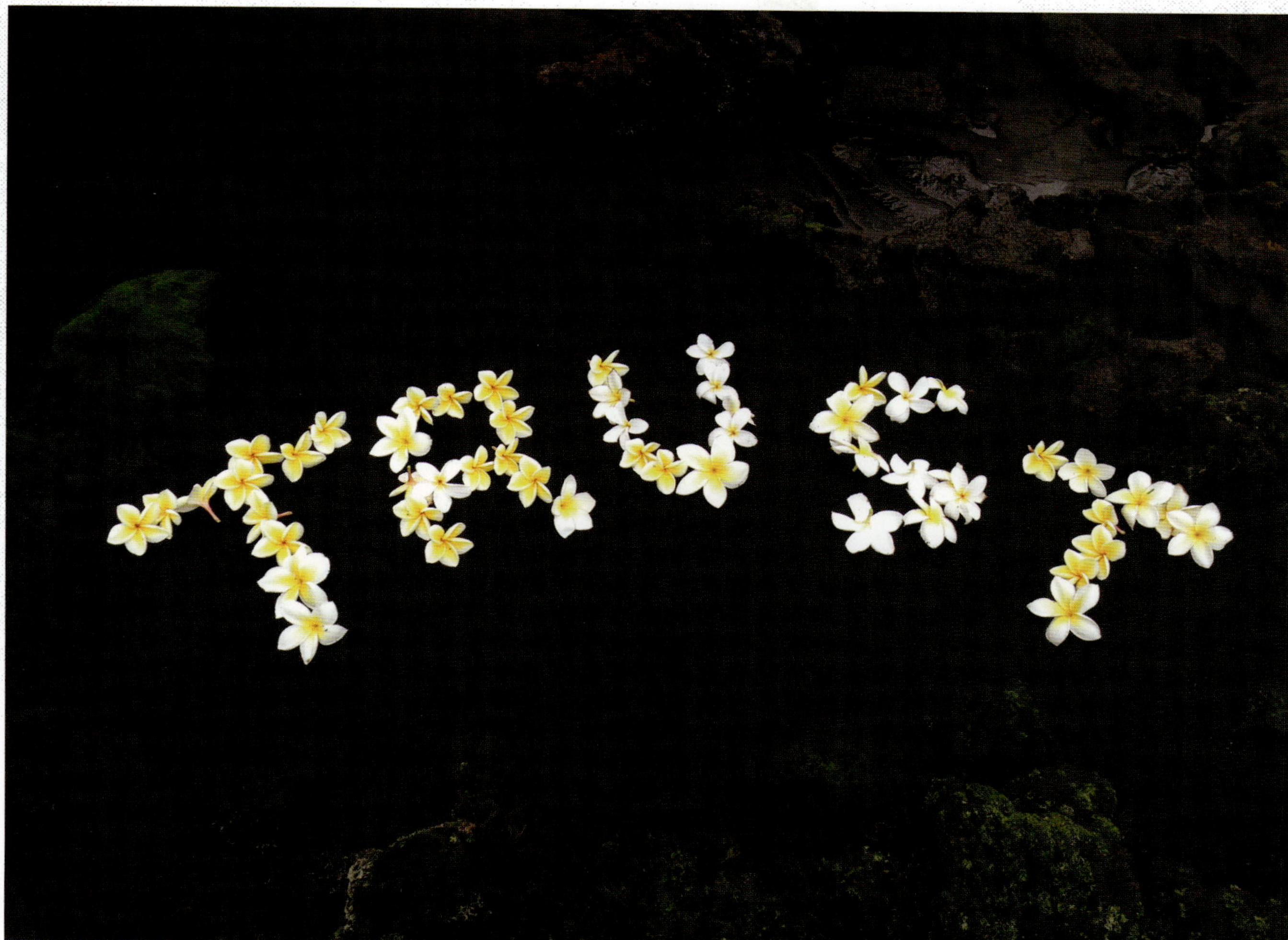


set to work to create, and almost instantly our inner critic wakes up and begins to inform us of all the things that are "Wrong" (with a capital W) with what we're doing. This is yet another thing that no one is exempt from! This time, the easy-peasy solution is *affirmation*. For every ugly message you hear while you are creating, you must respond. You must fight for your right to a happy and judgment-free creative practice. I suggest you keep a notebook nearby and actually write down the things that you hear in your head. Then write back. Sounds a little silly, but try it. Come up with a response that emboldens you and diminishes that voice. Every time you hear your inner critic lash out, respond immediately with your affirmations! Creativity is about the spirit of play, and there is no room for unhappiness in it! It won't happen immediately, but I promise that if you do this over time like a telephone salesman, with your persistence, he'll eventually give up. You can diminish that inner critic, and in doing so, you will find so much more happiness flowing through your creative time. Your happiness is in your hands.

# painted pages

**by Juliette Crane**

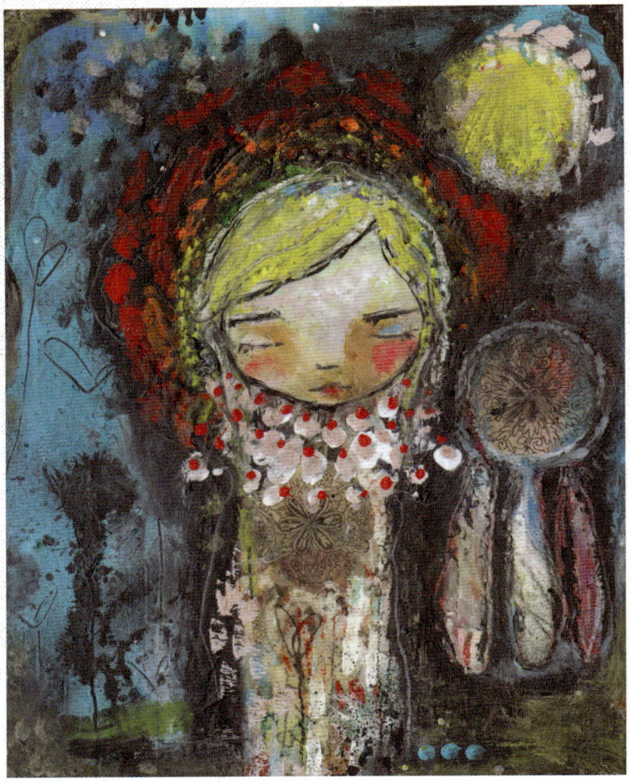

Whenever I paint, my intention is to have fun. I believe that joy gets infused into your artwork and makes anyone who sees it smile.

I have certain colors and techniques that I always go back to: turquoise and hot pink, fingerpainting and layering tissue paper on canvas. These things make me happy and help me spread joy to others through my paintings and in my everyday.

If I don't like something in my artwork, I cover it up, knowing that every mark is important. For me, it's all part of the process, and allowing those beautiful mistakes and false starts to happen, adds depth to each painting. It helps me express my story as an artist and to heal.

Outside of painting, I also find happiness and balance in morning meditation, yoga, healthy eating, starting my day doing something nice for someone and keeping a gratitude journal.

### What You Need

collage elements

favorite art supplies (I love bleeding art tissue paper, Cobalt Teal and neon acrylic paints, watercolors, colored India inks, Liquitex inks, Krink paint markers, Shiva Oil Paintstiks and water-soluble oil pastels.)

glue

music you love (I currently love to paint to the *Amélie* soundtrack. It always gets me in a whimsical mood.)

sketchbook

variety of brushes (foam, bristle, sponges, calligraphy)

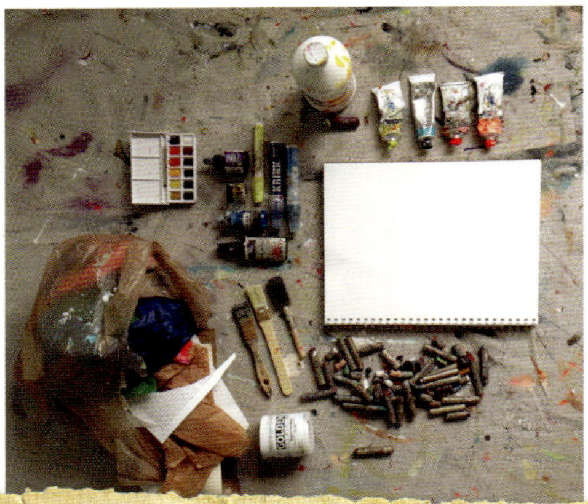

### RULES TO REMEMBER (OR FORGET!)

- Oftentimes my mind jumps in and says I can't use acrylics with oils, but then I try it anyway and realize it looks beautiful.
- If I feel like my background isn't pretty enough, it usually means I've stopped having fun and become too focused on the final outcome. That's when I start a new painted page or go back to using my favorite colors and techniques. I also cover up the parts I'm struggling with, with colors or papers I love.
- If my painted page looks too busy, I'll add in some solid areas with India inks or my favorite color acrylic paint.
- If I write something I don't want anyone to see, I cover it up with bleeding art tissue paper or a book page, then paint over it some more.
- If it seems like the page needs something more, I add a few of my favorite stamps or stencils.

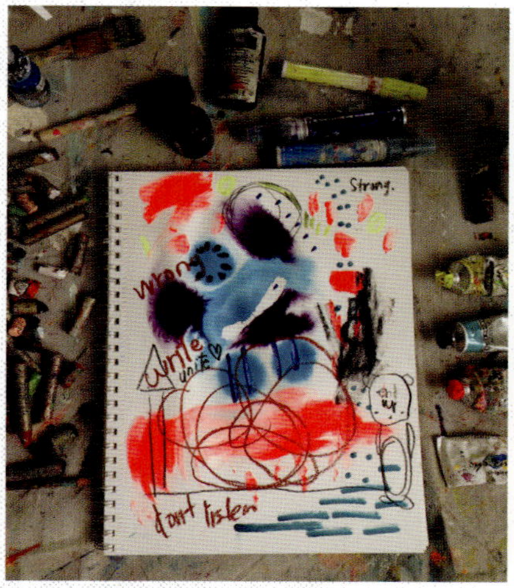

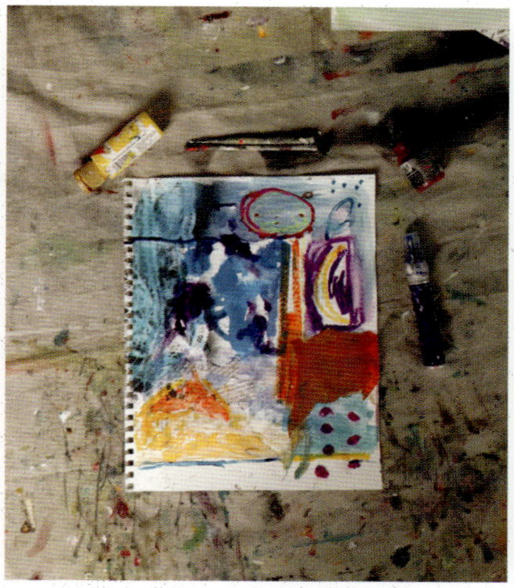

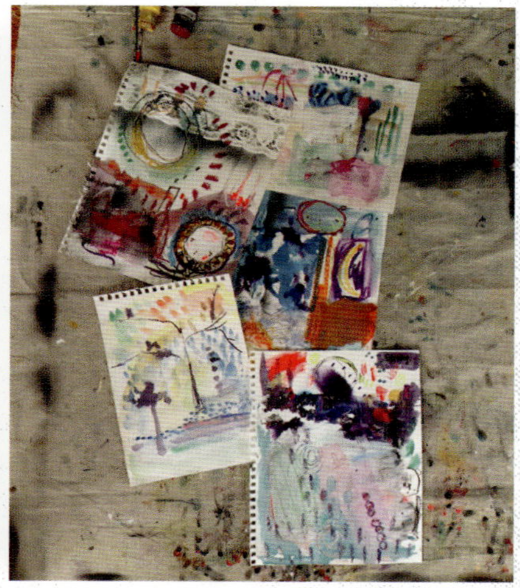

**1** Put on your favorite music and get out all of your art supplies. I like to set them up in rows like teachers did in preschool, so everything is ready to go.

**2** Grab whatever art supplies catch your eye and play in your sketchbook. At this stage, I work fast and follow my instincts. I scribble, smudge and let the color run all over and bleed if I want. I make silly marks with acrylics, doodle in pencil and then scribble over it with oil pastels. I write whatever words come to mind.

Work on a few pages at once. This phase is all about covering up the white space.

When I've covered most of my white space, I start another piece while the first dries. I always have five or six painted pages going at once. That way I never get impatient or too attached to just one.

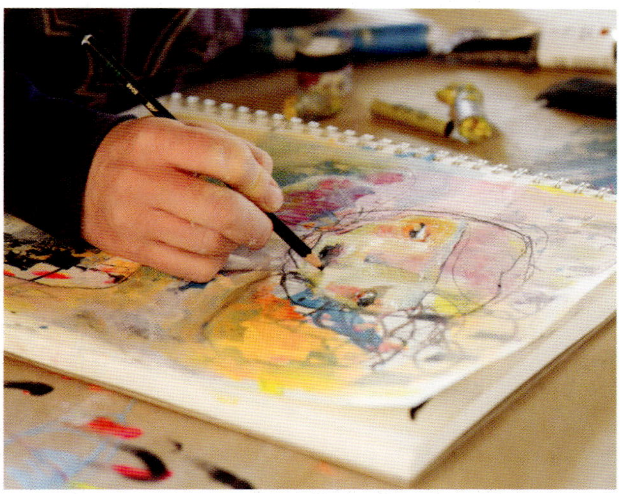

Photo by Kate Daniel

**3** Add a second layer to each painted page. Nothing here needs to be perfect. It's all about staying loose and having fun.

Sometimes I pull out sheet music and old children's books like *James and the Giant Peach* and glue sections down in strips. If I'm feeling sentimental and remembering how lovely it was to run through the flower garden in the summertime, I will be drawn to butterflies and birds on gift wrap and vintage postcards as well as tissue paper I've saved from favorite birthday presents.

Once I finish layering my papers, I use acrylic paints to fill in between the collage elements, popping out areas I like most while creating solid sections of color for the viewer's eye to rest.

To keep with the whimsical feel, I scribble with water-soluble oil pastels and wax crayons. This reminds me of coloring as a kid, spread out with all of my art supplies on a big blanket in the grass. That's the way I still love to paint. It makes me stay carefree and play in my artwork.

I often rip out the parts I love most in these painted pages and glue them back together again like puzzle pieces on canvas or wood to start a new background.

There is no right or wrong way.

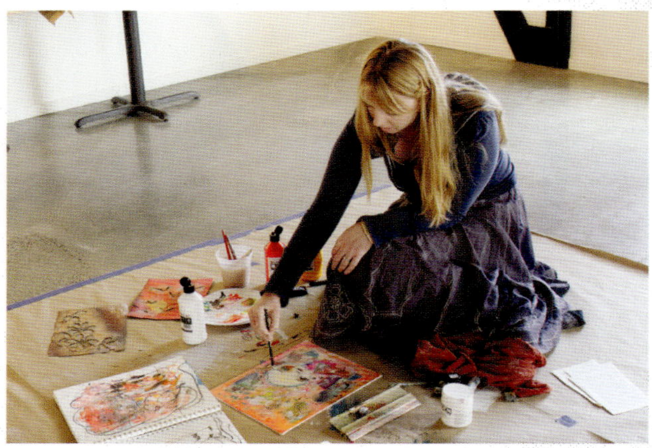

Photo by Kate Daniel

exercise

# inky sojourn

I have discovered that hours spent behind a computer screen are not conducive to a relaxed state of mind. And a relaxed state of mind is key to cultivating a state of happiness. Too many times I have felt that fuzzy, heightened, unfocused buzz of being glued to the screen too long, flitting back and forth from one of the many open tabs, trying to get everything done yet getting distracted time and time again, neglecting to drink water or go to the bathroom, trying to get just one more thing done!

Recently I have discovered that forcing myself to leave my office after a couple of hours, head on outside into the garden and then lying spread-eagled on the grass for at least ten minutes, taking in the sounds and beauty around, feeling the sunshine on my face and body, will bring me straight back into a grounded, relaxed, connected and far more focused state. A quick sojourn into my studio after a garden sunbath to play with colored inks adds even more to the happiness equation. I invite you to step away from the screen and join me in some inky exploration!

**What You Need**

- acrylic artist's inks
- eyedroppper
- foam brush
- skewer or other mark-making elements
- spray bottle with water
- viewfinder
- watercolor paper
- white oil pastel

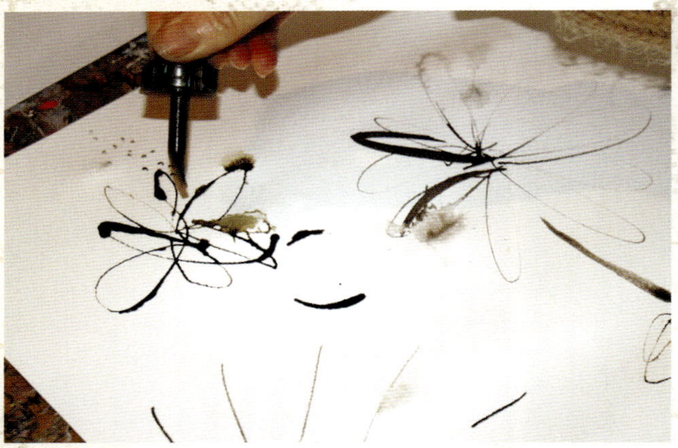

**1** Using your favorite inks (mine are FW Daler-Rowney Acrylic Artists Inks) and a large sheet of watercolor paper (feel free to experiment with different types for different effects), begin with black. Using the dropper as your drawing tool, begin to lay down images and marks inspired by the garden.

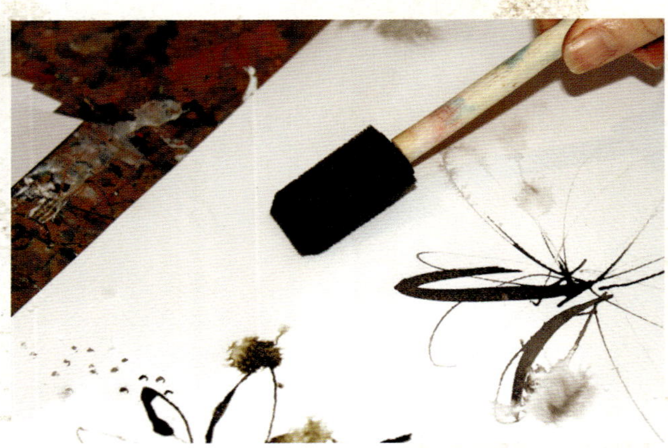

**2** Wet some areas of the paper randomly with drips, foam brushstrokes and a spray bottle and wait for happy accidents!

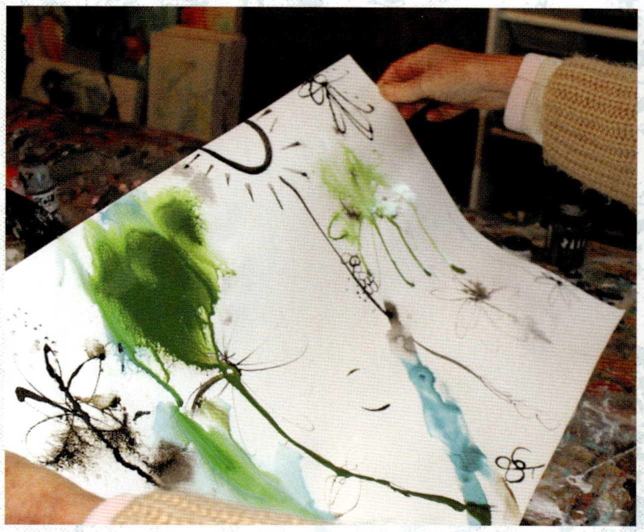

**3** Adding a couple more colors (I added Turquoise and Olive Green), play with sploshing, spraying and dripping the inks with no expectation of outcome. Can you see the little bluebird that magically appeared in a wet brushed area?

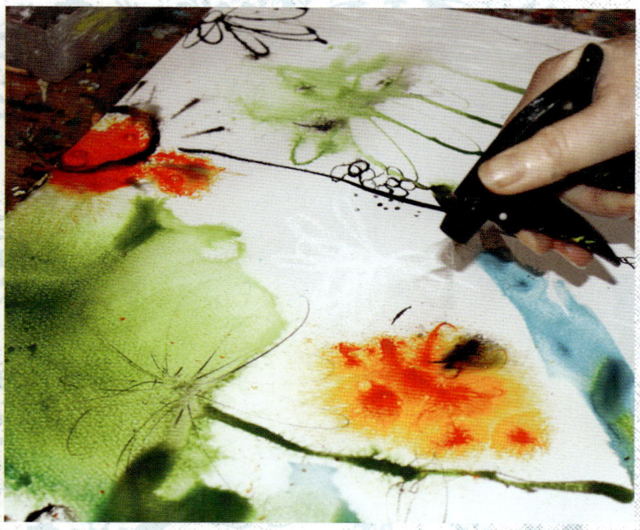

**4** I drew in some more garden-inspired designs and marks with a white oil pastel and then dropped and sprayed my Flame Orange ink into the mix.

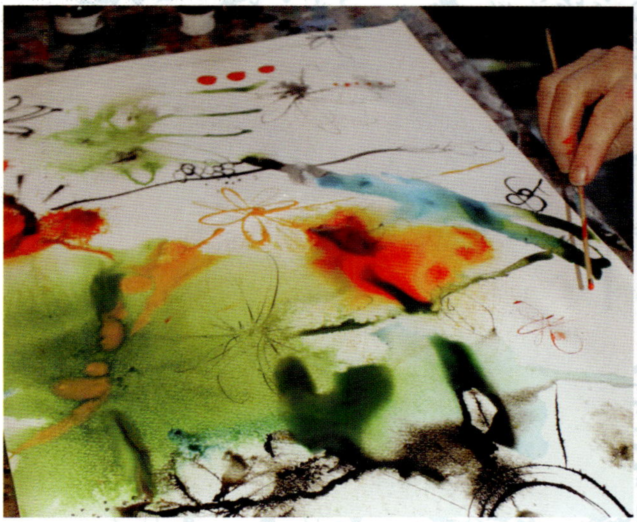

**5** With a bamboo skewer and/or your fingers, pick up some of one color and move it around the page, dabbing, dotting and drawing, balancing out the composition with broad swatches of color and more delicate marks. I work playfully and not too fast, leaving lots of white spaces for a balance in contrast. To further enhance the visual contrast, add in some swatches of darker areas. A big green love heart puddle formed in the middle here. So much fun!

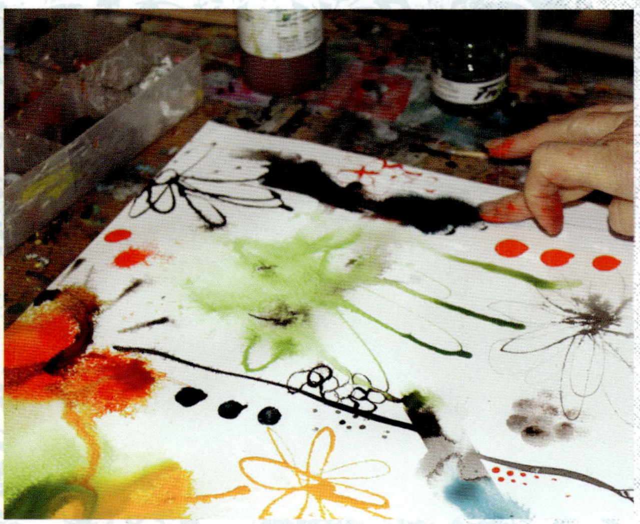

**6** I added some red and ochre into the picture, blotted the excess water with a paper towel and let the image dry.

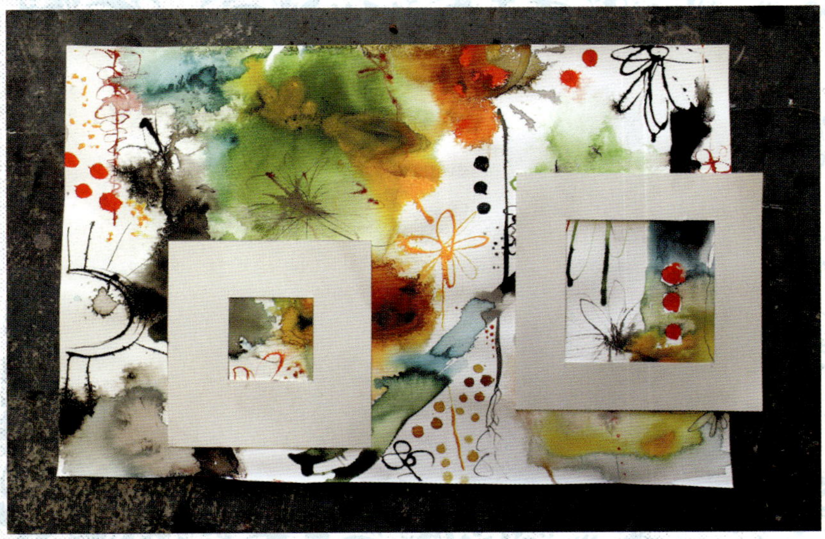

**7** When your image is dry, play around with a small viewfinder, looking for pleasing compositions—smaller images within the larger. I like to use a ruler edge to tear these smaller images from the larger exploratory piece. This way I always have a multitude of beautiful images in my inspiration stash to work into and create more art!

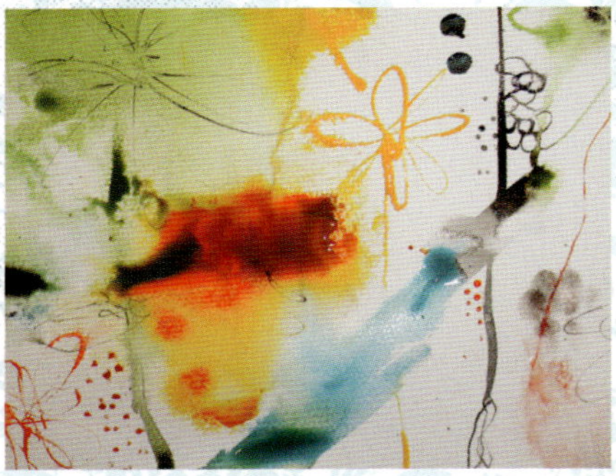

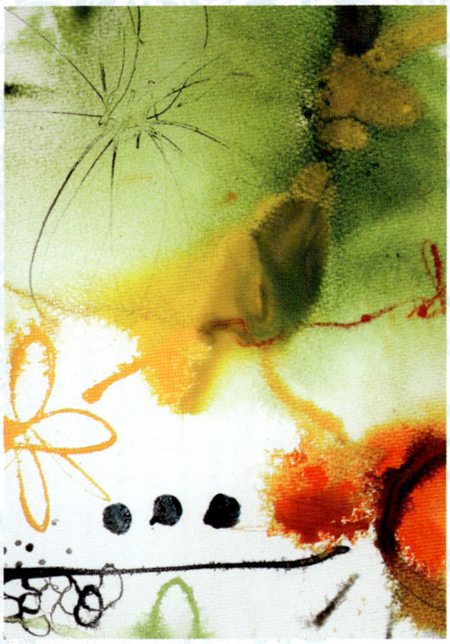

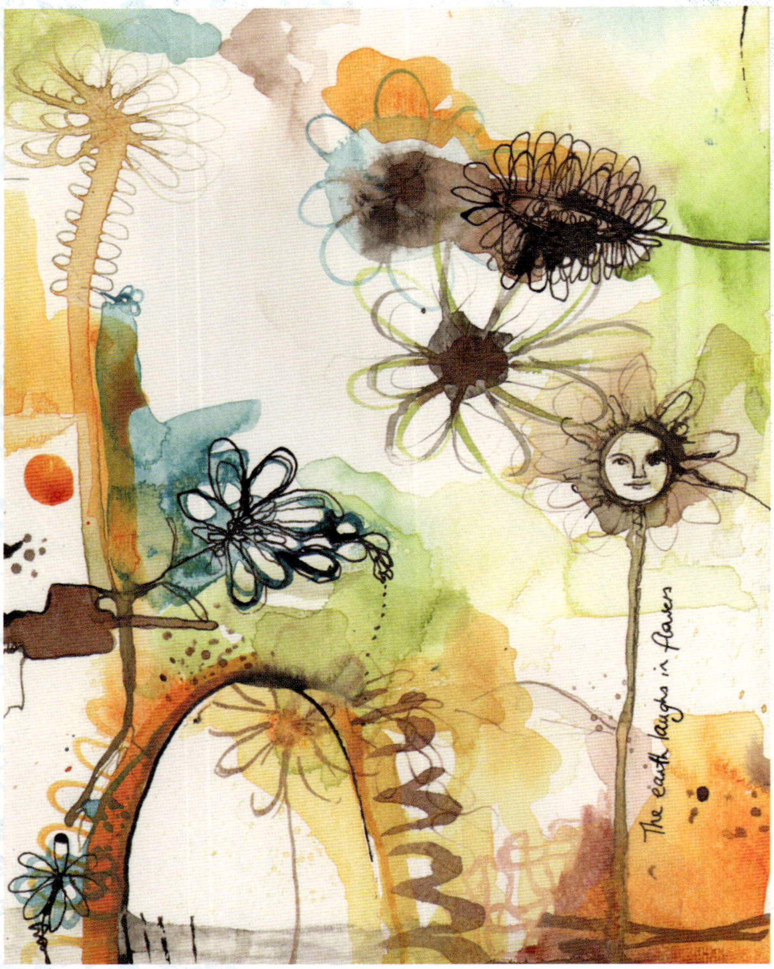

# happy, harmonic balance

**by Mary Beth Shaw**

Finding and keeping a "happy place" sometimes seems like a full-time job in and of itself. Like many artists, my most natural disposition tends toward extremes on both ends. I spent a lot of years thinking I somehow had to suffer or anguish to create powerful and moving art. Or, that I had to put myself into a mania to get anything done. However, I have most recently found these types of behavior ultimately end up causing me to spin out, which results in a waste of my precious (oh how precious it is!) time and energy.

It took me oh-so-long to get to this point and I guess I am sounding a wee bit like an old fogey in her fifties even saying it, but I think I might, just might have finally learned something. I perform best and am my happiest when I remain in some semblance of harmonic balance. This requires regular—as in daily—attention to my physical and mental state of being.

There are a number of things I try to do: exercise, meditation, a proper diet and quasi-normal sleep patterns definitely help. The days of all-nighters in the studio just don't cut it anymore. I mean, sure, I do it when absolutely necessary, but I generally try to be more disciplined. It may sound überbasic, but the fact is I function better if I take care of my physical self. My energy level soars!

Extras that contribute to my sense of well-being are yoga and time in nature, such as taking a walk on most days. Playing with my cats is an indulgence I allow myself every single day. As my husband says, "Time spent petting a kitty is never wasted." And being with my grandchildren is a tremendous joy. Not raising children of my own, these grandkids that I inherited are quite special and tend to naturally keep me very much in the moment.

This all being said, you are probably thinking, *When on earth does she have time to make art?* Well, guess what, when life is smooth, time for art reveals itself every second, minute, hour, well . . . all the time! There is an undercurrent of art that is constant for me and I love it that way. It sort of defies logic, but this is how I think it works. Ideas abound in joyful ways and I feel so lucky to live this life. Yes, making art is the cherry on top of the sundae, or maybe it is even the sundae itself because for me, art and life are inextricably linked in such a way I could never point to the division line. My art is my life is me. And this keeps me happy.

Which leads me to the final thing I do without fail each and every day. Before I sleep, I do a brief gratitude practice (prayer, whatever you like to call it). I remind myself of the abundance in my life and all the things for which I am grateful. Although it is a mental exercise only, it is a beautiful way to fall asleep.

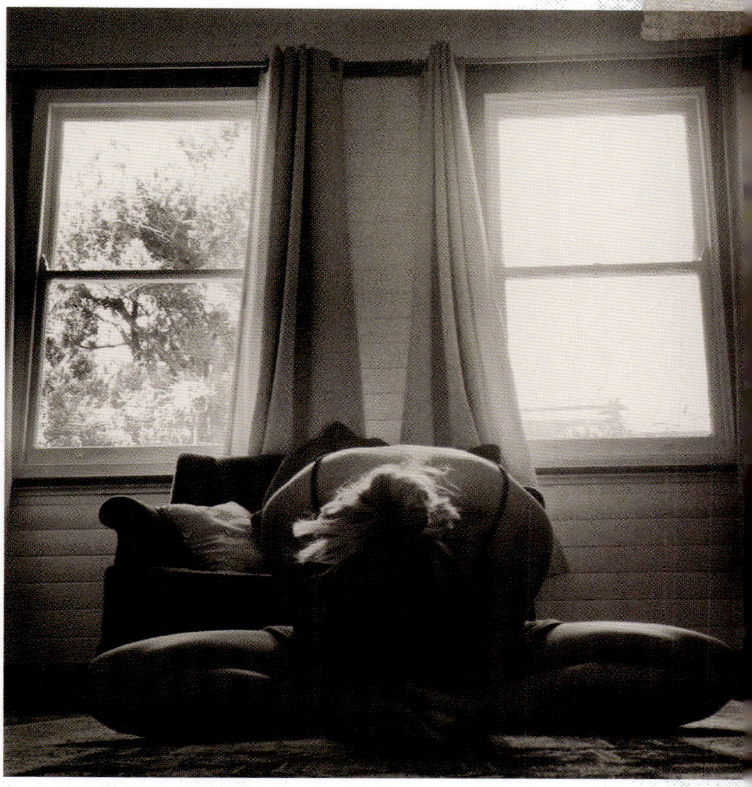

Photo by Santana Verdugo

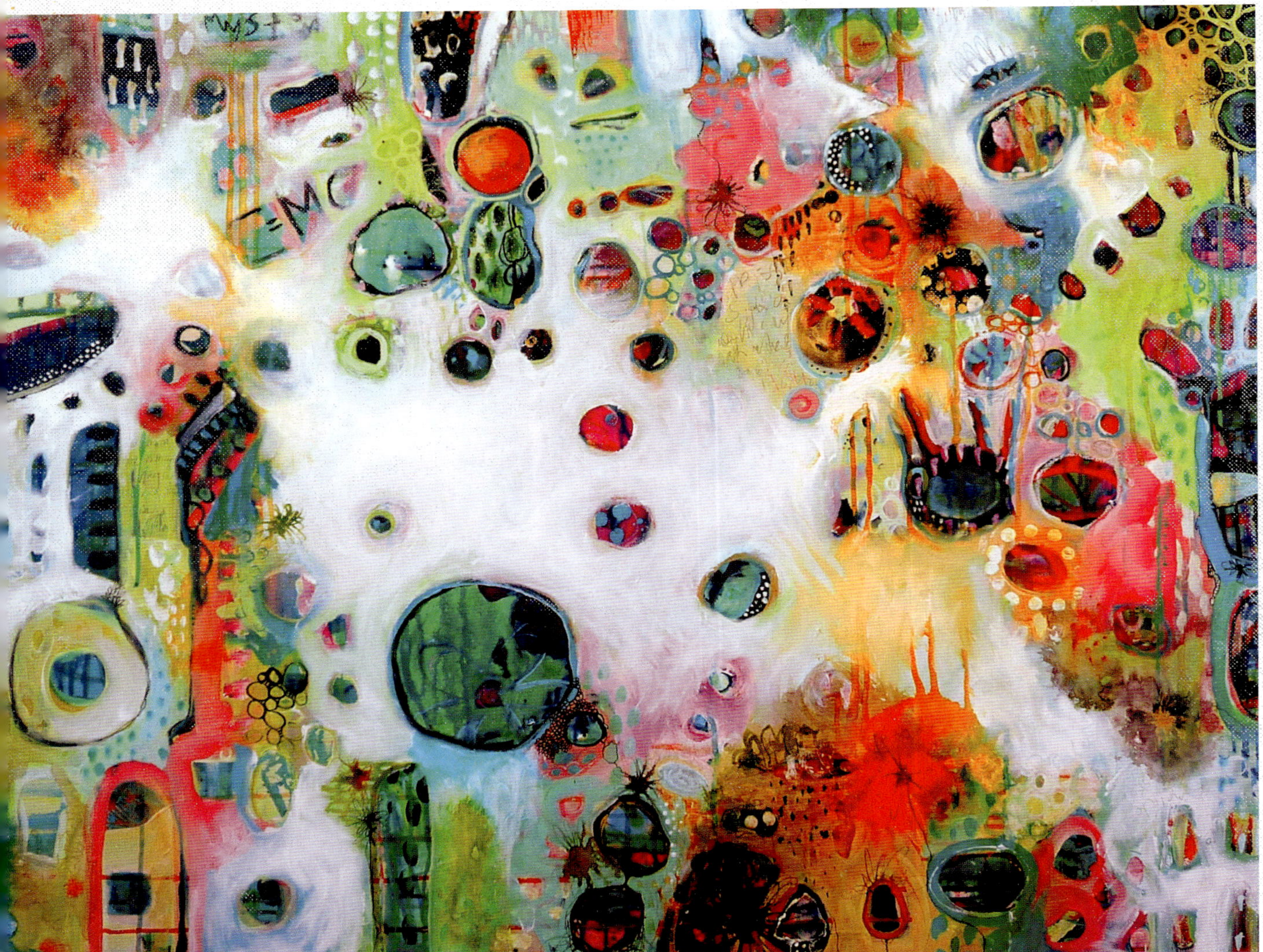

# chapter nine: come together

## Connecting with community

It is 1997. Sienna is seven weeks old, a peaceful baby already sleeping through the night. Santana is a precocious three-and-a-half-year-old. We have just bought a house and have moved from a bland rental on a one-acre rural block to a cottage in need of a lot of TLC, one block from the beach, with numerous makeshift additions and a backyard filled with aviaries. There are eight hundred people in this village by the sea. We know only one of them.

A mole on my left shoulder darkened during my recent pregnancy, and my doctor recommended we remove it after the birth, just to be safe. Amongst the busyness of moving and being in a cloudy-headed state of new mamahood, it had slipped my mind until I felt it itch.

A simple excision, one stitch, and then a phone call the next morning. Never a good sign. Dr. Harper, a jovial surgeon with a heart of gold, tells me it is melanoma, malignant, superficial, spreading. My heart sinks. He tells me he thinks we have caught it early; I cling to the optimism in his voice. The next day Marco drives me to the hospital. I try in vain to use the breast pump so Marco can feed Sienna, but nothing will come. The nurse assures me I'll be able to feed her in a few hours.

On the operating table I count backward. 100, 99, 98, 97 . . . I slip into oblivion, and then, I am awake again. A jagged line of stitches extends from my collarbone down my left arm in the shape of a lightning bolt. They are confident they have removed it all. I am sent home from surgery with my throbbing arm in a sling and strict instructions not to lift anything. I look at them blankly. I am breastfeeding a seven-week-old baby. "Maybe you can have a friend come to help. A family member?" they ask. There is no one. Marco is in the middle of a building job and can't take the time off.

The next day I notice Sienna's chest moving in a strange way. It is as though every time she takes a breath her rib cage sinks inward. She is struggling. We drive back to the hospital, and in the emergency room the TV is showing a news story about an epidemic of bronchiolitis

*Humankind has not woven the web of life. We are but one thread within it. Whatever we do to the web, we do to ourselves. All things are bound together. All things connect.*
—Chief Seattle

in the area. The baby on the news has a chest that is doing the same strange thing. Sienna is admitted and spends five days on oxygen. I am beyond exhausted. Spent. Worried for my life and my baby's life. The nurses are beautiful. They set me up for five days in what is supposed to be an overnight-only parent's room. They dress my wound and wake me when Sienna cries, helping me to her room and lifting her out of the cot and into my arms.

When she is stable we return home and I hold my baby close and cry as I listen to the wheeze that will linger for the next six months as her lungs slowly heal.

I have never felt so alone. I say a silent prayer, asking for community.

Several years later and I am in the company of a group of women who know each other well. They are so easy with each other, accepting, comfortable. There are stories and wine and laughter. I am an outsider, there with them for business. I long for a group of women friends like this. The conversation swings to the topic of head lice. It is rampant at school and they have all dealt with it at one time or another. One of the mums mentions she has had an itchy head, and immediately her friends check her scalp. It is decided that they will all get together the next day to wash and check each other's hair. I am astounded at their willingness to be open and vulnerable. I am also envious. Somehow in that moment, picking nits becomes a symbol for authentic friendship and community.

Several more years pass. I have begun my creative journey, I am painting and holding exhibitions and part of an interesting, flourishing arts community, helping out on the committee for the Winter Arts Festival in our beautiful Jervis Bay. The girls are in school and we are meeting new people all the time, finding our tribe and feeling at home in our small community. Relaxing around the BBQ after sailing one Saturday evening, my friend Katie tells me that the shampoo she is using musn't be agreeing with her. She can't stop itching, especially at the base of her neck. I take a look, an expert on the subject now that I have school-age kids. "Oh, Katie," I say, "you need to come over tomorrow so we can deal with this."

Next day in the sunshine, we sit on our back deck for several hours as I comb through her hair, strand by strand, removing the pesky little eggs. I tell her my story and how special this moment is to me. We laugh about nitpicking as a metaphor for friendship and connection, but I know that I have begun to build community, that I am beginning to let down my guard, to connect on a deeper level, and I know how important that is.

* * *

Ten years ago when I was still very early in my art journey, I wrote my first artist statement. It flowed as if it came from somewhere outside of me and revealed to myself my fascination with the interconnectedness of all things.

*The universal theme of connection underlies all of my work: connection to each other and the ways in which we express our humanity, connection with the natural world and the beauty that surrounds us, connection with the divine and a sense of something greater at work in our lives.*

I like to believe that we are all part of an intricate and breathtaking tapestry. Our only choice each moment is whether to be a part of the creating or a part of the unraveling.

I have never since felt the need to modify that statement. It still encompasses the way that I see and walk through the world, only as time passes my understanding deepens, reinforced time and time again by the connections I have made, friendships forged, lives intertwined, stories explored and shared. As I continue to paint and teach, I step with more openness into the endless possibilities that present themselves, accepting all with love.

# a garden grows

by Peter Perez

### Dartmouth Garden, Boston, Massachusetts

Everything is an art tool—a brush, a pen, a pencil, a hammer, a stove, a shovel, a plant, tree or rock.

The 1970s were a great chapter in Boston history, and I was a part of it.

My advertising history in Manhattan preceded me to Boston and paved the way for me to open my own design studio. It was the destiny of my many wildest of dreams: from the orange groves of Southern California; a one-way ticket to Madison Avenue, NYC, in the early sixties; and then to Boston.

"You have to buy a brownstone in the South End of Boston for a write-off," the financial advisor told me. Little did I know that it would turn into a twelve-year restoration art project, not only of the building but of the entire South End. It would also create the South End Historical Society, the Boston Center for the Arts, the First Night and New Year's Eve celebrations, Community Gardens and many other extraordinary projects, including the Dartmouth Garden.

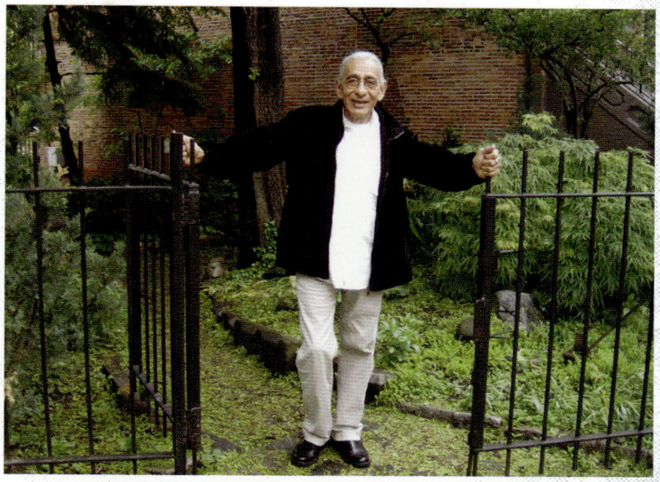

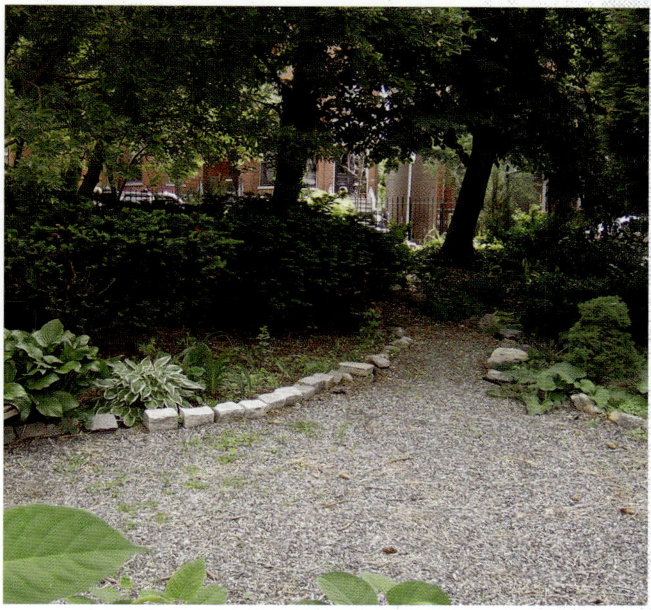

Three houses down from 19 Dartmouth Street, toward Copley Square, was a vacant lot next to the public school. The 1863 brownstone that once stood there had burned down many years before and the lot was waist-deep in trash and debris. Passing by one morning, I thought that it could be a nice sitting park one day. So each time I went by I filled a large yard waste bag and put it on the curb for removal. Eventually all the trash was gone. But then I realized that if nothing else was done, it would only fill with trash again.

Since no one had objected to my cleaning it up, I decided that no one would object to my planting a few things there . . . or a bit of excavation. I didn't ask who owned the property or get permission from the city to make a park, I just did it. I had the Boston Flower Market as a client, and they had a mountain of rejected plants and trees that I could help myself to.

Over time, I continued to add flower beds to the garden—tulips, daffodils, iris, climbing vines of heavenly blue and multicolor morning glories, honeysuckle, ferns and trees. The garden grew and flourished.

Each Mother's Day all the tulips and bulbs in bloom would disappear. The third year I put up a nice little sign that said, "Please wish your mother a happy Mother's Day from the Garden."

My best helpers were the homeless folks who adopted the garden as a safe place to sit and sleep. They also made sure that the rubbish and empties went in the can. One Christmas we decorated the pine tree with nip bottles hanging as ornaments and wrapped up six-packs of beer under the tree from Santa.

Of all the amazing art projects in the Boston chapter, I am most proud of this little garden that will always be a part of the South End history.

# community

by Jess Greene

Community can be hard. Really hard. Even gut-wrenchingly difficult at times.

And the creative community is not immune to all the difficulties. You will get nasty comments on your blog; you will have "friends" disappear; you will encounter cliques and feel excluded; you will send e-mails that will never be answered; you will watch others form lifelong bonds and wonder where yours are.

Despite all the difficult, often confidence-shaking examples of poor community that I have experienced, my mind is also filled with a plethora of pure, piercingly bright vignettes of solid community and creative connections. I can honestly tell you that while the creative community is not without its flaws, it is transformational as well.

When I think of the times I have experienced positive community, the following are stories that come to mind:

- In 2011, I applied and got into an artist residency in Spain. One artist friend had prompted me to apply in the first place and then another friend pushed me to come out of my shell enough to tell people about my acceptance at an event we were at. A few weeks later I launched a crowd-sourcing campaign to fund my experience, and a large portion of supporters came from the people I had met at that event. Those two artists believed in me and pushed me forward, which resulted in even more people supporting me—in a financial way—which blew my mind.
- Early in 2012, I decided I wanted to drive around the United States and Canada offering free art-making events and meeting the creative people I knew online. The wild idea was met with enthusiasm on Facebook, and I received enough "Come here!" requests to make the whole thing possible. I stayed in only four hotels during my three months on the road because the rest of the time, I stayed in people's homes—people I had only known online through the creative community. Sharing their lives and their homes was one of the most profound aspects of my trip. During the 2012 road trip, I was gathered in Big Sur, California, at a retreat called Matrilumina. I drew a word from a pile during an activity. The word was *adventurous*. Most of the women in that room burst out laughing when I read it, and in that moment I knew I was seen and known. Those women knew me enough to see the powerful serendipity in my choosing that word and shared that marvel with me.
- And just last week a friend sensed that I was trying to force a new business move. I was floundering and unclear but still trying to make a project work. She sent me a nice e-mail with her thoughts including a suggestion from her and from two of our other friends to rest, relax and instead focus on restoration. I cried. Then I called her and had a good conversation in which I revealed just how confused I was. Being understood and being led away from bad decisions and having my frustration heard and met are some of my most cherished benefits of community.

But one of the hardest things about community is finding it. It has taken me years to find mine. And community is not something you just arrive at; it evolves.

The biggest thing I have learned in my journey is to keep showing up. If you want the magic to happen, you need to be there. Go to the retreats, take the e-courses, comment on the posts, share what resonates with you, reply to the newsletters, reach out with a simple e-mail, get introduced to someone new, drive to meet people you only know online and have lots of phone dates. And don't just look up to those you admire; look around for those who are on a similar path as you.

If you keep showing up with your soul bared, willing to help others, the community that is meant for you will show up with a hello. Never stop seeking that which your heart wants, and others will notice.

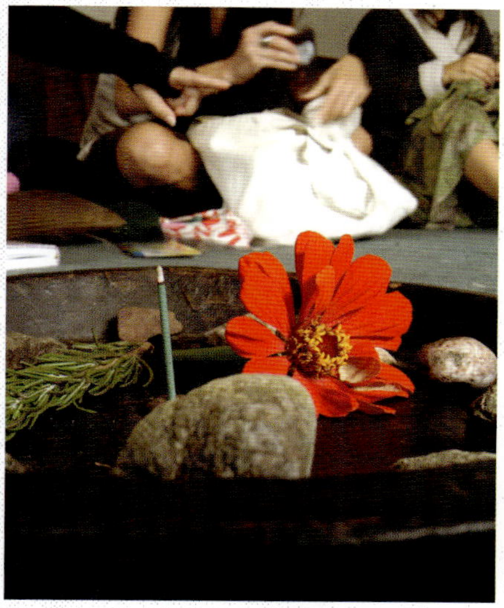

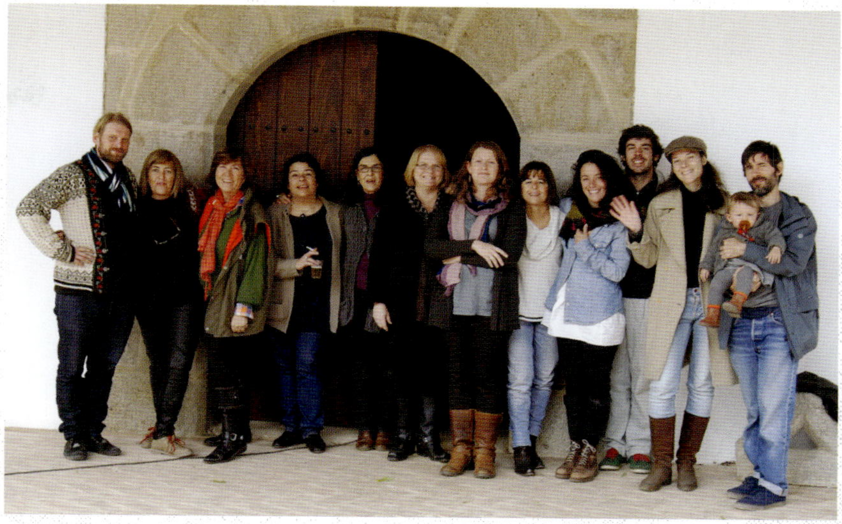

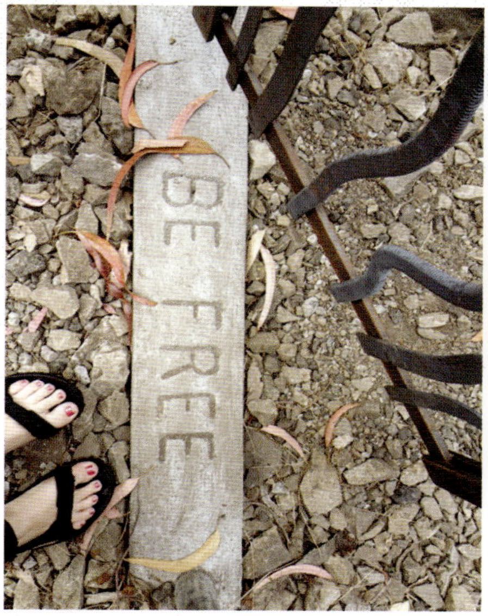
BE FREE

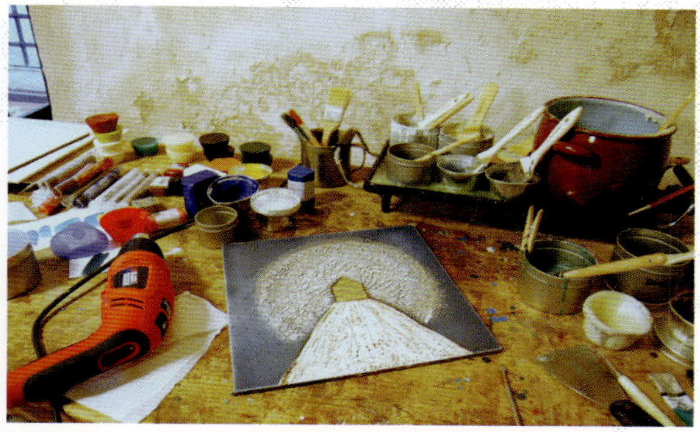

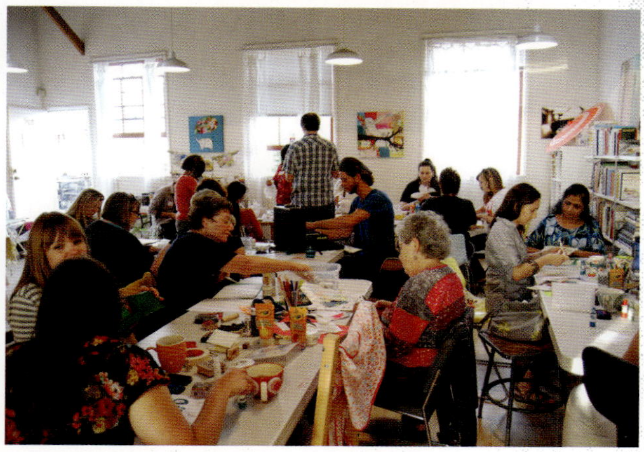

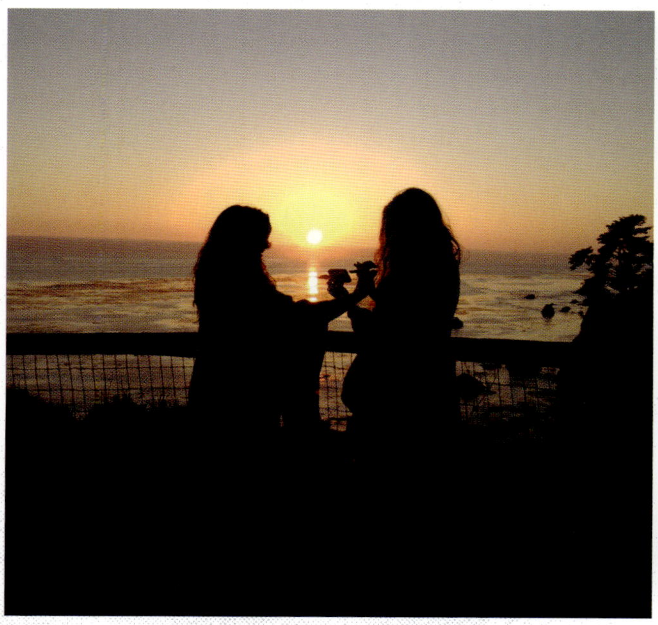

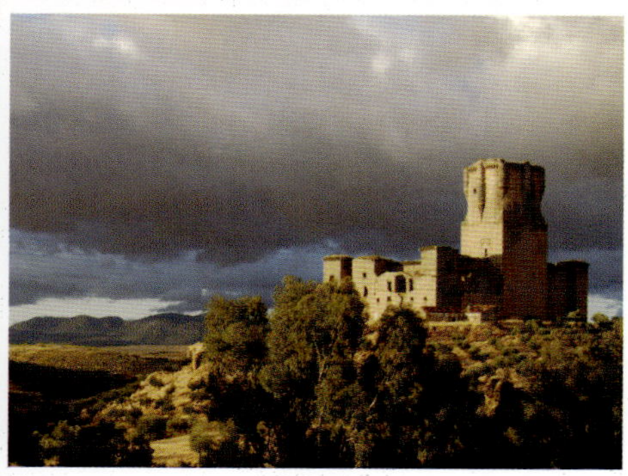

# we're all connected

by Mary Beth Shaw

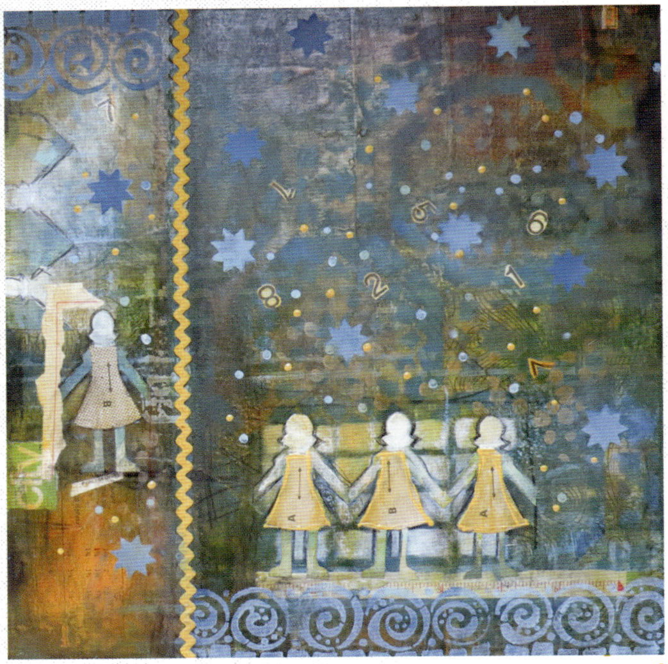

**What You Need**

- fluid acrylic paints
- gel medium
- gesso
- paintbrushes
- paper collage materials (assorted decorative papers)
- paper towels
- pencil, black
- scissors
- Scribbles Dimensional Paint
- stencils
- stretched canvas

I have explored the concept of community and connection for many years through several of my series. It is a strong belief of mine that no matter where we happen to live, it is possible for us to all find "our people."

This particular piece is symbolic of maintaining a sense of self while also being present in the tribe. Lots of personal topics may be explored by using simple paper doll imagery.

**1** Select hand-painted paper and fold it into an accordion shape. Draw half of a childlike paper-doll shape up against the fold side of the paper.

**2** Cut out the image and gently unfold.

**3** Select neutral-colored collage elements and tear into square and rectangular shapes. Using gel medium, glue these collage pieces to a stretched canvas, being careful to put gel medium under and over each element. Wet a brush and paint some diluted white gesso across your collage pieces.

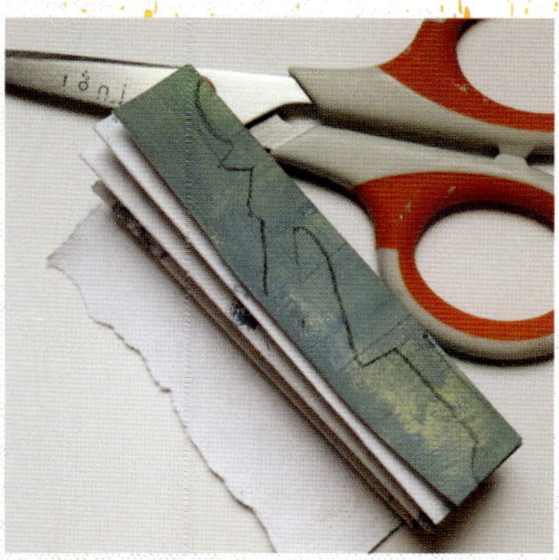

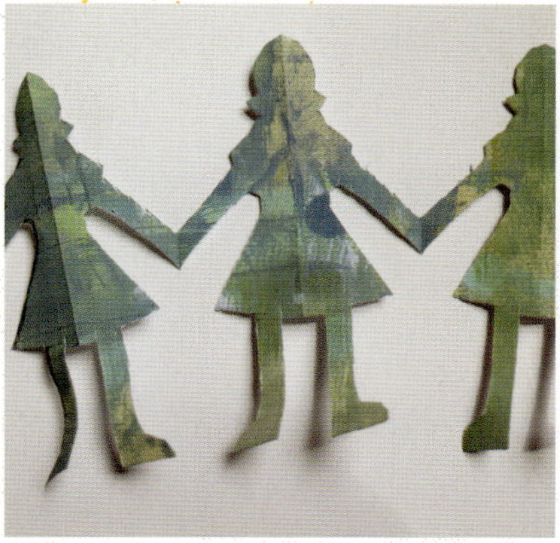

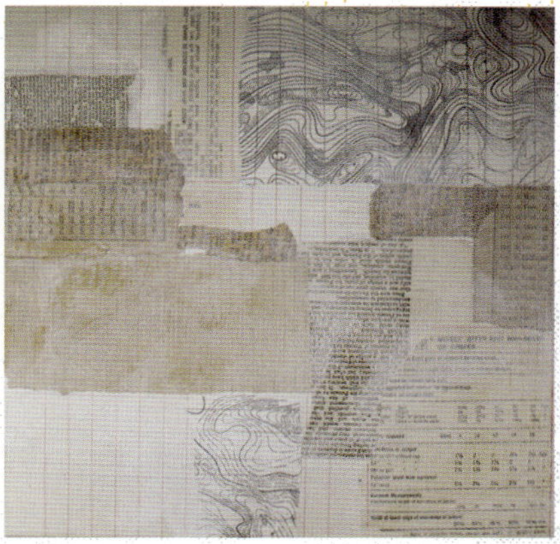

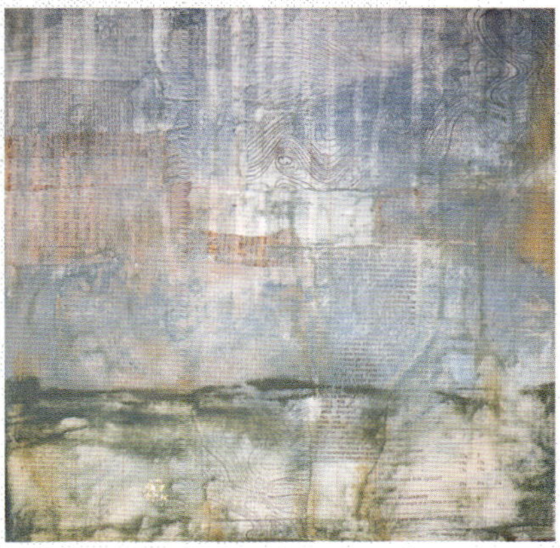

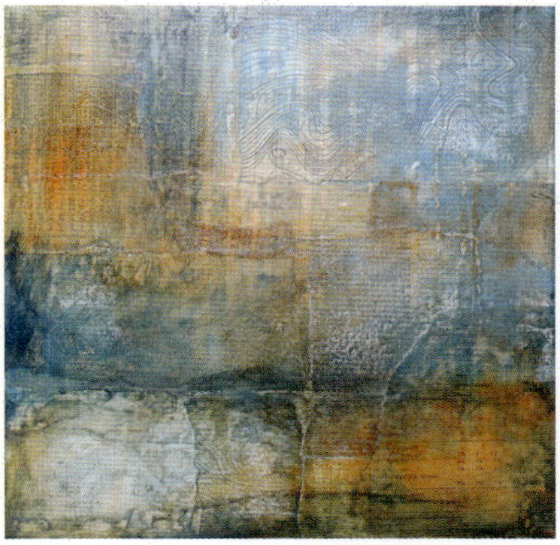

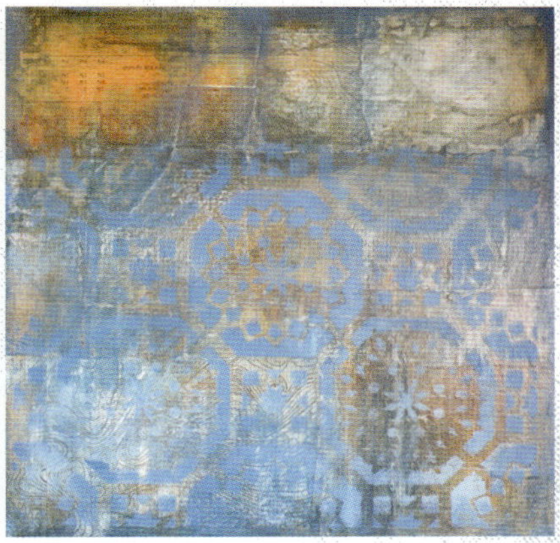

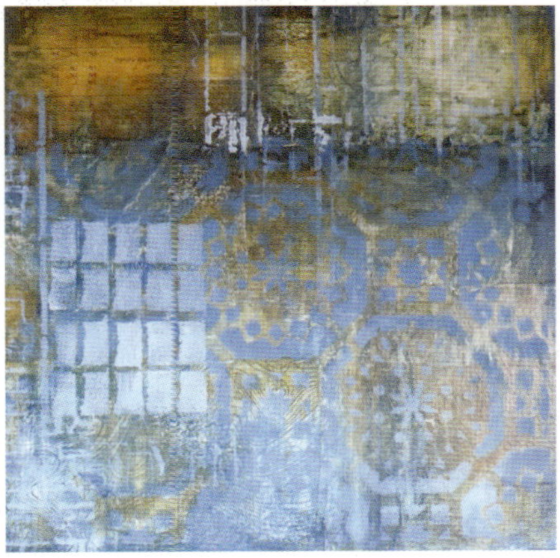

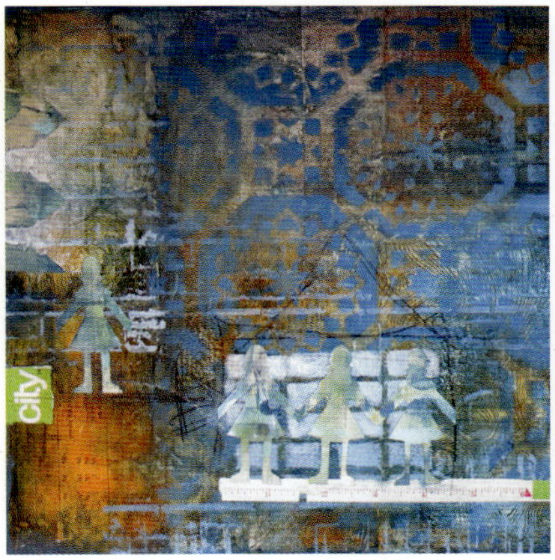


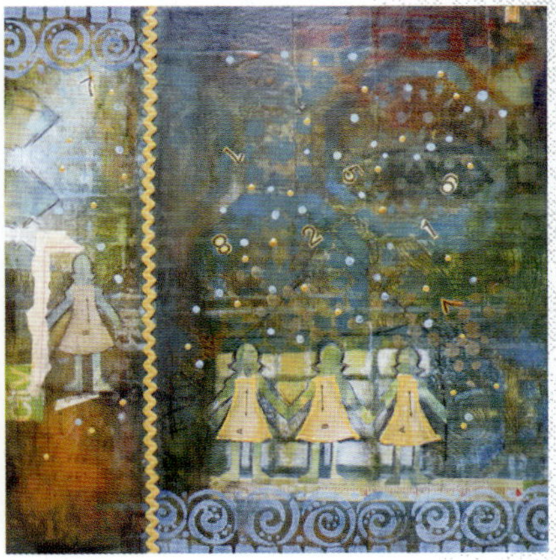

This unifies the background to some extent but still allows the underneath parts to be seen.

**4** Select a very limited paint palette. I used Prussian Blue, Transparent Orange Oxide and Titanium White. Keep the paints thin and wet, and blend and drip color across your canvas. Set aside to dry or use a hair dryer.

**5** Continue to add paint until you have achieved a pleasing look.

**6** Using a pattern stencil, apply paint over two-thirds of the canvas. Once you have removed the stencil, use a damp paper towel to gently blot the stenciled area, which blends it into the background.

**7** Continue to add stenciled areas to the piece as you start to consider possible options for composition.

**8** Add collage components. Take your time and move the parts around until you are satisfied. Using white paint and a black pencil, work on details to increase the contrast and pop the whites and blacks, for instance, around the paper dolls and other collage parts.

**9** Use a Scribbles paint to add dots and other features (outline of the girls' dresses) to the piece. Add more stencil effects if needed.

exercise

# putting it all together!

## Everything Is Connected!

In this final project you get to sneak a peek into one of my workshops and watch my demo painting unfold from start to finish using a combination of many of the techniques in the previous chapters! Remember to approach your painting with an attitude of curiosity and wonder and playful exploration. Feel free to mix the steps up, use your own symbols, poems, music and words to inspire you, and listen to your heart and your painting as it comes to life. All of the projects in this book are flexible, just like that part of you that yearns to loosen up and be less rigid. Let's see together how far we can push the boundaries of our art, breathing a life into our paintings that speaks our own authentic story. And most of all, don't forget to have FUN!

## A Note on the Symbolism of Deer

I never know what or who is going to emerge from a canvas, and I am always intrigued to find out the symbolism of an unexpected visitor to my studio. I am a big believer in synchronistic events and serendipity, so I was delighted to find out that this beautiful creature who has decided to grace the final pages of a book that I hope helps you to explore new creative territory is symbolic of gentle forays into enticing new adventures. The deer speaks of new perceptions, expansion and growth. And, like all of us, a deer has a multitude of personalities: strong and feisty, with a call to adventure; a cautious, protective side; but above all, a great sense of individuality. The deer asks, like I do, that you learn to trust yourself and your intuition as you journey on further in this wonderful creative adventure!

## What You Need

- acrylic artists inks
- acrylic paints (I used Golden fluids and heavy-bodied)
- collage elements
- large canvas, board or paper 30" × 30" (76cm × 76cm)
- mark-making tools: foam brushes, twigs, other brushes, bamboo skewer
- paintbrushes
- sketchbook paper
- spray bottle with water
- stencils
- water-resistant oil pastels, variety of colors
- water-soluble pencil, any color
- white chalk

### Change Your Perspective

To keep the flow going and your perspective fresh, turn your canvas often during steps 1–6 so the orientation changes.

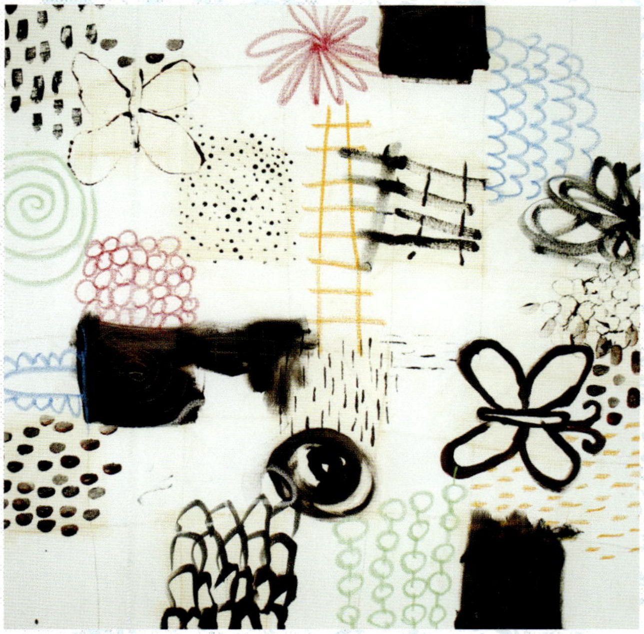

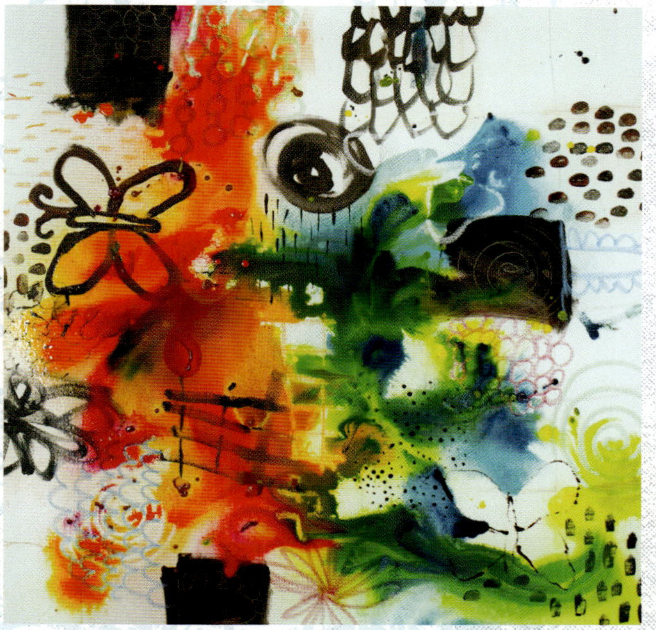

**1** Using a water-soluble pencil, divide your canvas, board or paper into a grid; no rulers allowed! We used forty-nine squares on a 30" × 30" (76cm × 76cm) canvas, but there is no set formula for an intuitive, playful art exploration. I think of the grid as representing our self-imposed notions of what is right and wrong, and instruct my students to jump out of the box and paint outside the lines as soon as possible. Maybe you would like to start with a spiral or concentric circles instead of a grid. Use your imagination and try several new starting points!

Use your symbols from Chapter One and practice painting them onto the canvas using as many diverse methods as possible! I used a dark paint mixed from Turquoise Phthalo and Quinacridone Burnt Orange to paint, and some colorful oil pastel to draw my symbols.

Paint your symbols using a range of different brushes, old, new, thick, thin; vary the pressure when applying paint, skipping lines, switching to a bamboo skewer to paint with, blocking in whole boxes with dark paint and scratching your symbols in. Raid your kitchen or the tool shed, the hardware store or the garden, and find new tools to bring diversity to your work!

Grab some oil pastels and draw your symbols onto the canvas. This will give some beautiful resist effects when you apply the first layer of paint! Experiment with your nondominant hand and your eyes closed. Make sure that one of your symbols is your own unique thumb- or fingerprint.

**2** Next, let's play with warm and cool colors, using Golden Fluid acrylic paints and Daler Rowney FW acrylic artists inks interchangeably.

Drip harmonious cool colors onto one end of the canvas and warm colors onto the other. Spray the colors with water and watch them spread and mingle. Notice which colors work well together and which ones create muddy tones. Store these things away in your memory for next time. Don't despair over a little muddy color; just be sure to keep some separation between the different colors for more visual interest.

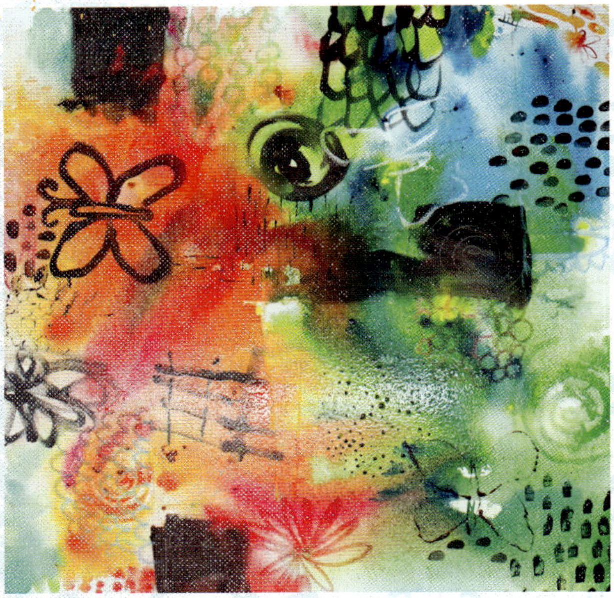

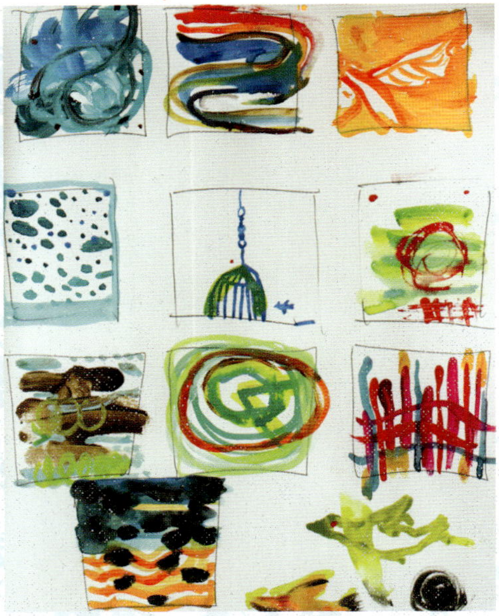

Student work: Andrea Henning

**3** Move the paint around now, using any of your tools, but remember to include a diversity of marks. If you want to make a swirl, make one and then make another, but don't cover the canvas with swirls. If you want to add some fingerprints, throw some in there and then maybe a few diagonally opposite, but don't fingerprint the whole thing!

Spread the paint with your foam brush for broad swatches of colors, then pick up some paint with the bamboo skewer and make delicate dots. Pick up a little of the cooler colors and move them into the warm area just to see what happens. Repeat some of your symbols in some areas. Spend at least half an hour to an hour on this step.

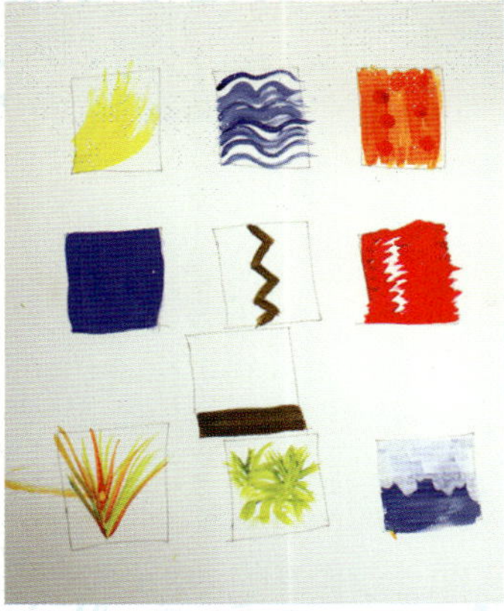

Student work: Beth Saxena

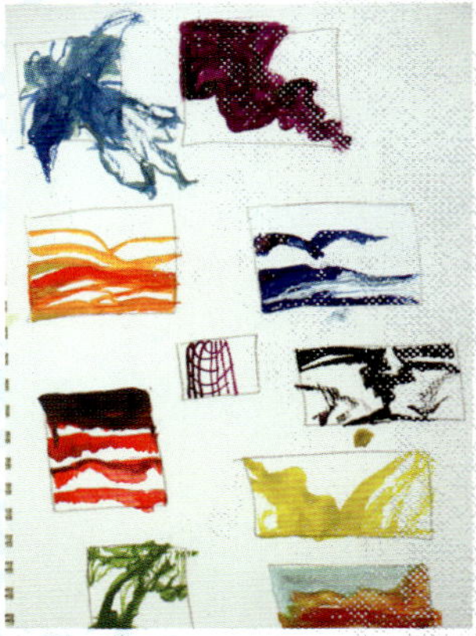

Student work: Pamela Beck

**4** Set aside your painting for a while to let it dry. While the painting is drying, we're now going to experiment on a blank piece of sketchbook paper, stepping outside of our left brain and painting entirely from emotion. This is where we can begin to cultivate a fearless approach to our painting. You may feel like you are messing things up, but when things are messed up it's important we learn to find ways to deal with that.

Draw ten little boxes and lay out a palette of five to seven colors, including white and Raw Umber as mixers. At this stage, I typically ask my students to listen as I read them the poem "I Know Why the Caged Bird Sings" by Maya Angelou. You could use any poem, song or prose that uses words to provoke an emotive response.

Slowly and deliberately, I read a line or two at a time to my students, and they paint a "feeling" painting inside one of the boxes. As you do this, do not overthink; just respond in the moment, choosing colors and making marks from a place of emotion rather than a literal response.

I read out lines such as:

A free bird leaps
on the back of the wind
and floats downstream
till the current ends

I then watch a range of responses: sweeps of blue, swishes of red, little black dots, each feeling different, brains disengaged.

Above are examples of three students' exercises.

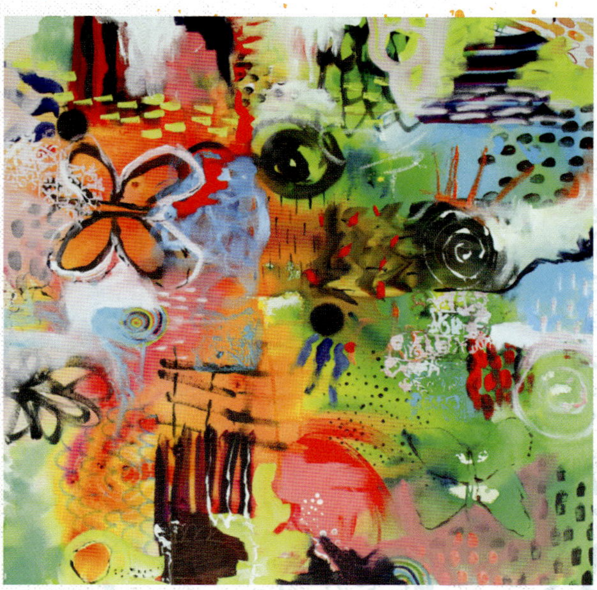

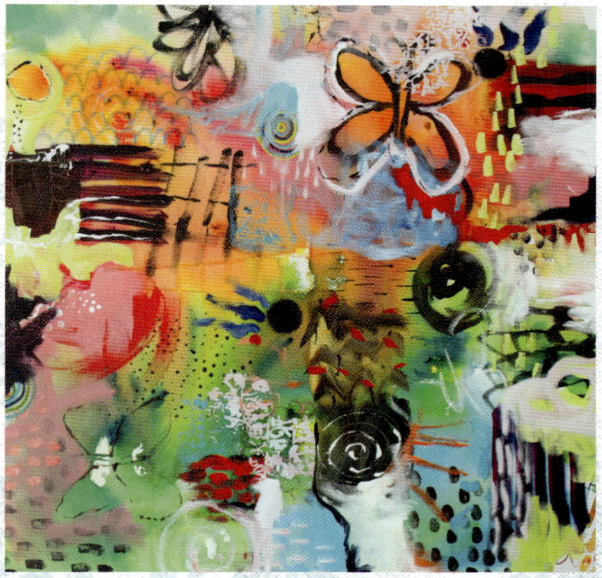

5 Now it's time to take these little feeling paintings and duplicate them onto your canvas. You will probably feel some resistance at this point. Maybe you don't like the colors you chose or the little paintings you created seem ugly to you. Give re-creating them a try anyway. Trust me. We will set ourselves up with some problems and find ways to solve them.

Get those little paintings onto the canvas and then try the following things to bring cohesion back to your painting:

- Repeat the feeling painting in another place, especially if you have just introduced a new color or a dominant bold design.
- Use white, pastel colors or a dark (such as Payne's Grey or Raw Umber) to scrub in some broader swatches of color. Try not to paint over areas that you dislike; instead, use the swatches of color to break them up, perhaps scrubbing over just a corner or linking two quite different areas with a swatch of color.
- Use marks such as dots, fingerprints and dashes to link one color to another (e.g., one red area on one side to another red area across the way). Stencils and painted words could also be used in this way.
- Use stencils to unify one area with another (e.g., a strong area of orange next to an area of lime green could be unified by adding a stenciled pattern over parts of both in a slightly lighter tone of either orange or green).

6 Spend some time now just looking at your painting. Lean it against a wall, turn it different ways and squint your eyes to see if anything sparks your imagination. We are not looking for an image to jump out at you, although sometimes that might happen. We are looking for something that might lead us in a certain direction.

After I began my elephant series, I noticed elephant potential in every canvas I started. In class, if I see a potential fish, for example, suddenly everyone in the room begins to see fish on their canvases. Our brains work well to find the things we focus on.

Think about composition when you find a possible bird, fish, giraffe, elephant, etc. Would it be well placed on the canvas or squashed toward the bottom or falling off the side?

One of my favorite tools at this point is a plain, white piece of chalk. Make lines on your canvas where you see possibility. Draw in a crazy creature around something that reminds you of an eye. Does that curve look like the side of a dancing woman? Roughly draw it in and see how it might look. You can adjust your drawing or get rid of it completely with a damp paper towel; just make sure the paint is dry before you start this step.

Looking at my painting this way I decided that I could see the beginning of some kind of animal with the bold dark dot toward the center as an eye (with blue eyelashes maybe?), the spiral below as a snout and a definite suggestion of a neck and shoulder line. Could it be a giraffe with a butterfly on its head? Maybe, but then what would I do with the other half of the canvas, and doesn't a giraffe need a very long neck to look, giraffe-like?

I played with the chalk a while longer and suddenly it hit me: A deer! With plenty of room for big, beautiful antlers!

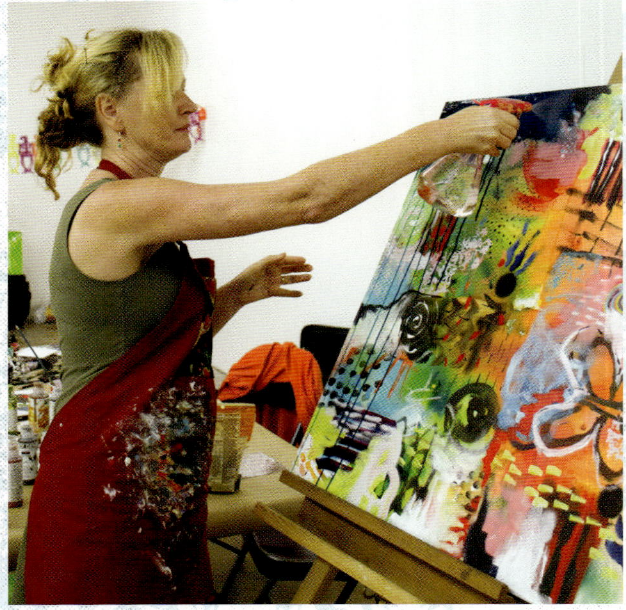

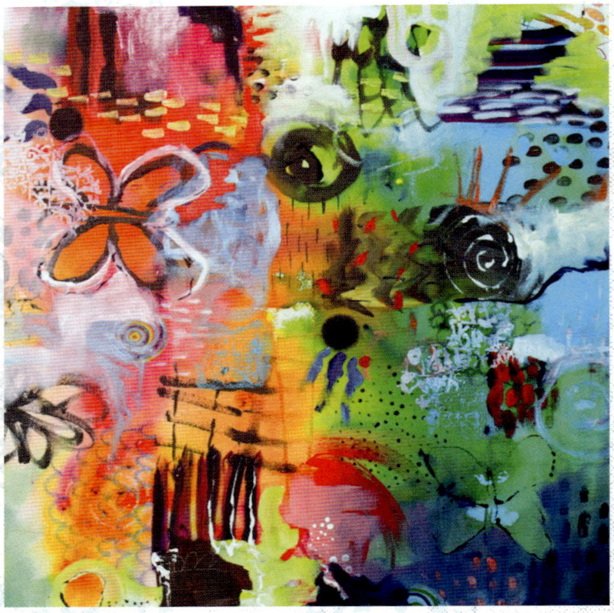

7 At this point, it's common for several of the students to feel that their paintings are still quite disjointed, busy or jarring, and I often want to unify my painting a little before proceeding to the next stage. Glazing over the whole painting or sections of the painting with one or several harmonious colors is a great way to pull things together!

Glazing effects can be achieved with glazing mediums, but I find water also highly effective, especially when using paints like Golden with intense pigment quality.

Pouring a line of Turquoise (Phthalo) across the top of the canvas, I proceeded to spray it with my water bottle, allowing the paint to drip down and used a foam brush, my hand (you may want to use a disposable glove when painting with your hands and fingers) and paper towels to move and control the flow and drips. Alternatively, you can glaze with your canvas flat on a table to have more control over the consistency of the glaze in different areas.

Using a paper towel, I selectively blotted areas to allow some intensity of color to show back through.

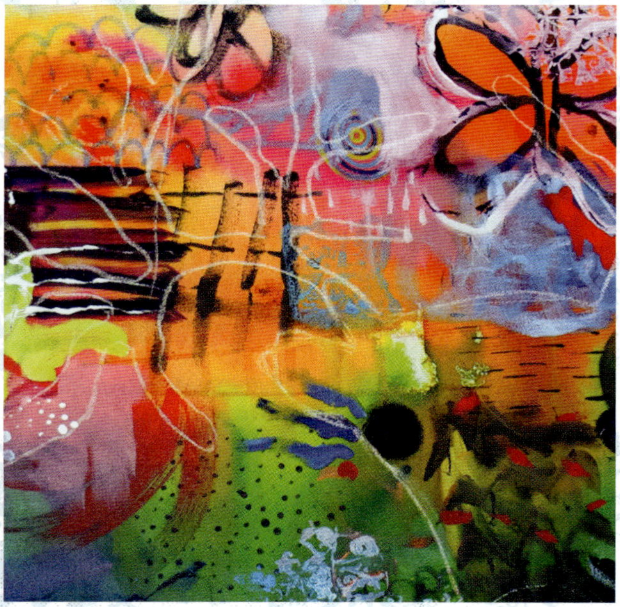

8 Using the white chalk, I draw in the outline of my deer, adjusting and readjusting as I go. Using Payne's Grey I add in another eye. Feel free to add in any elements such as this to your own painting to complete the image you are visualizing.

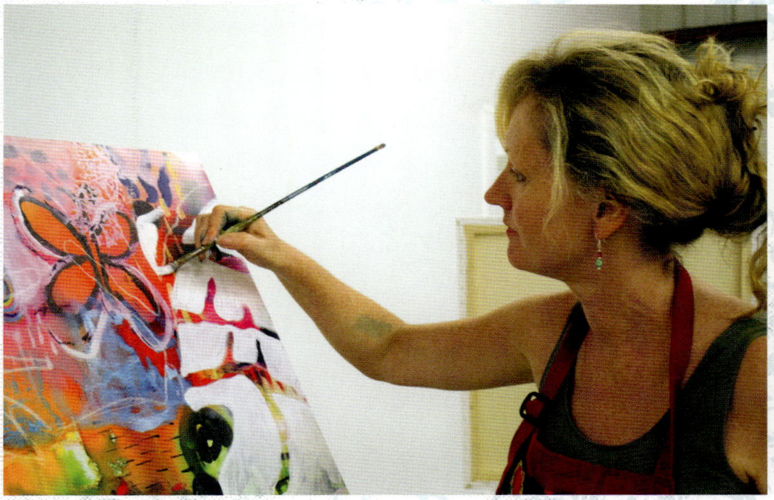

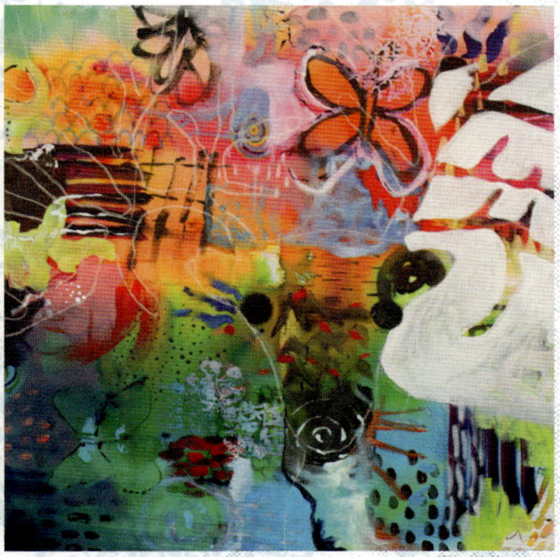

**9** With Titanium White and a small flat brush, paint in all the negative spaces around the form you sketched with the chalk. As the deer emerged I made more adjustments now that I could see the balance of the form against the background better.

You may decide to use a color other than white around the form that emerges from your canvas. Play with different colors in both opaque and transparent applications.

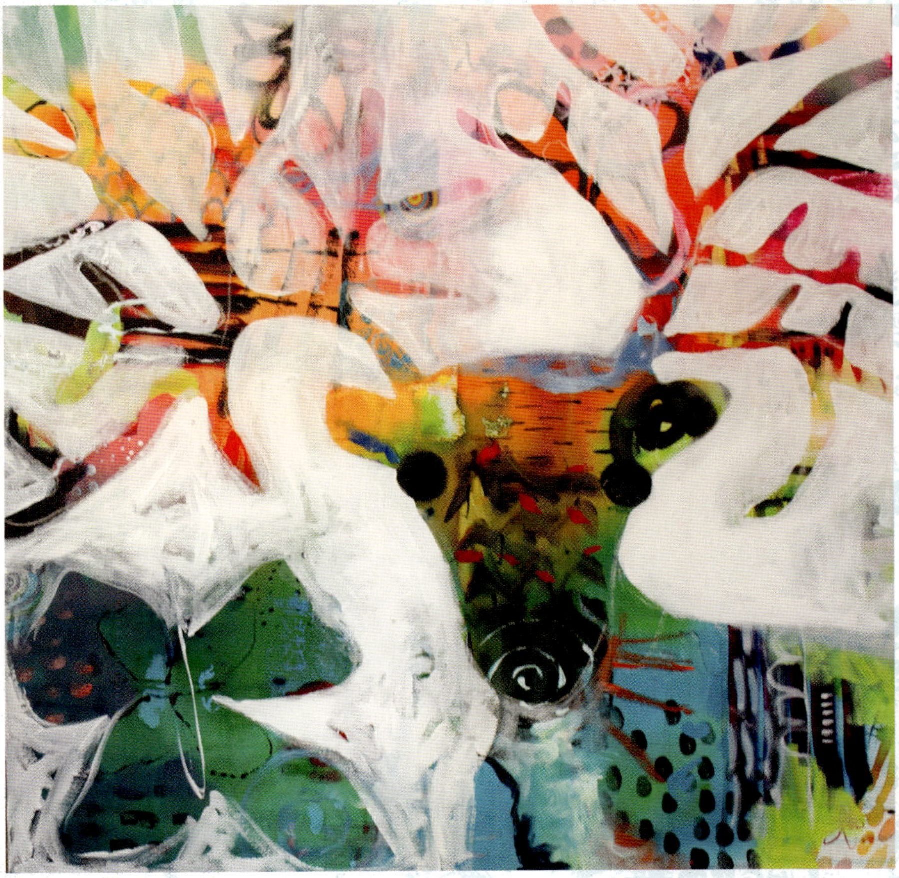

**10** It's nice to leave the transparency of the white in some areas, but you may decide to vary the paint opacity level in others. Using my fingers I scooped out some heavy-bodied white and applied it thickly to several areas around and above the head.

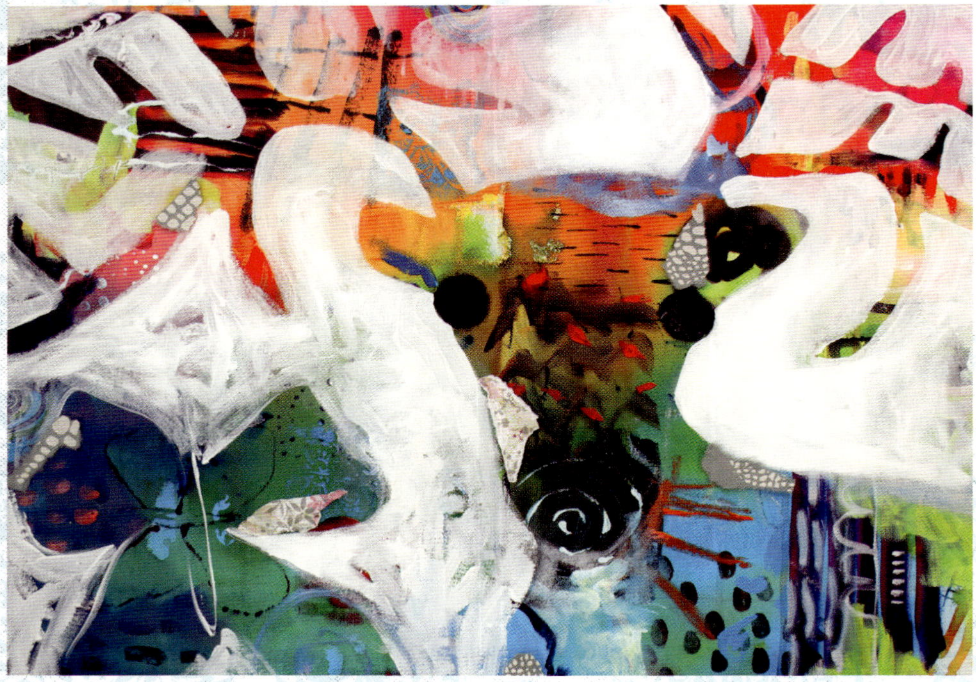

**11** Experiment with the addition of collage in your painting, either in the early stages or toward the end as I have here. When adding a collage element, be sure to repeat patterns in several areas for cohesion. To push the patterns back you can glaze over areas with a unifying color.

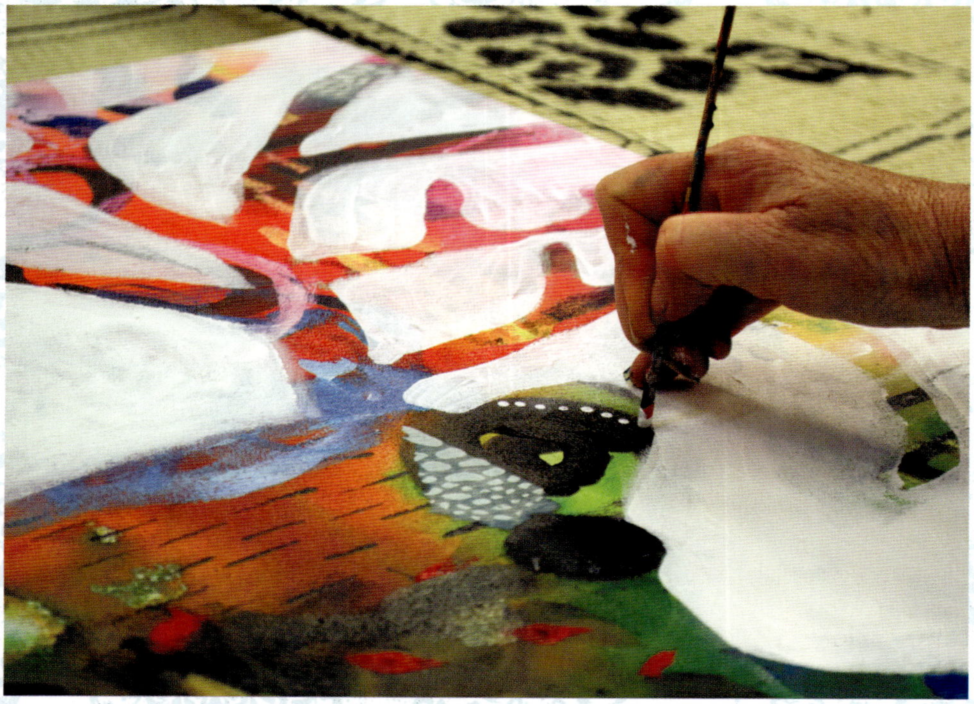

**12** Complete your painting by adding in small areas of detail within the form using a fine brush.

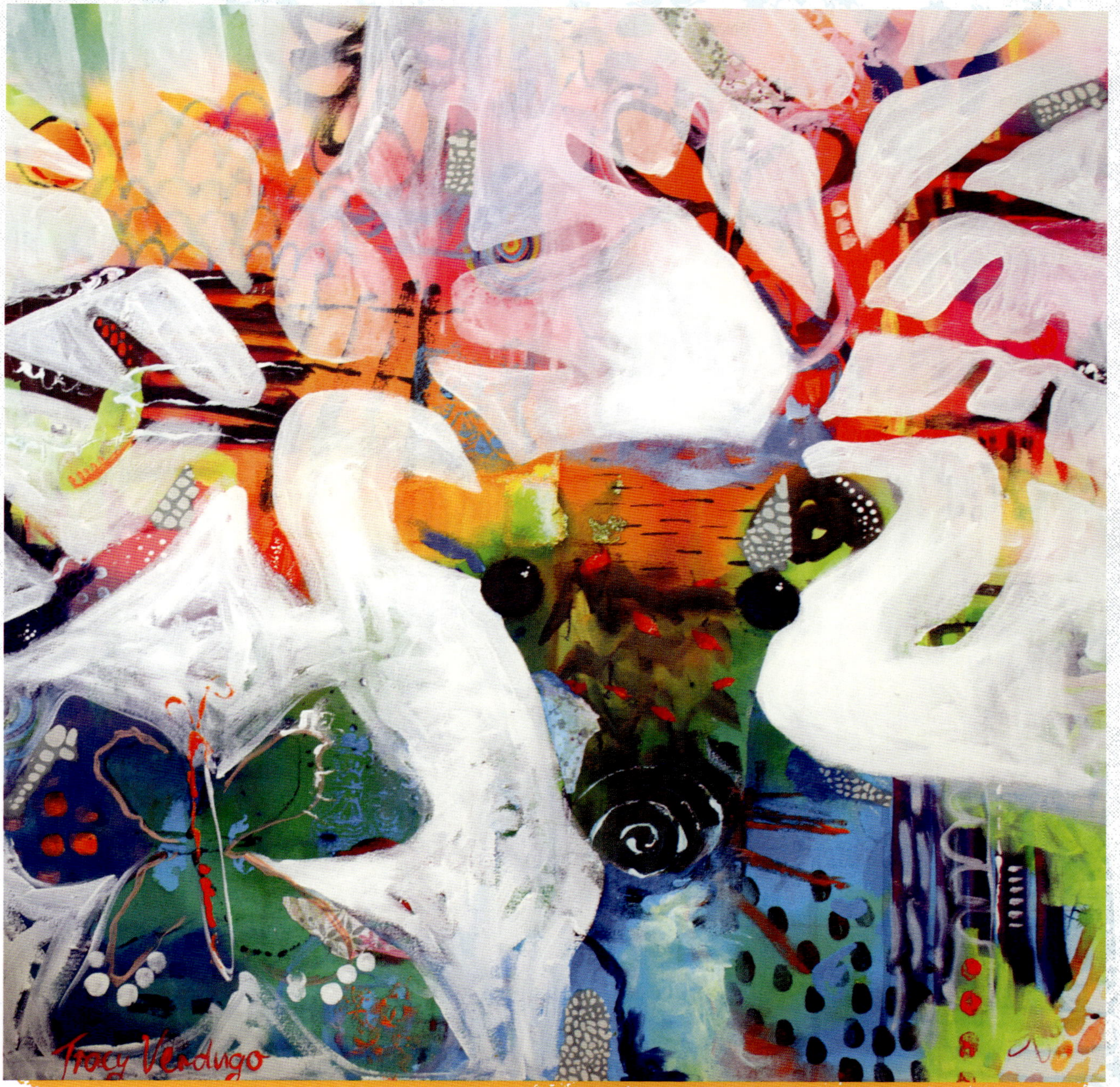


## Some Parting Affection

I hope the stories and projects in this book, shared generously by a group of fabulous imperfect, human, creative beings, just like you, give you the confidence to explore, a willingness to let go and make mistakes. I hope this book is the impetus to defining your own authentic art-making practice. May you shine your creative light on high beam so that others are entranced and inspired by its glow!

# contributing artists

### Erin Faith Allen

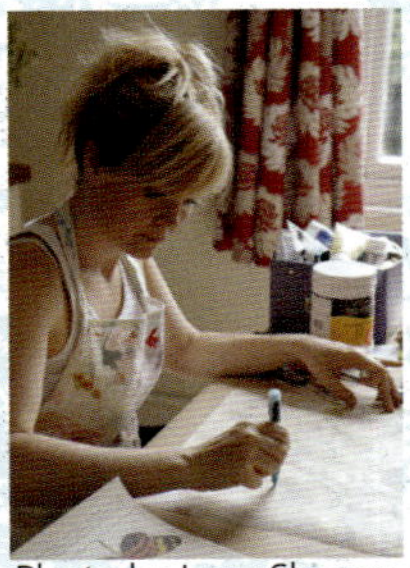
Photo by Lucy Sharpe

As an artist and empath, I experience the world on a supernatural level. I make art to understand and process my self, life and the planet.

Feeling the strong and undeniable presence of universal womanness, I conjure female legacy and story through words and pictures.

I spill out my world in color, texture and stream-of-consciousness writing in an endless dance between photography, painting, illustration and text.

My art conveys the delicate dance between light and shadow. We must howl in wild, stark exposure at the moon to know true bliss in the glow of the sun.
erinfaithallenart.com

### Seth Apter

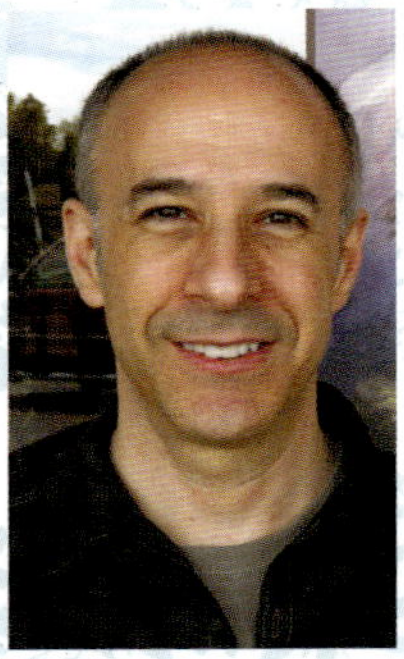

I am . . . happiest in those moments when I lose all sense of time because I am so completely engrossed in making art. I am . . . always excited when the first coat of gesso is brushed on. I am . . . able to see the beauty in an endless array of objects that others have tossed aside. I am . . . thoroughly convinced that there is magic to be found in every tube of paint. I am . . . an artist.
thealteredpage.blogspot.com

### Orly Avineri

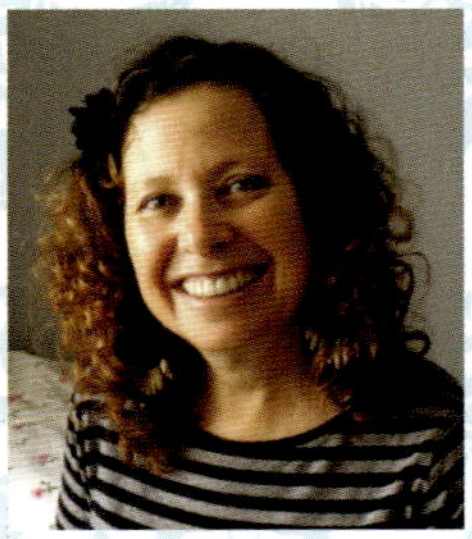

I am surrounded by possibilities: to stretch my own canvases—at all times, at all places—to make many papers that have colors, patterns and textures—papers that are raw and have words on them, printed or scripted, bound into art journals. Journal pages constantly and consistently provide me with canvases on which to depict my newer narratives. These visual stories make me feel that I am complex, not complicated; that I am visible and indivisible. Blank pages, lusciously filled, make me yearn for the next blank page.
oneartistjournal.com

### Lisa Sonora Beam

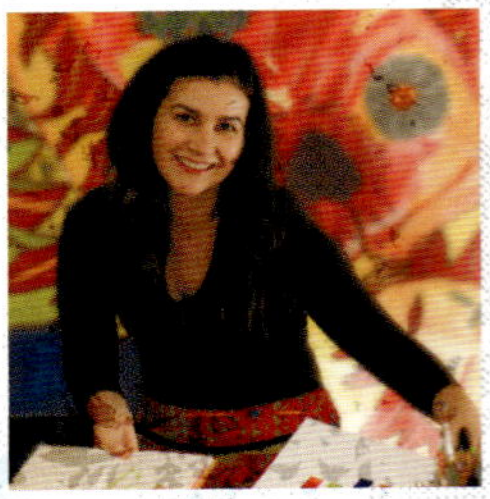

Lisa Sonora Beam is an American artist, therapist, business owner and strategist. She is passionate about the healing and transformative powers of creative expression, and about turning a creative calling into a viable business. Lisa is the author of *The Creative Entrepreneur*, the award-winning and best-selling visual guidebook to creativity and business. An avid traveler and keeper of visual journal sketchbooks, she teaches workshops globally. Her latest book is a memoir: *Sketchbooks: My Personal Creative Practice*.
lisasonora.com
creativeentrepreneur.biz

### Jessica Brogan

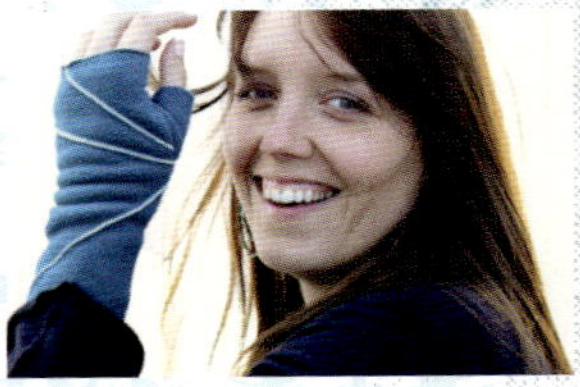

Jessica Brogan is a nationally published writer and photographer, a popular blogger and a guide, showing women how to live a passionate life from the inside out.

Little known facts: She collects soap, has lived in Europe four times and dreams of being a barrel racer on horseback and of splitting her time between Hawaii and Italy.
jessicaleighbrogan.com

### Juliette Crane

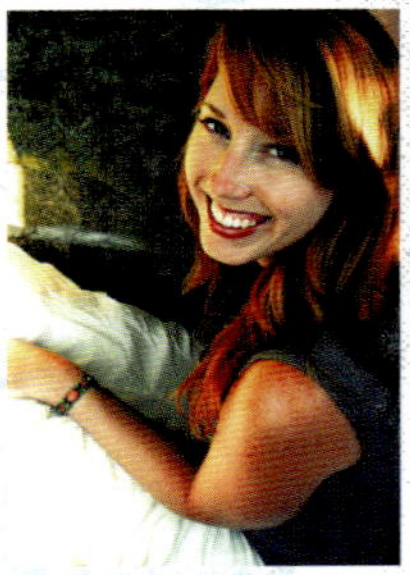
Photo by Stephanie Claire Birr

I'm an artist, teacher, storyteller and adventurer. As often as possible, I paint outside, mostly in the grass, surrounded by flower gardens and the tallest trees.

I'm the creator of a series of online courses that encourage thousands around the world to let go, to get creative and live their dreams.

My work has been published in *Glamour* magazine UK, *Somerset Studio, Somerset Studio Gallery* and *Artful Blogging*.

When I'm not teaching, traveling, cooking and painting in gardens around the world, I live with my bluegrass-singing husband in Madison, Wisconsin.

juliettecrane.com

### Kecia Deveney

Kecia Deveney has a vintage soul, and she loves the individuality of found objects. With her passion for making and displaying gifts and home décor, Kecia found her connectedness to the art community by blogging, selling her beautiful art online, teaching and through the creation of her website. Her work has been published in magazines and she enjoys working in a diversity of art mediums reflected in the free-spirited, gypsy nature of her artwork.

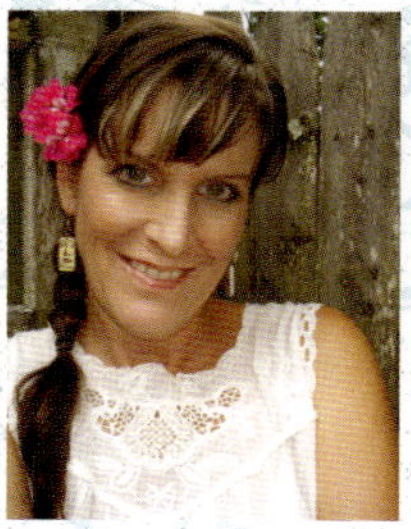

lemoncholys.blogspot.com

### Louise Gale

Louise Gale is a British artist with a passion for color, nature, pattern and energy.

Louise spends her days creating, running creative workshops and assisting other creative souls with their businesses. After eight years in a corporate job, she found the courage to pursue a life filled with more creativity and freedom. Now she walks barefoot in the sand every morning as the sun rises and has a secret obsession for sacred geometry.

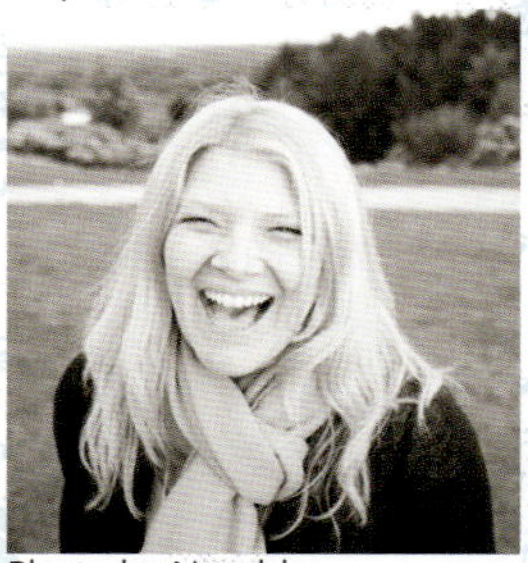

Photo by Navyblur

Her mixed-media series Sew Hoboken is a permanent collection at the Hoboken Historical Museum in New Jersey, USA, and her work has been published in *The New York Times* and featured in *Inc.* magazine as well as other publications.

louisegale.com

### Jess Greene

Jess Greene is an adventurer, artist, teacher and experience designer. After spending years assuring middle schoolers that despite being a sex cell, pollen can't get you pregnant, Jess has now expanded her focus to writing and guiding others through transformational experiences. As the founder of SeekYourCourse.com, Jess inspires adults worldwide to engage the creativity inside their minds and to craft inspired lives.

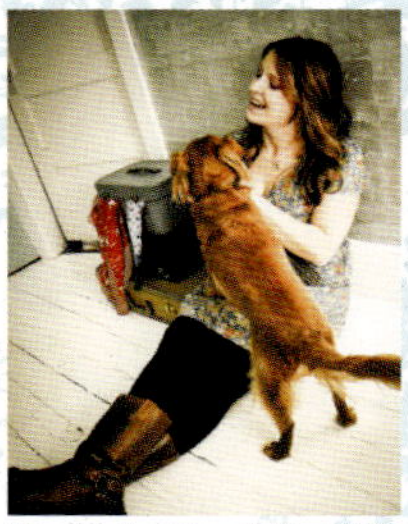

Photo by Danielle Intile

jessgreenestudio.com

### e'Layne Koenigsberg

e'Layne Koenigsberg is a mixed-media collage artist, business owner, artist empowerment coach, author, teacher and mother. Her mission is to create inspirational art and to support women to thrive spiritually, emotionally, physically, artistically and financially. She founded Tribe Wild Women, an online community where women can come to nurture their soul and creative spirit, and share their empowerment journeys in the light of truth, sisterhood and love.

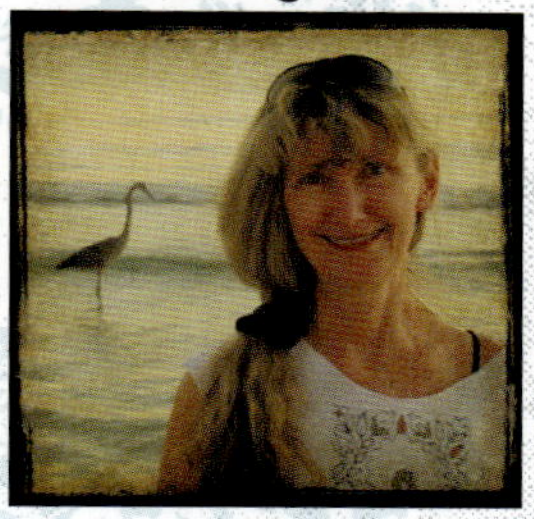

artbyelayne.com

### Laurie Mika

Laurie Mika is an artist, instructor and the author of *Mixed-Media Mosaics*. Over the last two decades, Laurie's work has evolved into an original and easily recognizable style of mosaics and assemblage. Her unique approach combines handmade polymer clay tiles with beads, jewelry pieces, charms, glass tile and found objects. She feels very fortunate to be able to combine her love of travel and passion for art through teaching at art retreats both in the United States and abroad.

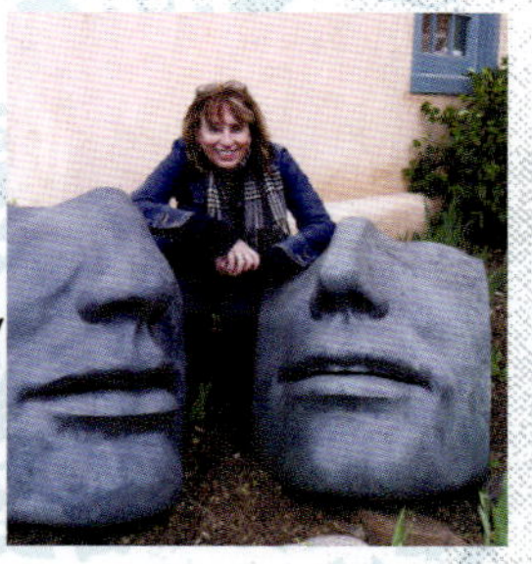

mikaarts.com

### Peter Perez

I am a graphic designer, painter, curator, cultural historian and a national and international recipient of several design awards and recognition.

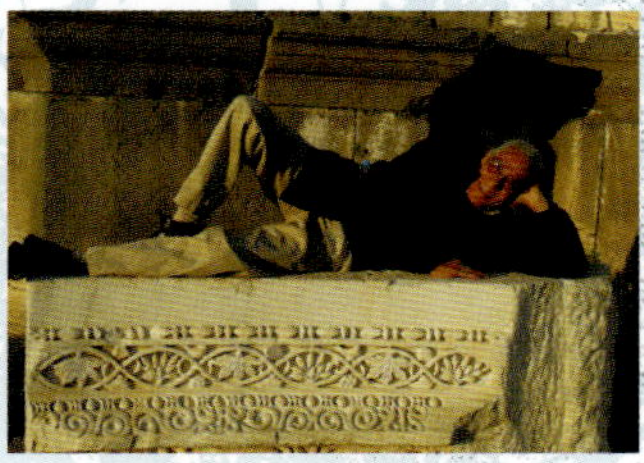

I chose to be an artist at a very young age (1949 in Mrs. Howard's fourth-grade class). No one thought it was a very good idea, but I knew it was my calling. At fifteen I set off on my own to be an artist, and since that time, I have enjoyed a forty-year art career and my own design studio.

To me, everything is a possible art tool and palette: Food is art on a plate; gardens are a living palette; anything can be a brush to enhance the world around you, and this approach makes it all taste better.

For the past thirteen years I have been on the road painting, curating and promoting Day of the Dead celebrations. The recognition of this important cultural tradition has gained popular acceptance and is an opportunity for all people to celebrate their cultural roots and pass family memories on from generation to generation. Art paves the way to the next adventure in the next dimension.

It is what we do while we are here that makes the difference.

facebook.com/peter.perez.31508

### Jesse Reno

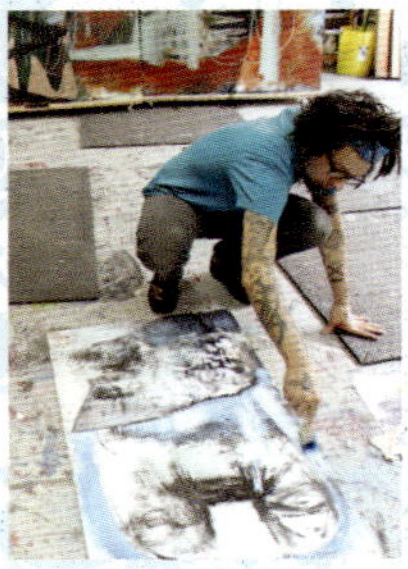

Jesse Reno is a self-taught mixed-media painter. He has been drawing since he could hold a pencil, and painting and exhibiting his works since 2000. Jesse has amassed over three thousand paintings in the last twelve years and has exhibited his work extensively across the United States and Canada as well as France and Mexico. His work has been covered in various art publications including *Juxtapoz*, *ARTnews*, *Artension*, *dpi* and *Somerset Studio*, just to name a few. One of Jesse's largest works can be seen in Winnipeg, Canada, where he was commissioned by the Province of Manitoba to create a 25' × 40' (8m × 12m) mural as a reminder of the cultural importance of the Native American people in the region.

jessereno.com

### Mary Beth Shaw

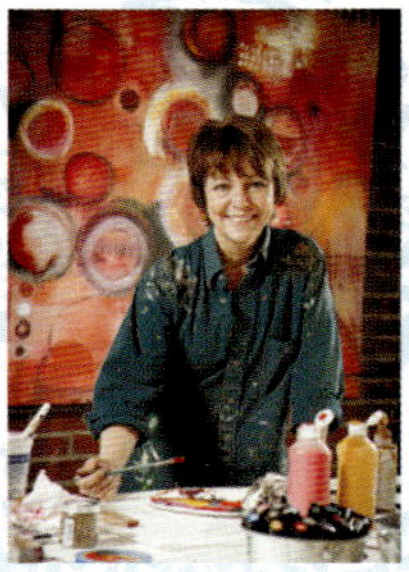

Mary Beth Shaw works in mixed media because she loves to play with art supplies. She contends that mixed media is for artists who can't make up their minds. The owner of StencilGirl Products, she uses stencils on anything and everything. Her spontaneous process utilizes pastel, ink, marker and acrylics, layered with various collage, texture and three-dimensional materials. She welcomes so-called mistakes because they lead to wonderful opportunities and discoveries.

She is author of *Flavor for Mixed Media* and *Stencil Girl*, both published by North Light Books, and is a columnist for *Somerset Studio*. Living in Wildwood, Missouri with her husband and three cats, Mary Beth is passionate about every moment of life.

mbshaw.com

stencilgirlproducts.com

### Roxanne Evans Stout

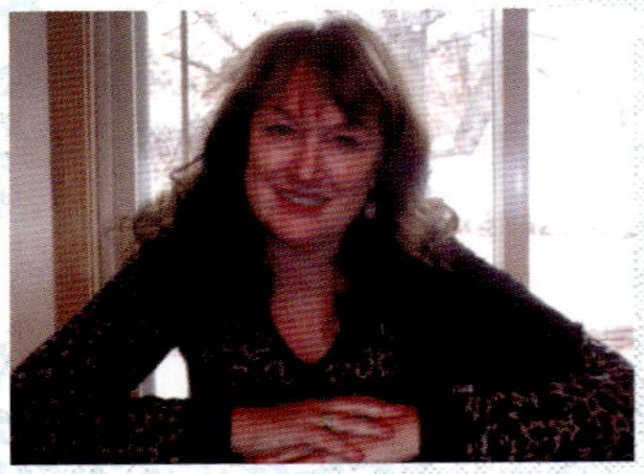

Roxanne Evans Stout is a mixed-media artist who lives and creates in the Pacific Northwest. She teaches art workshops and has had her work shown and published nationally. Roxanne is constantly inspired by natural history, the mountains and the river lands surrounding her home. This inspiration has always been an integral part of her art. Book arts, art journaling, encaustic painting and collage are her favorite ways to express herself.

rivergardenstudio.typepad.com

facebook.com/roxanne.evansstout

### Judy Wise

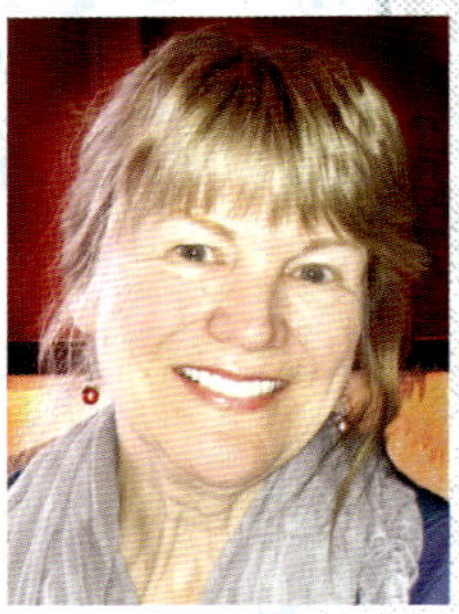

Judy Wise is a lifelong painter who loves to stare at things, play with unfamiliar materials, daydream in her journal and think about existence. She loves to teach and travel and has been lucky all her life.

judywise.com

# index

# dedication

For Marco, Santana and Sienna . . .
I love you all the stars and every grain of sand in every Universe.

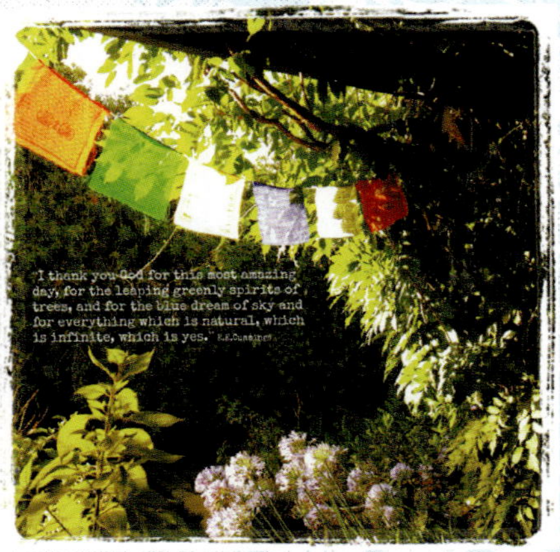


 Published by North Light Books, an imprint of F+W Media, Inc., 10151 Carver Road, Suite 300, Blue Ash, Ohio, 45242. (800) 289-0963. First Edition.

Other fine North Light Books are available from your favorite bookstore, art supply store or online supplier. Visit our website at fwmedia.com

fw a content + ecommerce company

23 22 21 20 19 5 4 3 2

DISTRIBUTED IN THE U.K. AND EUROPE
BY F&W MEDIA INTERNATIONAL, LTD
Brunel House, Pynes Hill Court, Pynes Hill, Rydon Lane
Exeter, EX2 5AZ, UK
Tel: (+44) 1392 797680
Email: enquiries@fwmedia.com

ISBN 13: 9781440301186

Edited by Tonia Jenny
Designed by Geoff Raker
Photography by Santana Verdugo (except where otherwise noted).
Production managed by Debbie Thomas

# thank-yous

What a beautiful unfolding journey I have undertaken these past few years. I feel deeply grateful to so many for all that has led me to write this book.

To Marco, Santana and Sienna for wrapping me in your warm love while giving me the freedom to pursue the BIG dream even when it meant being without your wife and mama for extended periods of time. I am one lucky woman!

To my family, friends and community, both online and in the flesh, for supporting, encouraging and always cheering me on.

To my hosts around this beautiful planet who have extended their hospitality and friendship, welcoming me into their homes and hearts and enriching my life in a multitude of ways.

To my incredible students who show up eager to learn and who teach me new and wondrous things . . . every single time.

To my gorgeous contributors for sharing their wonderful stories, advice and art on these pages. You have made this such a joyful collaboration.

To the many artists who have inspired me by being brave enough to be out there doing their thing in the world, spreading beauty and creativity and not subscribing to the starving-artist myth. May we all be paradigm shifters for each other.

To the best editor in the world, Tonia Jenny, for making the whole process seem not so daunting and for standing beside me each step of the way, even when I floundered.

And to two women with hearts of gold, Sallianne McClelland and Ellen Legare, who took a chance on a cheeky, enthusiastic Aussie girl and catapulted me into the life of my dreams.

Endless gratitude to all.

# about tracy

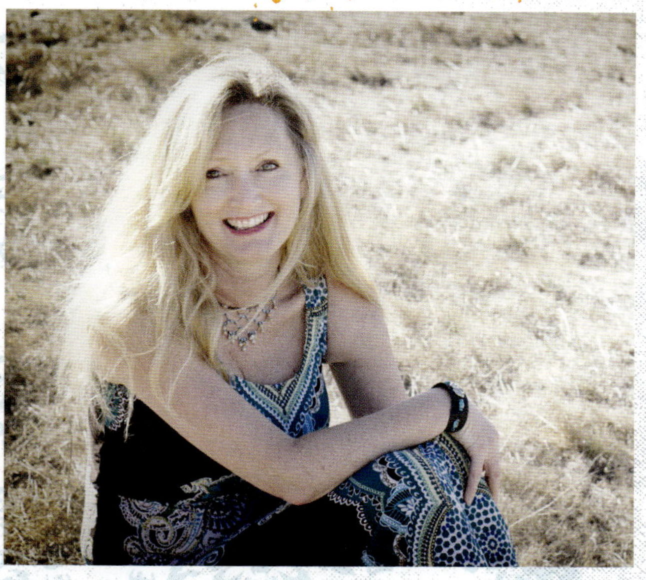

Photo by Stacy de la Rosa

If Tracy Verdugo were given the opportunity to coin a term for a new art movement based around what she teaches, she might call it "curiosity and wonderism" or maybe "loosen-upism" or "endless possibilitism."

When she is not hanging out with her family in their artsy adobe home in a small village on the shores of Jervis Bay, Australia, or throwing paint around in her little purple studio in their backyard, you may find her wrangling with two large suitcases attempting to board the BART in San Francisco en route to teach at an art retreat or sitting in a circle on St. Pete Beach, Florida, listening intently as women share their stories of creative longing.

Tracy is an inspiration instigator, prolific painter, singer/songwriter and lover of the written word, smitten traveler and soaker-up of all that is beauty-full. She teaches her Paint Mojo and other creative workshops all over this amazing planet and reminds her students of the wonder that already resides within them.

Mostly, though, she is Mama Bear to two gorgeous, zest-filled daughters, Santana and Sienna, and co-adventurer-in-life with her *amor* of thirty-three years, the talented and brilliant Marco.

www.tracyverdugo.com
artoftracyverdugo.blogspot.com
facebook.com/tracy.verdugo
instagram.com/tracyverdugo
Don't be shy! Come say hello :-)

*What I really, really want is to paint the world in rainbows of possibility.*
—Tracy Verdugo

# contributing photographers

## Santana Verdugo

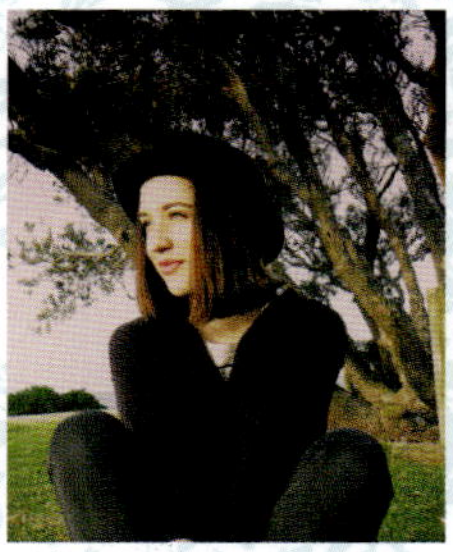

Santana Verdugo is captivated by light, the beauty of cultural difference and the natural environment. She lives on the pristine shores of Jervis Bay and is inspired to tell the stories of her adventures in the world with her camera and an eye for the beauty of the ordinary moment.
santanaverdugo.com

## Beth Saxena

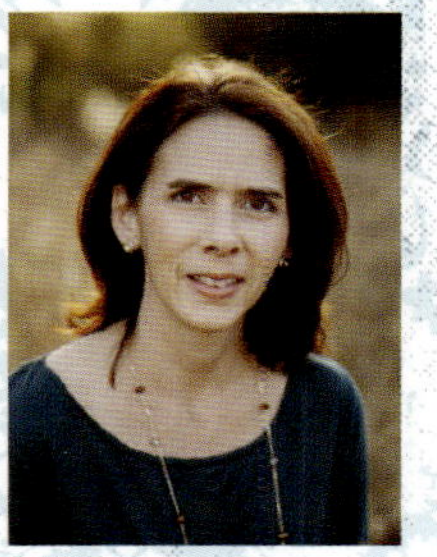

Beth Saxena is a mixed-media artist and photographer living in Austin, Texas. In her paintings Beth uses layers of rich color, expressive mark making and hand-painted collage elements. The end result is a painting rich in texture and history. She is inspired by the intricate patterns found in nature as well as the patina of aged surfaces and graffiti. In her photography, Beth focuses on capturing the fine art of nature.
bethsaxena.com